STRATEGIC CHURCH

Everyone committed to being part of today's Church should read this book. From the lead pastor to the congregant, we all *must* understand the importance of strategy and how it relates to culture. Dr. Damazio unpacks the key elements to becoming a *strategic church* that will have a sustaining impact on your congregation.

RANDY ALWARD
President, Marantha Music

Frank Damazio has given a blueprint for building a ministry of integrity that can stand the test of time. These principles of structure and outreach can be applied to anyone's life, whether he or she is a new believer or an established church planter. *Strategic Church* is a daring challenge to the kingdom of God to do greater things in His name.

MATTHEW BARNETT
Pastor and Co-founder, The Dream Center, Los Angeles, California

Today's changing and complex world calls for strategic leaders to impact culture and lead with passionate purpose. This book will inspire the vision to build an enduring and biblical church, with principles of vision from a person who has lived and led with vision for more than 40 years.

MARK BATTERSON
Lead Pastor, National Community Church, Washington, DC

As a leader and advocate of the local church, I'm excited about this book from Frank Damazio, one of the great champions of the Church. This book is a powerful read that clearly outlines practical and spiritual tools for every ministry leader who wants to build an enduring and biblical church.

CHRISTINE CAINE
Founder, The A21 Campaign

Pastor Frank's wisdom and insight have personally helped me as a leader for many years. His latest book is brilliant! The principles he outlines have greatly assisted the growth and development of our church team. I highly recommend it for any church leader.

PHIL DOOLEY
Lead Minister, Hillsong Church, South Africa

Frank Damazio has written a masterpiece of strategy for the Church. This book uses Scripture and the Lord's own ministry to teach the men and women of God how to make disciples of all nations. Salvation is tremendous, but it is just the first step in becoming a true disciple or follower of Jesus Christ. Growing up into the image of Jesus Christ is the goal of every true Christian, and it is what is needed in making fruitful disciples of Christ. Please read this wonderful book and be blessed and inspired to make disciples, bring new strategies into your church, and to bear much fruit for the kingdom of God.

Yonggi Cho
Chairman of the Board, Church Growth International

Frank is an outstanding Christian author and has a passion to see the Church of Jesus Christ move forward. *Strategic Church* will not only challenge and encourage you but also inspire you to build the Church that Jesus wants you to build in your local context. This book will give you a fresh insight into biblical strategies, principles and vision that will move your church forward. It's a great read for everyone that is passionate about the local church.

Gary Clarke
Lead Pastor, Hillsong Church London

Strategic Church is a dream come true for any leader who is serious about building a prodigious church. Pastor Frank Damazio has done this in City Bible Church, and now he is showing us how to do it in ours. When Pastor Damazio has something to say, I am quick to listen. Get ready for growth!

Chris Durso
Pastor of MISFIT NYC, Christ Tabernacle

Frank Damazio has good insight and experience into strategic church leadership. Those who read this book will draw from the revelation he has been given in his many years of experience building a great church.

Russell Evans
Senior Minister, Planetshakers

Frank Damazio is a leader's leader. His new book *Strategic Church* will challenge you to break through the barriers and embrace the possibilities. Read this book and dare to lead!

Jentezen Franklin
Senior Pastor, Free Chapel, Gainsville, Georgia
New York Times Bestselling Author, *Fasting*

Frank Damazio's writings on leadership are outstanding! *Strategic Church* is equally outstanding. Reading this book will give you the tools to lead with strategic vision and provide you with the blueprint to hit the mark of excellence.

MARILYN HICKEY
President, Marilyn Hickey Ministries, Englewood, Colorado

Strategic Church is incredibly insightful, theologically sound, practical and uplifting. This book is unique because Pastor Damazio writes from his personal experience as an outstanding church leader who has tested and proven the concepts in the book. Every pastor and church leader who wants to be effective and lead the local church to the next level and beyond should read it.

CHIN DO KHAM
Church Consultant
President, Global Outreach and Community Development

Frank Damazio is well known as a leader and strategist. As a church planter and pastor, he is one of the first people I go to for insights on people, church and the Bible itself. With this book, he is essentially picking up the phone and offering wisdom that could help you change the world.

CARL LENTZ
Pastor, Hillsong NYC

Frank is such a powerful and passionate communicator. I have had the opportunity to see firsthand the work he has been able to accomplish here in Portland, and I have had the joy of working alongside him on several occasions. I know Frank poured his heart and soul into this book. It is clearly the product of several years of research, prayer and "in the trenches" experience. It is sure to challenge many with its biblically based insight and wisdom.

KEVIN PALAU
President, Luis Palau Association

Frank Damazio is a man committed to seeing the cause of Christ established on the earth in an ever-changing culture. In *Strategic Church,* he has not only identified and outlined the essential elements needed to plant and grow contemporary twenty-first-century churches but has also researched and defined the different types of churches and leaders required who will do that. This book will help pastors refocus and re-fire their leaders and congregations toward their true north.

PHIL PRINGLE
Senior Minister, C3 Church, Oxford Falls, Sydney, Australia

Strategic Church is, without a doubt, one of the best books I have ever read on leadership, vision and strategy. As a leader serving more than 250,000 churches around the world, I was informed, inspired and renewed in the passion of my vision. Clear, convicting and challenging, this book is a *must-have* for every church leader.

HOWARD RACHINSKI
President/CEO, Christian Copyright Licensing International, Inc. (CCLI)

In *Strategic Church,* Frank Damazio has given an overall strategy for church building that can apply to the traditional church, the emergent church, or the small neighborhood church that has never grown. The great thing about this book is that it shows a pastor does not have to be a "10-talent guy" to lead a church that can be used greatly of God—He can use any pastor, anywhere, at any time, to make a significant influence in the life of His followers. This is a great book coming from a great pastor and church revitalization authority.

ELMER L. TOWNS
Co-Founder and Vice President, Liberty University, Lynchburg, Virginia

Frank Damazio has written a book that every pastor should read. His years of experience as a successful leader are the foundation of this compelling book, and it will help pastors gain clarity on how to build the church and the vision God that has placed in their heart. I love this book!

PHILIP WAGNER
Lead Pastor, Oasis Church
Author, *How to Turn Your Marriage Around in 10 Days*

Frank Damazio's insight into Scripture and love for the Church will inspire and challenge you as you read *Strategic Church*. He draws from years of experience building the local church and planting churches. I'm so thankful for His love for today's leaders and the next generation's leaders! *Strategic Church* will focus your church's vision for genuine impact in your city.

RICH WILKERSON, JR.
Senior Pastor, Trinity Church, Miami, Florida

As a pastor and church leader, I'm always looking for books that inspire, inform and instruct me in becoming a more effective leader. Frank Damazio has done just that in this book. *Strategic Church* is packed full of practical information that, when applied, will lead to positive transformation. It is a must-read for every forward-thinking pastor.

BILL WILSON
Lead Pastor, Oregon Assemblies of God

STRATEGIC CHURCH

A LIFE-CHANGING CHURCH IN AN EVER-CHANGING CULTURE

FRANK DAMAZIO

a division of Baker Publishing Group
Grand Rapids, Michigan

Published by Baker Books
a division of Baker Publishing Group
P.O. Box 6287, Grand Rapids, MI 49516-6287
www.bakerbooks.com

Baker Books edition published 2014
ISBN 978-0-8010-1762-9

Previously published by Regal Books

Printed in the United States of America

The Library of Congress has cataloged the original edition as follows:
Damazio, Frank.
The strategic church : a life-changing church in an ever-changing culture / Frank Damazio.
p. cm.
Includes bibliographical references (p.) and index.
ISBN 978-0-8307-6376-4 (trade paper : alk. paper)
1. Church development, New. I. Title.
BV652.24.D36 2012
253—dc23 2012006090

14 15 16 17 18 19 20 7 6 5 4 3 2 1

This book is dedicated to my dear friend Jack Louman,
a man of amazing character, integrity, faith and Christlikeness.
He has been my armor bearer, my Jonathan in all the years of my ministry.
He is a prayer shield, a warrior with unbending faith,
a builder and a strategist. This gifted man has impacted our church
and many churches. Thank you, Jack. You are the model leader.

Contents

FOREWORD

BY PASTOR TOMMY BARNETT

When I first started pastoring at Westside Assembly of God in Davenport, Iowa, I had no idea the church would grow from 76 people to more than 4,000 members in a few years. What we experienced was truly supernatural. But there was also a strategy. There was a plan for making the dream of winning thousands of souls a reality for us.

This book is about the dream you have from God and the strategy you need to create if you want to live that dream.

The strategic church is a world-impacting church. It's infectious. There's a certain buzz and excitement in the air. There's real change. The broken are restored, prayers are answered, miracles abound, and people give time and resources generously. Does this sound like the kind of church you want to be a part of? Do you want to experience more of God's presence in your worship services? Do you want to build an effective team of leaders from your own house who will train and disciple others to build a life-changing church? It's possible, and there is a divine strategy for fulfilling the God-given destiny for your church.

I can tell you for certain that thriving churches do not grow by accident. There's a dream, and there's a team. That team has a plan for reaching the city and for experiencing the presence of God in a profound way each time the church gathers. If you want to build a church that not only grows but also endures when the world changes—and changes the world—you need a dream and you need a plan.

Maybe you're a seasoned church leader, or maybe you're just starting your church-planting journey. I guarantee that there's more for you. If you don't know where you want to go or how to get there, *Strategic Church* will help you. If you're already on your way to fulfilling your dream, *Strategic Church* will greatly help you get there.

I've held many conferences for pastors and I've listened to many questions, hopes, fears, lacks and dreams from pastors around the world. This book answers many of those questions I've been asked, and it builds hopes and dreams for pastors. How do you discover biblical vision? How can you have healthy and lasting church growth? How can you create an attitude of faith that says, "Yes, we can do this!" And how can you build a dynamic atmosphere in the church?

Let me urge you—pastors young and old, new and mature, church planters and church growers—to get this book and use it. Take your staff through it. Train your interns and send this book to your missionaries. Its message will work anywhere at any time. It is a winner.

Frank Damazio is a gifted communicator who has diligently studied the biblical pattern for church leadership. This book is so practical in its layout and content. You're going to learn how to build an enduring church, just like Frank has learned in his 30 plus years of ministry. I love this book, and I believe you will love it also. Make sure you have a pen with you while you're reading, because you'll want to take notes on what you're doing now and what you should start doing in your church. Get ready to lead a strategic and world impacting church!

PASTOR TOMMY BARNETT
Senior Pastor, Phoenix First Assembly
Co-founder, Los Angeles Dream Center

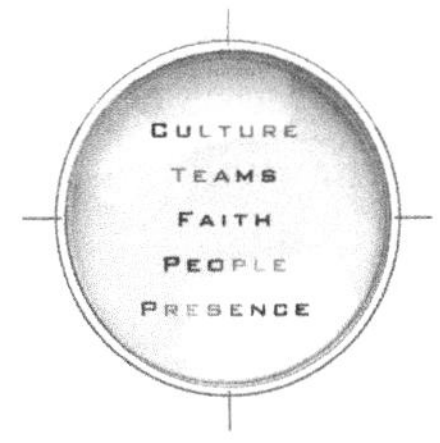

FOREWORD

BY PASTOR ROBERT MORRIS

In this complex day and age, the Church desperately needs leaders who are strategists—men and women who can anticipate the future and keep the church on course . . . leaders who truly have an "understanding of the times" (1 Chron. 12:32, *ESV*). I believe *Strategic Church* is the perfect book to help you think differently and gain a unique perspective on how you and your church can thrive by overcoming obstacles.

During my years of pastoring Gateway Church, I have experienced many challenges but countless blessings as well. I've had to go through what all pastors go through: casting vision, raising resources for that vision, reaching our city, identifying and training up-and-coming leaders to pastor people—the list goes on. I've spent my life serving and building leaders who can build the Church. And I've learned that in order for a great church to have enduring fruit, it has to have a great team who works together and builds together.

Strategic Church is not just another "how to" book or a collection of abstract theories; it is a book about healthy team-building that will help you galvanize your leaders together with clear focus. These are solid principles Frank Damazio has lived out in his 30-plus years of ministry. These pages contain engaging analogies, dynamic truths and proven strategies based on a firm foundation from the Word of God that will spur you and your church to more effectively build fruitful disciples of Christ and transform lives!

If you're new and just starting out as a church builder, *Strategic Church* is an excellent resource to help you establish a strong, healthy foundation and build right. If you've been on a journey of building a church for several years and could use some inspiration and encouragement, *Strategic Church* will hit the mark. This is an ideal read for your leadership team, your entire staff, the interns at your college, your small group leaders and all of your church members . . . because *each person* builds the Church. I wholeheartedly recommend this book to you as a strategic blueprint for building a healthy church that will make a lasting impact in your city and around the world!

ROBERT MORRIS
Senior Pastor, Gateway Church
Bestselling author, *The Blessed Life, From Dream to Destiny, The Power of Your Words* and *The God I Never Knew*

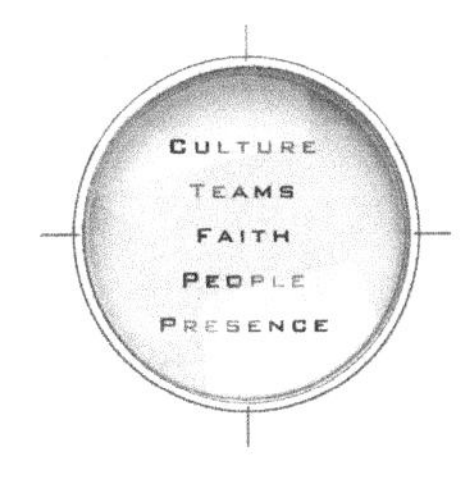

Introduction

It was over 30 years ago that I stood at the altar of Bible Temple and clearly heard the voice of God call me to plant a church in Eugene, Oregon. I was on staff with the church and actively teaching in our Bible college, but I knew that I had to go where God called me. Eventually I would come back to my sending church, now called City Bible Church (CBC), and serve as lead pastor. Thirty plus years and we are still going strong! But there was a moment where I had to decide: *Do I leave the comfortable place where I am now and take a risk; or do I stay here, still do ministry, but not be totally fulfilled and obedient?* I took the risk and it took me on quite a ride! The moment I decided to leap was a pivotal and strategic moment for me.

There is no doubt in my mind that ministry is made up of very strategic moments that shape leaders. Some moments can be bad or dark; some are puzzling; some are moments of inspiration where dreams take wing and begin to live; and others last only seconds before the dreams die and fade into obscurity. Out of such moments arise a new you and a new day. Your moments affect your ministry, your church and the world around you. You must stand ready for the God moment that is the turning-point moment.

God is the master orchestrator of moments. He packages things in such a precise and opportune way that you would never think of doing in your own limited ability. He is concerned with every moment of your life and every moment of your church. He keeps careful watch over everything. He has your back and side doors. In Isaiah 27:3, He is called the waterer of our gardens: "I, the Lord, keep it, I water it every moment; lest any hurt it, I keep it night and day." One moment is all it takes to change the course of your life and put you on the road to something unique and impacting. Your influence on people flows from what has impacted you. Joshua was so full of encouragement from Moses and the Lord that he had the confidence to inspire an entire nation to march through the Promised Land and conquer Israel's enemies. He drew on that moment where the Lord had spoken to him and told him to be strong and courageous, and he took that moment with him throughout the campaign for the Promised Land.

Strategic moments have incredible power. They can be moments of supernatural encouragement where you were drained in the wilderness and in need of refreshment—and it came. Maybe you worked long and hard to win your neighbor to Christ, and after 15 years there still seemed to be no apparent progress. In that season, however, the word came to you to not grow weary or fatigued in doing a good thing, because at the right time and the right moment, you *will* bring in a harvest if you "do not lose heart" (Gal. 6:9). Along that same vein, there are moments that revive your calling. There is nothing more important in the Kingdom than for you to know your calling. One moment can redirect your path and clarify your future. You don't have to see, but you do have to believe. God had to tell Abraham to "get out of the tent" and look around (see Gen. 15:5). When you're "in a tent," that is your whole world. The power of a strategic moment causes you to lift your vision so that you open your eyes and look at the sky. You start believing.

Strategic moments can open pivotal windows of divine opportunity. What starts with a disappointment or hurt turns out to be a divine occasion that forces you to enlarge your borders and receive more. A lot more opportunity than you ever thought was possible appears before you. When your vision is lifted, belief sets in. Strategic moments are dream-encounter moments. You receive the grand dream for you that God has in mind, or you remember the dream that had been buried. If your dream has been hidden or delayed, you need to recapture it and believe that it can be fulfilled. God is the God of fulfillment. Have faith for your promises and then wait for that moment when prophetic words are fulfilled as you step into your miracle. At the pool of Bethesda, the first person who stepped into the stirred water received a miracle (see John 5:4). You need to step into the miracle in order to receive the dream. This is the principle of capturing the strategic moment.

I believe that the church and her leaders today are at a prophetic moment that calls for a prophetic response. Although we can discern the season, we don't create it; and while we can't change those seasons, we can adapt. There is a purpose for every season, and we need to capture that opportune time if we are to build strategic churches and fulfill the dream that God put in our hearts (see Eccles. 3:1). Just remember that the church is not about buildings, money and staff. The Kingdom purpose is always fulfilled in people. You are called to build people and change lives.

The future we face consists of events and conditions over which we have little or no control. Turnarounds in economy, property loss, demographic changes in neighborhoods and the like comprise the future we face. On the other hand, the future we make is the one that is directly related to our quality of choices. We choose our leadership process, our vision, the team with which we work, and the budget priorities. It could be said that every leader is in the process of picking a future. That future can be a strategic future or it can be a chance future; a future with a great vision to achieve, or one with little or no vision; a future with a church that is stagnant or a church that is growing. I choose to believe that a healthy, growing church is a church led by strategic leaders who are following a strategic plan and are committed to a strategic vision. We work with a strategic God who calls and equips strategic leaders to do strategic things.

The strategic church is a focused church with a clear vision and mission. The book you hold in your hands is meant to complement your God-given call and purpose with tools to build a strong, relevant, life-changing local church. Strategic leaders who have the ability to anticipate the future and prepare and position themselves for it build the strategic church. It takes all levels of people and leadership functioning to their full capacity of skill and wisdom to build the strategic church.

In order to build this church, however, we must understand where we are now: What is the condition of our church? What are the challenges facing our church, and what are the opportunities that lie ahead of us? We must have a clear picture of where we want to be, our ultimate goal. What is the model we should follow? What does a strategic, God-centered church look like? And, finally, how do we build a strategic church?

We will explore all of these topics and more as we discuss what a church should look like in today's world according to the model seen in Scripture and as we profile the leader who builds it. As we do, keep this in mind: *The strategic church is focused on a biblical blueprint and has an intentional design and clarity of purpose that builds an impacting, vibrant and enduring church.*

I have been a church leader for more than 30 years, taught five years in a Bible college, and earned a master of divinity degree and a doctor of ministry degree from Oral Roberts University. I am presently lead pastor of a sizable multisite church and am chairman of a fellowship of hundreds of churches. I say this only to frame my words in this book. They are researched words, proven words and words with tangible, visible fruit. I am totally committed to building strategic leaders who build strategic churches. This book is the heart of the strategy I see and the strategy I use. We have built a strategic church that has been fruitful and healthy for over 60 years, that has planted dozens of churches and that has sent dozens of missionaries around the world. We serve our metro area with passion, and I humbly say our city respects our church.

I believe that the material I provide in this book—material that has been proven to work—will inspire you to greater vision, encourage you to focus and build with biblical simplicity, and move you to engage the culture around you today. We *can* build strategically and successfully.

Strategic Leaders Build Strategic Churches

More than four million bricks. Thirty-seven thousand tons. That is the composition of the dome of the Florence Cathedral in Italy, dubbed the greatest architectural feat in the western world. Its story and its architect are as fascinating as the building itself.

Filippo Brunelleschi had a way of seeing things that was different from his peers. He looked at the world with a unique perspective and with an eye that was always innovating and pushing the boundaries of what could be done. He was an architect. The problem he faced was that after 100 years of construction, there was a massive cathedral that was missing its dome. The original architect designed it to be the largest structure of its kind ever made, rivaling the Pantheon of ancient Rome. Brunelleschi looked at the unfinished building and had a vision to see the dome raised to new heights, defying the conventional methods of architecture and engineering of his day.

To win the commission to build the dome, Brunelleschi had to present his blueprints to the cathedral authorities, who would select the architect for this monumental project. Not wanting to totally unveil his designs, he challenged the competitors to stand an egg on its end. When they failed to do so, Brunelleschi broke the egg and it stood upright. The men protested that the solution was so obvious, to which Brunelleschi replied that it *was* obvious, and so would be the solution to the dome. He won the commission.

To develop his strategy for construction, Brunelleschi turned to the architecture of ancient Rome, particularly the Pantheon. Simplistic and classic in its design, the Pantheon gave plenty for Brunelleschi to study. He observed its proportions, its raw materials, and the structure that made this magnificent building stand. From his observations, he devised a plan to use bands of sandstone rings that would hold the dome together like the rings of a barrel. One part of the strategy was complete.

Now that he had this great strategy, it was time to gather the materials and workers. To illustrate the end product, Brunelleschi made a small wooden and brick model of the dome that served as a guide for all the craftsmen. They would lay brick upon brick according to the model. The design was innovative and had never been attempted by any builder. Most people who saw the plan said it was undoable, yet Brunelleschi was undaunted, and he stuck to his blueprint in the face of unbelief and near impossible engineering challenges.

One engineering challenge was that scaffolding could not be used during construction of the dome. There was not enough timber in the local area to build such a structure. So Brunelleschi had to design a way to raise the hundreds of tons of materials over 200 feet high. To overcome this obstacle, he developed totally original machines to hoist the bricks and beams to the construction site. He devised a gear system with a reverse mechanism so that the oxen driving the hoist would not need to be unharnessed and turned around after lifting the beams and bricks, as was the current method. Efficient, innovative and focused. Another obstacle overcome.

There also was the issue of preventing the bricks from falling inward as the dome rose higher. With each brick laid, the angle of the dome increased. But along with there not being enough wood to build scaffolding, there was not enough wood to build forms for the bricks to stay in place while the mortar dried. But how was the dome to support itself throughout construction? To solve this problem, Brunelleschi again devised an inenious solution. He created the herringbone pattern that redirected the weight of the bricks outward toward the supports instead of downward toward the floor. By carefully observing the curve of the dome as it took shape, Brunelleschi was able to place the bricks in key areas. He did not observe from a distance; he was hands-on and active during the entire project. He inspected bricks and even laid them, all the while inspiring the workers to keep building, even when they thought the dome was going to collapse.

Brunelleschi also looked after the physical condition of his workers, and he made sure the builders were fed and had plenty to drink. Finally, in 1436, 16 years after he drew the blueprints, presented the vision and began construction, Brunelleschi completed the massive dome over the Florence Cathedral. This massive culmination of a vision fulfilled, a course maintained and obstacles overcome sparked an architectural revolution throughout Europe.

In 1438, this cathedral served as the meeting place for the Council of Florence, a global meeting that brought the religious views of east and west together under the vision of a man who dreamed big, worked hard, took risks, found solutions and did not give up on the vision. Brunelleschi's dome is larger than the domes of the Capitol Building in Washington, DC, St. Paul's Cathedral in London, the Pantheon in Rome, and St. Peter's in Vatican City. The cathedral takes up three city blocks and is visible to the whole of Tuscany. Yet without the vision, the strategy and the leadership of this one man, the building would be another story of an ambitious project that had a great beginning but hit too many roadblocks to succeed and make its mark on the world.

Strategic leaders are vision leaders who have the capacity to see and face the future, unafraid of what it may look like. They have a global vision—they see the scope of the world but recognize and understand that despite great cultural diversity, the world is now a global village. In the middle of a new economic environment, strategic leaders understand finances and resources and how to manage and multiply them. They also know how to master technology and bring new opportunities to the church through communications, networking and other technological innovations. All these elements will be needed in the strategic church, or SC, as we'll call it.

Yet while new opportunities and innovations are introduced, strategic leaders keep the church on a mission course: be the instrument of God, expand His kingdom and see lives transformed and people realigned to God. These leaders create and pave a smooth freeway from the church services to the city streets. They direct a gospel-taking people to serve and transform the people in their communities. They build using the nonnegotiable biblical ingredients that we will uncover in this book. At the end of the day, strategic leaders see what they are to build, have a strategy for getting there, and clearly communicate that picture to their churches.

The Complexity of Today's Church World

The pressing need today is for leaders to think strategically and then build strategic churches—churches that are biblically based and that spiritually transform people into fruitful disciples of Christ. This is no small task in today's complex church world. It seems as if leadership preparation has not equipped leaders to face today's theological challenges, organizational changes and tremendous pressures to succeed.

Church leaders today are expected to provide effective leadership in the middle of a changing context that faces a massive cultural shift in people's attitudes toward God, the Bible, the church and church leadership. And inadequately trained leaders are vulnerable to the many strong voices teaching numerous church models to follow and various success stories, all of which influence leaders' thinking and actions at all levels. Pastor-leaders can easily become unfocused, confused, double-minded and clouded when trying to identify what kind of church they are commissioned to build. Like Brunelleschi, leaders face seemingly insurmountable obstacles to building churches for which they have a God-vision.

All these pressures can hinder leaders from becoming strategic, aim-and-hit-the-mark leaders. They may lose heart and a clear vision for the church and, consequently, not have faith to make future plans and hard changes. Therefore, it is vitally important for every leader to see clearly and to confidently build the kind of church that is a right and biblical model, a model that can engage the heart and soul of the pastor-leader.

Different Views of "Church"

What comes to mind when you hear the word "church"? I posed that question to the congregation I lead, and the responses were quite interesting: family, worship, teaching, friendship, people, exciting, awesome, giving, serving, prayer, hope, caring, forgiveness, fun, receiving, grace, connecting, opportunity, learning, laughter, Jesus, God, passion, holy place, touch my life, can't miss it, healing place, and unconditional love. You can feel some of the love the congregants have for church in these words. But did you notice that no one mentioned the word "building"? The concept of church seems to simply be a community and a safe place to do life.

Christ loved the church—God's community—so much that He gave His life for her. In His three-and-a-half-year-long ministry on earth, Christ interacted with all sorts of people—He got into their world, healed them, delivered them and ultimately died for them. His church is a place of freedom from sin and oppression, of faith and victory. It is a community of God's people thinking and acting as God intended and inviting others to join the family. Christ still loves His church! Today, we have the authority and awesome responsibility to help Him build His church, of which He is the foundation (see Matt. 16:18-19; see also 1 Pet. 2:4-6).

When He left this earth, Jesus gave His disciples all the tools they needed to construct a church worthy of His name. Fitted with a toolbox packed with the Holy Spirit and Christ's teachings, the apostles did build a vibrant church, as we see in the book of Acts. It is their example and teachings, along with Christ's, that we follow when we conceptualize and plan our churches today. As leaders, our call is to be Spirit-empowered strategists who build Christ's church according to the biblical pattern described in 1 Corinthians 3:9-11:

> For we are God's fellow workers; you are God's field, you are God's building. According to the grace of God which was given to me, as a wise master builder I have laid the foundation, and another builds on it. But let each one take heed how he builds on it. For no other foundation can anyone lay than that which is laid, which is Jesus Christ.

The foundation we are building on is Christ, and our blueprint is the Bible. I use the term "strategist" when referring to a church builder because I am convinced that Christ did nothing without a specific purpose and strategy in mind. The most effective way of accomplishing anything is using a strategy, a game plan. Coaches do it, school teachers do it, military commanders do, and so should we. An architect does not build any project without a blueprint being drawn first.

The Blueprint of a Strategic Church

In their book *Transformational Church: Creating a New Scorecard for Congregations*, Ed Stetzer and Thom Rainer give this insightful and sound advice about drawing the right church blueprint:

> The Word of God is always the best place to begin. God's Word always speaks with greater clarity and truth than anything we can muster up. That which has been inspired by the Holy Spirit thousands of years ago speaks to us today with startling immediacy. While we and our churches shift from fading relevance to relevance, the Bible is always relevant, in every second of every century.[1]

It's true! The Bible is living and always relevant. Even though it is relevant to all times and cultures, it never changes. Its principles never change. In a constantly changing context, we have the enduring Word of God to guide us in our endeavor to build Christ's church.

It's the Word of God that is our basic blueprint. To build the SC, you have to envision the SC as described in Scripture and then build from that basic outline. When you do, the church will have clarity of purpose, and it will focus on that biblical picture to build an impacting, vibrant and enduring church. Do you believe that you as a leader can find this blueprint, discern it and build it? I do believe it's possible. It may sound too simple or even a little presumptuous to say we can find a biblical model for church. I'm not claiming others haven't; but I do seek to encourage and to add another voice to the search, and I say we can find a biblical model and biblical principles for building strategic, impacting churches.

The Bible not only shows us the model church, but it also contains all the principles and guidelines for building a powerful, life-changing, impacting church. It's like a recipe book, complete with the directions for making a dish: a list of the ingredients, a guide to putting the ingredients together and a picture of the end product. Every cook, though, will adjust the spices according to his individual taste. Similarly, every pastor and leadership team will mix the ingredients and build the church according to the biblical model, adjusting the fine points based on their specific giftings, geographic location, demographics and application of the principles. So the churches may differ in the fine points, but they will all be built on the biblical model so that the end products are all strategic churches.

I see the SC and its basic ingredients recorded in the book of Acts and explained and enlarged in the New Testament Epistles. There are several undeniable characteristics—what I believe are nonnegotiable factors—that distinguish this SC:

- Has a strategic vision
- Exhibits growth
- Sustains a dynamic atmosphere
- Reflects a unique culture
- Champions a team of teams culture
- Fosters an emerging-leadership culture
- Demonstrates life-changing worship
- Has powerful praying

- Pursues the supernatural
- Blends the Spirit and the Word
- Nurtures a culture of generosity
- Reaches cities, regions and the world
- Learns important lessons

THE FIRST CHURCH AS A MODEL

The first church is our model church because it is the first time we see what Jesus meant when He said "I will build My church" (Matt. 16:18). The sum total of Christ's ministry—His death, burial, resurrection and post-resurrection teachings—culminated in the establishment of the church at Jerusalem, as this diagram illustrates:

FIGURE 1.1

THE DEVELOPMENT OF THE FIRST CHURCH

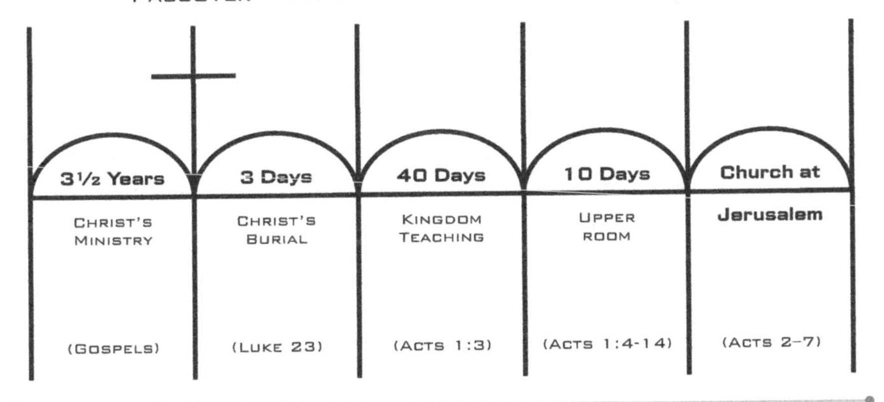

The church was inaugurated with a powerful and intense period of prayer in the Upper Room. This is the beginning of the church that Christ first built, so it becomes important to every church builder.

The true SC builder is Christ, and He has given us glimpses of His church throughout the book of Acts. The SC is patterned after the model seen in Acts and other snapshots throughout the New Testament of what church should look like. As a church builder, I have this church in mind when I lead, preach, teach and cast vision for our church. I am not double-minded or moving three steps forward and two steps back every time I cast vision or make a decision. I move forward with confidence, because I have a solid model and strategy from Scripture. This is the church Christ built; therefore, this is the same mark I am going to try to hit with our church.

THE DEFINITION OF "STRATEGY"

Now that we have a general idea, a picture of what we are shooting for when we think of the SC, the next step is to have a plan, or strategy, to get there. So what is a strategy? The word "strategy" means the art or science of leading. It originated as a military term, coined in 1810, and comes from the Greek word *strategia*, which means "of the general." *Strategos* is a leader or commander, a chief person. Strategy, then, is the means by which objectives are consciously and systematically pursued and obtained over time.

A church cannot become a strategic one without a strategic-thinking leader. The leader, therefore, must be a strategist. Strategists have a unique perspective, a style of thinking different from most people, and an intense implementation system. Brunelleschi had a unique perspective that allowed him to find ways of overcoming obstacles so that the vision could be met. He also introduced the technique of linear perspective in art, which allowed pictures to give the illusion of being three dimensional. Beforehand, drawings were done in one dimension. Now, there were depth and layers. This idea revolutionized not only art but also the way we see things. Strategists have a way of seeing the world in a different way and motivating others to alter their perspective to match that of the strategist.

There is an identifiable difference between today's pastor and today's pastor-strategist. Pastors and pastoral teams are trained in and focused on pastoring people, not on strategies. Please be assured that I value pastoring people; I value the shepherd's heart and the shepherd's work. I'm not throwing that out at all. I am seeking balance. Along with pastoring people, the pastor-leader is called to lead, cast vision, set a course, manage the vision movement forward, and rally teams of people to fulfill the vision.

A baseball manager has a similar challenge. He or she has to not only focus the team's energy on winning ball games but also develop the individual players. Joe Torre, manager of the New York Yankees from 1996 to 2007, is one of the most successful managers in baseball history because he was able to strike the balance between "shepherding" his players and rallying them to the vision, which was winning championships.

He was not much for long, motivating speeches right before a game. The majority of his coaching and motivating was constant, one-on-one interaction with the players. He studied the body language of each player, he knew what made each of them frustrated and what made each of them excited, and he always knew the current condition of his players. Therefore he knew when to drop the right word at the right moment to give each of his players the extra boost of confidence he needed.

Torre had a goal: to win championships. And his primary strategy for getting there was to know his players and make sure they also knew what the goal was. After those pieces were in place, they moved forward. In every game and at every inning, he constantly kept his players focused ahead. He didn't let them stew over past mistakes. Instead he focused them on the future, on getting better for the next game.

While manager of the New York Yankees, the team won four World Series titles, and they did it because Torre was a strategic leader who knew his players and rallied them to the goal.

It's possible for us to do likewise. We can meet our goal of becoming a thriving SC by being leaders who pastor and shepherd the people, constantly knowing the state of the flock and then utilizing that awareness to know what to say and do to unite them to the vision. Today's SC leader must balance being a pastor-shepherd and a leader-strategist.

The Nine Components of Strategic Leadership

The pastor as strategist not only has to know the nine components that are part of strategic leadership but also put them into action.

1. Strategy

You the leader must be skilled in developing a strategy. You are the one who will answer the important questions of what is to be done, for whom it is to be done and how to excel at the work. You must know and implement the plan and process and establish organizational structure, allocate resources and communicate vision. You need to see and build a church for the present day and culture and also build with the future in mind. Because you believe that great churches can and will be built, you construct your church with wisdom, upon biblical principles, to win people to Christ and then turn those converts into disciples.

2. Analysis

You the leader know the state of your church spiritually and organizationally. You carefully consider demographics, various strengths and weaknesses, changes in leadership, state of church programs, growth momentum and staff changes. You determine the overall atmosphere and culture of the church. And you recognize the internal strengths and weaknesses as well as external opportunities and threats.

I have learned over the years that you cannot make strategic decisions without intelligent information. There have been many times that I have sensed a need for adjustments in our church strategies, but I knew that my gut-sense needed to be validated with objective analysis. This key leadership principle has allowed our leadership team to make wise decisions in turbulent times.

Over the past few years, we have worked hard to discern the new challenges we face due to the volatile economic climate in our country. I knew that our previous approach to facilities needed to be reviewed and that we might have to change our strategy from owning assets to a leaner strategy of leasing facilities. We developed a team of key church leaders and outside business consultants who had considerable experience and skill in real estate. Then we began a course of action to gather information in order to make intelligent decisions. This process, although laborious, pointed us in the right direction of releasing critical assets to further advance vision. Winston Churchill, one of my favorite strategists, said, "However beautiful the strategy, one should occasionally look at the results." As you face challenges, make sure to take the time to gather the proper information before making decisions that will change the course of your future.

3. Vision

You the leader define the biblical target intended for the future, the church's fundamental objective, why the church has a purpose. Paint a vivid, clear picture of the thing you are seeking to build. It is imperative that the vision you can see in your mind is understandable and contagious. If others do not catch the vision, it simply becomes a fantasy or, at best, a frustrated dream. I have been challenged in recent years to simplify all that I communicate so that all who hear me have the best chance of retaining the message communicated.

Recently, our leadership team at City Bible Church went to great lengths to simplify our vision, mission and values so that every member of our church would know what we are building, why we exist and who we are. Let me give you an example. Our previous mission statement was, "We exist to build fully devoted followers of Christ, who in turn are reaching out and impacting their communities, cities, and nations for the Kingdom of God." Pretty impressive? I thought so too, but it's not very memorable. It contained the critical components of why we existed, but it wasn't really easy to remember or repeat. So we changed it to read, "Live like Jesus. Share His Love." Simple, clear, contagious and compelling. It contains the great commandment and the great commission in just six words. In a matter of months, the entire church has been energized to fulfill this mission. This is how you add clarity to the thing you are seeking to build.

4. THINKING

Your thinking must be of the kind that is based upon the core values and beliefs that you the leader hold as convictions, causing you to think in a specific way about everything involved with your strategy. Such thinking will make you aware that specific actions must be taken to close the gap from idea to reality. Such thinking is ahead of the curve and anticipates all circumstances and problems. Thinking without clear vision and a plan for getting there is not strategic and will cause detours, delays or stagnation.

5. PLANNING

As a strategic leader, you need to become an expert at planning. You define the strategy and direction and make difficult decisions in order to achieve the goals. This calls for building team communication and team discussion about where you are going and how you all will achieve the strategy.

6. DIRECTION

To achieve your strategy, you assess, analyze and then set the direction in order to achieve the strategy. You are the one who must choose models, teams, values and methods, and it is you who determines the pace of forward movement. Once you determine the direction, those you work with can move ahead to design, align and build the SC.

You the leader should have regular time set aside to think strategically. This requires clearing your schedule and allowing ample time for prayer and meditation regarding important decisions you are facing. I have built time into my regular routine to assess the major decisions I face. I don't allow other meetings, projects or appointments to invade this critical time of assessing the strategic direction. Most of my best decisions have come out of this special time where I was able to devote hours of prayer and meditation to the subject at hand. If you don't have this regular time in your routine, today is a great day to start.

7. Culture

The SC creates a learned and shared pattern of thought and behavioral characteristics within the group of people being led. The beliefs, morals, habits and values of the group you lead all combine to become the spiritual DNA and definable spiritual culture of the church.

8. Execution

You need to learn the art of linking strategy to operations and synchronizing people and their various contributions to the goal. You will have to discipline yourself to systematically process everything, rigorously discussing the hows and whats, always questioning, tenaciously following through and ensuring accountability. This may be one of the most difficult tasks that you face.

9. Team

You the leader should become an expert at leading a team of team leaders. No single leader can provide the full extent of leadership required in any local church to be strategic and successful. Effective leadership requires bringing together and blending all the talents and types of individual leaders into one dynamic, unified team. You the lead pastor are directly responsible for motivating, empowering and casting vision, but it takes a team of leaders to become strategic with attention to details and being efficient, careful and organized.

It's all about teams! Each team leader must be a champion of the team being led and must master the art of listening, developing empathy and the ability to come up with win-win solutions. You will build best by partnering, collaborating, cross-pollinating and forming coalitions for the good of the cause. With the other components of strategic leadership in place, you and the leadership team can develop a strategic quality in the team that will be effective. (Because team leadership is so important, we'll spend more time talking about teams in chapter 6.)

LEADERSHIP WITH INTEGRITY

Along with exhibiting the nine components of strategic leadership, you must also pay close attention to your character. In today's world—and in the church—people are looking for leaders with integrity. They want to trust leaders who are honest, self-confident and loyal to principles. Integrity trumps skill every time. It is at the core of every action, attitude and thought. Remember that our model church builder is Christ, and He has incorruptible integrity and character. When we lead with integrity, we imitate Christ and, therefore, we are building Christlikeness in our church. Our character deeply influences the church culture. If your character is sound, then the same flavor will be in your church. If integrity is lacking, then it will also be lacking in the church. Yes, be a compelling preacher and be skilled with your gift. But the bottom line is that your character level is more important than your skill level.

A few years ago I heard a story about Richard Wurmbrand. This Romanian Christian minister of Jewish descent publicly denounced communism and said that it was not compatible with Christianity. Due to his unwillingness to compromise his convictions, he experienced imprisonment and repeated torture for his beliefs. Despite his almost unbearable hardships, he never made a negative statement about those who persecuted him. In fact, he was known to pray for each communist guard on a daily basis.

At one point during Wurmbrand's imprisonment, one of the other prisoners confronted him in the middle of the prison compound. He said that the way Wurmbrand had been imprisoned and tortured proved that there was no God. Wurmbrand is said to have quietly responded, "If I can show you God, would you then believe?" The man retorted, "Of course, but look at you, look at us! You can't show me God."

Wurmbrand looked at his fellow prisoner and said, "God is like me." Instantly the man fell to his knees and gave his life to Jesus.

Leaders need to have Wurmbrand's type of unbending integrity. We also need to complement our character by developing resiliency. Learning how to recover from setbacks, take risks, be willing to fail, admit mistakes, learn from mistakes and move on is a vital leadership quality. How do you handle disappointments? Do you bounce back or do you beat yourself up and refuse to try again? The great inventor Thomas Edison once said, "Many of life's failures are experienced by people who did not realize how close they were to success when they gave up." Strategic leaders are committed to the goal and do not abandon it until they see it achieved.

Models of Various Churches

Although the blueprint for the strategic church can be drawn from the Bible, we would never know that from the many different church models that are in operation today. Even today, there are churches that hold the same doctrine, but the way they present the gospel or the way they structure their corporate worship services is different. There are also differences in where services are held: one church might be a multisite church while another operates only a single site. Or maybe the church meets for each service in a different house instead of one central location.

To pose afresh the question of church models suggests a self-critical awareness that we are practitioners of a particular model that may not be the only one or the best one and that other church models are indeed worth considering. Church models must not be dictated by cultural reality, but they must be voiced and practiced in ways that take careful account of the particular time and circumstance into which God's people are called. I have found at least 18 twenty-first-century church models that are discernable and definable.

Evangelical Church

The Evangelical church, or Protestant Christian movement, began in Great Britain in the 1730s and gained popularity in the United States during the Great Awakening of the eighteenth and nineteenth centuries. Its key elements included the need for personal conversion, or being born again; actively expressing and sharing the gospel; a high regard for biblical authority, especially biblical inerrancy; and an emphasis on teachings that proclaim the saving death of the Son of God, Jesus Christ.

Pentecostal Church

The Pentecostal movement is a child of the Holiness movement, which in turn is an offspring of Methodism. The period between 1901 and 1906 marked the beginning of this movement that had a theological division with the Holiness movement over the evidence required to prove that one had been baptized in the Holy Spirit. The 1906 outpouring of the Spirit with the evidence of tongues in Los Angeles marked the beginning of the modern Pentecostal churches. The groups that grew from this included the Assemblies of God, the Church of God, the Church of God in Christ, the New Testament Church of God, and the International Church of the Foursquare Gospel.

Latter Rain Church

Latter Rain, also known as the New Order, had its origin in the 1940s, with one of its great outpourings being the 1948 revival at the North Battleford Church in Saskatchewan, Canada. The revival outpouring of the Spirit continued from 1948 to 1960 and was called the Latter Rain. This Latter Rain movement established a new dimension of praise and worship where the sacrifice of praise included the lifting of hands and spontaneous singing of free praise. It emphasized relational networks over organizational structure and was rejected by classical Pentecostal denominations.

Restoration Church

The restoration church model is based on the belief that God is restoring the church to the New Testament order and position as seen in the book of Acts. It maintains that the church has gone through a decline and is now being restored to its full glory. Restoration churches are those that implement the worship model of the Tabernacle of David, the church structure with elders, and a belief and practice of the fivefold ministry (apostle, prophet, evangelist, pastor and teacher—mentioned in Ephesians 4:11-12). In addition to the Tabernacle of David, they espouse the power of the Holy Spirit, healings, church government, worship, laying on of hands, and prophecy.

Word of Faith Church

Although who exactly set the major doctrines of the Word of Faith movement may be disputed (some believe the doctrines derived from the teachings of E. W. Kenyon, while others believe Kenneth Hagin's teachings were foundational), the Word of Faith church has classic Pentecostalism and healing revivalism in its roots. Its five central doctrines are revelation knowledge, identification, faith, healing and prosperity. Also central to the church is the "positive confession" doctrine, widely known as the "name it, claim it" faith position. In "Jesus Appears to Me," the first chapter in his book *How to Write Your Own Ticket with God,* Hagin describes the formula that Jesus gave him for receiving whatever one needs from God, a formula he must share with all people: "Say it, do it, receive it, tell it."

The Word of Faith church numbers in the hundreds and has many great churches of influence and balanced truth.

Charismatic Church

The Charismatic model is an international, cross-denominational, nondenominational Christian movement, in which individual historical mainline congregations adapt beliefs and practices similar to Pentecostals. The baptism of the Holy Spirit is the main doctrine of the Charismatic church. This movement has been criticized by theologians for its lack of biblical depth, its emphasis on private revelation, leaders with faulty character, and undue importance given to the manifestation of signs, wonders and healings. Overall, this movement has had an astounding positive effect on mainline churches, with lasting fruit and positive impact.

New Apostolic Church

The New Apostolic church model is largely associated with the Pentecostal and Charismatic movements. Its main doctrine is based on the belief that God is restoring the governing church offices of prophet and apostle. Some believe that this is leading to the New Apostolic Reformation. In this model, spiritual warfare, spiritual mapping, territorial warfare, city reaching, and prophetic ministry are emphasized.

House Church

The house church is a largely hidden yet growing phenomenon that is changing the face of Christianity in the West and is profoundly affecting the way in which Christians are choosing to practice their faith. Disillusioned by the lack of New Testament realities, by abusive authority, and by spreading apostasy within large segments of institutionalized Christianity, thousands of Christians across Australia, Canada, New Zealand, the United Kingdom and the United States are gathering in homes to experience the simplicity of Christianity. Surveys estimate that 6 to 12 million people in the United States attend house churches. In their research, the Barna Group found that 9 percent of American adults attend house churches.

Revival Culture Church

The revival culture church model focuses on keeping a perpetual revival culture in the church, because, according to this model, revival is what normal Christianity should essentially look like. These churches enter into revival seasons and then structure themselves around the atmosphere engendered by the revival. Followers of this model actively pursue an atmosphere of the supernatural and emphasize healings, miracles, gifts of the Spirit, and Holy Spirit activity. It is a movement of churches without a headquarters or a specific leading church in charge of the group.

SEEKER FRIENDLY CHURCH

The seeker friendly church is a model that seeks to connect to the present generation by adjusting how church is conducted and modifying the communication of the gospel message in order to reach the unsaved and unchurched. Participants in this movement believe the unchurched are not rejecting Christ but are rejecting stale and unappetizing forms of church, disconnected methodology, and an out-of-step-with-culture church.

G12 CHURCH

The G12 church model, developed by Pastor César Castellanos of Bogotá, Colombia, has at its foundation the belief that Christians reach the world for Christ by following Jesus' example: every Christian disciples 12 people, who in turn will disciple 12 people. The main steps of the strategy are (1) win—evangelize to reach nonbelievers; (2) consolidate—new disciples attend an Encounter with God retreat; (3) disciple—new disciples are trained to lead others; and (4) send—new leaders start new groups of 12.

MISSIONAL CHURCH

The missional church model is not, strictly speaking, the church; rather, the church is the messenger, the vehicle and the pipeline that takes God's mission into the world. The goal and purpose of this model is to mobilize every believer and every person who becomes a disciple or agent of the kingdom of God to carry the God-mission into every sphere of life. In effect, we all are missionaries sent into a non-Christian culture.

EMERGING CHURCH

The emerging-church model describes a renewal movement of existing churches seeking to contextualize Christianity for a postmodern generation. It holds that biblical fundamentalism is narrow and out of date and must be replaced by new postmodernism. Because postmodernism rejects universal absolutes, it is difficult to define and enforce truth, because the individual constantly redefines meaning.

Vintage Church

The vintage church model begins by focusing on the person and work of Jesus and moves to exploring the confessional, experiential and missional aspects of church. The Vintage model takes timeless truths from Scripture and blends them with aspects of contemporary culture in order to reach the current generation. It emphasizes the church as an organic, authentic community, not a building.

Transfusional Church

Many churches attempt a transition in order to become something different as a church. Transition implies modifying a model or a system, but structural and mechanical changes alone do not transform, or change, a church at its core. True change involves a transfusion of DNA at the church's core. The transfusional church retrains its leaders so that the DNA of discipleship is at the core. Leaders are encouraged to train and release their disciples to replicate the principle, and thus a transfusion of discipleship DNA takes place.

Multisite Church

The multisite church model is one church that meets at multiple locations, expanding geographically and demographically beyond otherwise set limitations. There are now an estimated 3,000 multisite churches in 46 American states and 6 Canadian provinces. Two-thirds of multisite churches are denominationally connected. One in three added a campus through a merge with an existing congregation or acquisition of a site from a recently closed congregation. Video church, digital church, extension sites, video café, multiple campuses, and satellite ministries all play into this way of doing church. Some multisite churches are now facilitating house churches by using the same idea as a campus church, where the house is the campus. Multisite churches have a 90 percent success rate for church growth.

Internet Church

The Internet church is a community of people using the Internet and social media to develop spiritual relationship. Participants may have abandoned the local church because they dislike a church government structure or traveling to a brick and mortar church is inconvenient, but they still want to be part of a spiritual community. People can tune in to a video stream of a worship service and on occasion connect with a pastor via phone conversation. All other communication, however, is done mostly through social media, discussion boards in the video stream interface, websites, blogs and other similar electronic modes. The Internet church is a fairly new and emerging way of doing church. It attracts mostly those in the 18- to 22-year-old range who come from Protestant backgrounds.

Contemporary Relevant Church

The contemporary relevant church model is based on a movement that strives to create a leader who will build a church for people who don't like church—a church nonbelievers love to attend. The goal of contemporary relevant church leaders is to influence leaders to rethink the way they do church. Rather than compromise, they seek to update today's church for today's world. The core beliefs of Christ's redemptive work, discipleship, authenticity, missions and social justice are major items on their agenda. They work with various styles of worship, evangelism, sermon communication, and connecting people by using today's technology. They also believe that anything edgy can become distasteful, and creativity can result in a gimmick. There is a strong push back toward exegetical preaching through the books of the Bible, expository sermons, emphasizing theology and using creeds.

The Challenge Before Us

Now we see our challenge! Most leaders will use pieces from the various models just described. This is obviously well and good—if the foundation and core values of what you see as a pastor-leader are clear. Future stability hinges on building upon what is unchangeable, nonnegotiable and, clearly, your vision. Thus, we need a blueprint on the drawing table to which we can always refer:

The strategic church is focused on a biblical blueprint and has an intentional design and clarity of purpose that builds an impacting, vibrant and enduring church.

With this framework in mind, let's unpack the details of that blueprint and identify the various components of the SC that you, the strategic leader, can build into your church.

Strategic Vision

A vision-driven church is indeed a strategic church fulfilling a very clear and articulated vision. The vision principle is core to building a strategic leadership team and a strategic church. Casting and managing vision is one of the greatest challenges for all lead pastors and all leaders who recast vision to the teams they lead. Within the context of the church heritage, history, spiritual journey, age, culture and demographics, the vision must be grasped, processed, established, guarded, implemented and balanced. Vision is what brings passion, and the leader must be the first owner of both vision and passion. When people sense the leader's personal commitment, they will willingly follow.

When I planted our church in Eugene, Oregon, I cast vision differently from when I returned to a church that had been going 40 years and already had fulfilled many parts of its vision. When we started the church, the vision was Vision 101, the basics of what a church should be according to the church founder, Jesus, and according to the church builder, the apostle Paul. I cast vision from Matthew 16:16-18, the "I will build My church" passage. This vision was clear and basic and one on which we built the church vision. In this Vision 101 series, I taught messages on what the church is; who the builder is; how to build with perspective and balance; building with the keys, with unity, with Jesus in the church and with forgiveness; the Holy Spirit; and building a vision to confront darkness and impact our community. Later, I added more specific pieces to the vision: a house of prayer and worship, a place for relationship and ministry development, gifts recognized and respected, global missions, church planting, city reaching, and more.

But the foundation of the vision was not made of things I wanted to do or things I could see. The foundation was formed with this question in mind: What kind of church does Jesus want to build? When I became lead pastor of a 40-year-old church, I built upon the foundation already there because it was biblical and right. They had a Matthew 16:16-18 foundation and they had many pieces already in place: global missions, church planting, and ministry development. I then conveyed new ideas to update the vision, bringing new life and fresh faith to see it happen. This also added new ways to enlarge the vision and brought additional pieces to the already biblical picture. I didn't start over. I built upon the current vision, and now it is deeper and wider than ever. I did need to challenge the status quo, believing what John D. Rockefeller said: "An organization is a system, with a logic of its own, and all the weight of tradition and inertia. The deck is stacked in favor of the tried and proven way of doing things and against the taking of risks and striking out in new directions."[1]

The vision leader is a vision builder. A vision builder is a person who highly regards, respects and esteems God, His Word and His principles. That means the builder places high value on what God values and builds according to God's plan without wavering. A builder uses the architect's drawings to guide what he or she builds. For us, the architect is Jesus, and the blueprint is the Bible. We start with the Word of God, not with our desires, ideas, creativity, culture or people. We must first see vision as a biblical guide for the churches we are building. Vision is the art of seeing God's great plans.

SEEING THE TARGET

What is the church Jesus desires to build? It is a New Testament church, or strategic church, as first seen in the book of Acts and developed throughout the New Testament Epistles (see chapter 1 to review the characteristics of a strategic church). We are on safe ground when we build according to the principles clearly given us in the book of Acts and the New Testament. Once we see the goal, we are on our way to a great future.

In the poem *Paracelsus*, Robert Browning tells the story of a man who, at one point, is traveling toward a city that is surrounded by a swirling mist. The man thinks he must have taken the wrong road and lost his way, but then the mist opens and for an instant he glimpses the towers of the city in the distance: "So long the city I desired to reach lay hid, when suddenly its spires afar flashed through the circling clouds; you may conceive my transport. Soon the vapours closed again but I had seen the city." Just a glimpse of the city gives the man the strength and the fortitude to press forward.

Seeing and grasping the vision is so important to living and building well. In Habakkuk 2:2-3, the Lord gives these instructions to Habakkuk: "Write the vision and make it plain on tablets, that he may run who reads it. For the vision is yet for an appointed time; but at the end it will speak, and it will not lie. Though it tarries, wait for it; because it will surely come, it will not tarry." The vision is something far off, something in the future. But it needs to be recorded now so that you can remind yourself daily of what you are aiming at, why you are aiming at it, and what you need to do to get there.

The vision we need is rooted in the eternal purposes of God and passed on to each generation. It is a comprehensive vision that can't be fulfilled in one lifetime and can't be fulfilled by one person. When I teach on vision, I use a simple diagram that shows the important ingredients of a comprehensive vision:

FIGURE 2.1
A HOUSE CALLED VISION

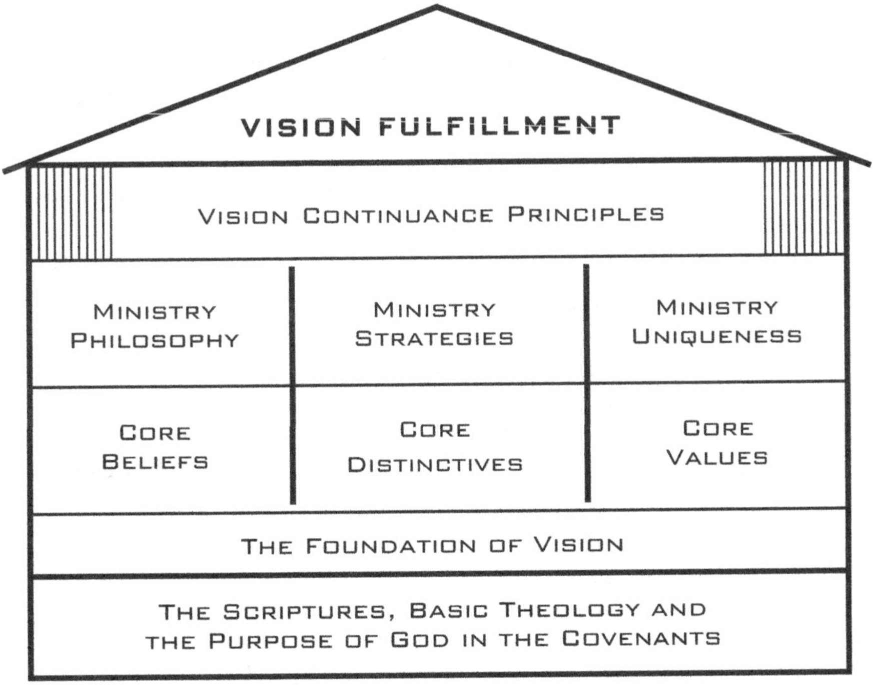

VISION FULFILLMENT

VISION CONTINUANCE PRINCIPLES

MINISTRY PHILOSOPHY	MINISTRY STRATEGIES	MINISTRY UNIQUENESS
CORE BELIEFS	CORE DISTINCTIVES	CORE VALUES

THE FOUNDATION OF VISION

THE SCRIPTURES, BASIC THEOLOGY AND THE PURPOSE OF GOD IN THE COVENANTS

Vision Components

Let's break down the components of a house called vision:

- *Purpose of God/foundation of vision*—God's plan is progressive, and it continues throughout the ages. The kingdom of God is the purpose, and the church is the divine vehicle to achieve that purpose. I believe the church will reap a harvest of souls from every nation and people group prior to Christ's Second Coming. The church is the final instrument of God that will reveal God's wisdom and glory to this world.

- *Core beliefs*—The core beliefs arise from the church's basic theological foundation. The foundation is grounded in our historic Protestant theology of all the basics: creation, redemption and the doctrine of the Holy Spirit. We hold strong core beliefs in the person, power and personal presence of the Holy Spirit. The Spirit is God's way of being powerfully present in our lives, our churches and our communities.

- *Core distinctives*—The core distinctives arise from the church's basic theology and beliefs found in Acts and the New Testament church. Thus these become the foundation for the development of the core distinctives.

- *Core values*—The core values are a combination of basic beliefs and distinctives and what the church deems worthy of merit. We value those things that we discern to be our convictions, our nonnegotiables, and an expression of our uniqueness. As values set vision implementation, they are clarified and confirmed by the leadership team and then owned by the congregation.

- *Ministry philosophy*—Philosophy asks the why question. It begins with a proper perspective that the Lord is the center of our lives and that the self, with all its rights and demands, has been nailed to the cross. The importance of and love for the Body of Christ overrides personal ambitions, hurts, offenses and trivial beliefs that may harm the Body.

- *Ministry strategies*—Each strategy is part of the how component. The leadership team sets a ministry strategy with a unified approach as to what and how the church will fulfill its vision. Strategies are consistent with honoring the core beliefs, core values and ministry philosophy.

- *Ministry uniqueness*—The uniqueness of your ministry is the who element. What sets your church apart in regard to geographical placement, demographics, or the specific kind of person you are seeking to reach? Each ministry has a unique time, setting and culture in which to grow its ministry. And every means possible should be used to reach every unique person in that ministry area.
- *Vision continuance principles*—The vision will continue on course if certain principles are honored continually: wise decision making, pacing, keeping the main thing the main thing, unity, communication and resources.
- *Vision fulfillment*—The vision can be fulfilled only if there is a clear vision stated with specific goals to be accomplished. The complete vision will find its ultimate fulfillment only in Christ's return. Therefore, we must set goals so that we can see and celebrate the progress toward the ultimate vision fulfillment.

Every vision leader must be able to define each of these components as the vision is being built. The vision we cast should include strong beliefs and values in a church spiritually alive with the presence of God and focused on a clear mission and purpose. The church should be willing to change in order to meet new challenges, welcome and initiate innovation, intentionally attract people of all ethnicities, and be contemporary, relevant and totally filled with Jesus and His grace, mercy and character. Vision should be cast with a spirit of faith that is confident in the greatness of God. As D. L. Moody once said, "If God be your partner, make your plans big!" Great vision is as big as our great God. When we see the future, we should look "for the blessed hope and glorious appearing of our great God and Savior Jesus Christ" (Titus 2:13).

God is a God of abundance and amazing miracles. He is a God who does great things and desires to do good things for you. We know this, but we must believe this and put that confidence into our vision. God is up to something so big, so unimaginably good, that our minds cannot contain it. What we see God doing is never as good as what we don't see. Great vision is Ephesians 3:20: "[He is] able to do exceedingly abundantly above all that we ask or think, according to the power that works in us"—exceedingly, extreme, surpassing, going beyond all the limits, more than enough, abundantly above all you are thinking! God has enough of whatever you need and much more to spare. His supply is plentiful, superabundant in quantity and superior in quality. It's unusual and overflowing. Build your vision with this in mind!

Vision Defined

Helen Keller was once asked what would be worse than being born blind. She quickly replied, "To have sight and no vision." If you ask successful people what has really helped them get where they are in life, invariably they will talk about a goal, a dream, a mission or a purpose—something that has been motivating them throughout the years to become what they have finally become. They achieve because they have a goal to accomplish.

Tragically, our world is full of what I call mundane men and women, people who see only what is immediate. They reach out only for things they can tangibly put their hands on. They go for the convenient, never looking beyond themselves and never looking at what they could be. These people lack depth because they lack vision. Mundane men and women can be found in every profession and in every walk of life. The young adult who is comfortable with the status quo has made the same choice to stay stagnant as the older professional who is content with his or her position, never wanting to budge or achieve something more than is convenient. Both lack vision and both are mundane. The poorest person in the world is not the person who doesn't have a nickel. The poorest person in the world is the person who doesn't have a vision. If you don't have a dream—a goal and a purpose in life—you're never going to become what you could become.

Vision is the art of seeing the invisible. The Hebrew word for vision is *chazon.* It is the ability to see something that does not exist as of yet. A visionary is a seer. He or she sees something becoming reality as if it were already there. God is the author of vision as it is His nature to be purposeful in everything He does. His counsel "stands forever, the plans of His heart to all generations" (Ps. 33:11). Vision connotes a gaze, a mental perception, and a contemplation with pleasure of things of the future. The Greek word for vision, *skopos,* connotes a mark on which to fix the eyes just like the goal line toward which a runner looks (see Phil. 3:13-

14). If you looked up "vision" in the English dictionary, you would find something like "the act or power of sensing with the eyes; the power of anticipation and expectation." These definitions illustrate that vision is something that one sees in the mind, dials into and shoots for, just as an archer shoots at a target.

Conceptually, vision is the ability to see into the future, to have foresight into or about something that is attainable to a person or a group. It may be defined as "a clear and precise mental portrait of a preferable future imparted by God to His chosen servants, based on an accurate understanding of God, self and circumstances."[2] For the church, vision is that which a congregation perceives by the Holy Spirit as pertaining to God's purpose for them. When they perceive it, a wave of spiritual momentum results, bringing spiritual advancement that is maintained through spiritual passions. Vision is the product of God working in us. God creates the vision, we receive it, and the vision becomes a rallying point toward which we, His chosen people, move.

VISION BASICS

Vision begins with the Word of God and a leader who knows how to build with and on the Word (see Isa. 28:13; Heb. 1:1-2). Healthy biblical vision must be biblically accurate, spiritually grasped, balanced in order to deal with the now and the future, and progressive (see Gen. 21:19; Matt. 9:29-30; 1 Cor. 1:10-16; 3:8-11; Eph. 1:18). Vision should be anchored to the rock but geared to the times. Pursuits to be relevant should never violate clear biblical commands, yet we should understand the unique setting in which vision will be implemented. The most difficult part is not just interpreting the Bible, but also interpreting the culture around you and your unique setting for the vision. Understand your place, your culture, your demographics and the dominant views of the generation with which you are dealing. Vision has to fit where *you* are, not where someone else is.

THE THREE APPROACHES TO VISION

As a vision leader, you can take different approaches in establishing the vision you see to cast:

1. *Analyst approach*—The analyst studies many different available models. For church, this may be user friendly, multisite, seeker

sensitive, contemporary relevant, miracles and power, evangelism, or whatever you can find. Study the model or models, draw from one or many, and then create your own model. You analyze and then absorb and then apply.

2. *Revelation approach*—The revelation approach is simply to follow whatever God has shown you to build while you were praying and fasting, taking a walk on the beach or doing something else. You see the vision and you know that it is a God-given vision (see Num. 12:6; Joel 2:28; Eph. 1:17). This approach may be difficult to prove and difficult to adjust because it is directly from God, according to the receiver of the revelation. There is no doubt that vision leaders need a personal Holy Spirit visitation that inspires their hearts to build their visions. The revelation approach combined with other checks and balances does seem to be what many great leaders have identified as their starting point of vision.
3. *Hermeneutical approach*—Hermeneutics is the study of the principles of interpreting the Scriptures. These principles are those of the first mention, election, covenant, Christocentric, progressive mention, comparative mention, full mention, direct statement, and so on. This is the grid by which the vision leader studies the Scriptures using correct hermeneutics in order to establish a solid biblical vision based on the purposes of God in the Scripture. What is God's plan? What is God's purpose? What is the place of the church today in God's timetable? What does the Cross mean to this vision? This is a safe and lasting way to establish a solid, biblical vision that will not be pushed into weird interpretations of Scripture that mold an unbiblical and harmful vision.

Extreme authority, extreme prosperity, extreme prophecy, extreme privileges of leaders—visions that exploit people and bring reproach on the name of Jesus are dangerous visions; this includes cultish visions that arise from extreme or improper interpretations of Scripture. Such visions require people to sacrifice everything for the vision—all their resources, their relationships, and sometimes their lives. They are extreme and harmful and so sad.

One example of a dangerous vision that comes to mind was that of the Heaven's Gate cult. Their vision was the result of extreme interpretation of Scripture. In 1997, 39 members of the cult committed suicide together, each helping another member drink a lethal concoction of barbiturates and hard alcohol. The members did this because they believed the earth was about to be "recycled" by a group of aliens. They believed that "human physical bodies are only containers (suits of clothes) for the souls" and that in order to enter the kingdom of God, they had to shed their container (body) to board the spacecraft that would take them to the "Next Level."[3] Observing an unusually bright comet, Heaven's Gate members believed the comet was a sign that the spaceship was near and their doom was inevitable. Under these conditions, they made a "willful exit of the body" and committed suicide.[4]

The people who taught this cult used Scripture and gave convincing arguments about the validity of their perspective, but they took the truth and stretched it to the extreme. Sound hermeneutics may not solve all the extremes in vision leaders, but I would dare to say that it slows down and solves some, if not all, of the problems. Jesus interpreted the Old Testament Scriptures as He taught principles and cast a vision of the kingdom of God: "beginning at Moses and all the Prophets, He expounded to them in all the Scriptures the things concerning Himself" (Luke 24:27). When we start building vision, let's do what Paul told Timothy to do: "Be diligent to present yourself approved to God, a worker who does not need to be ashamed, rightly dividing the word of truth" (2 Tim. 2:15).

If you can combine all three approaches–analysis, revelation and hermeneutics–then you will have a strong and safe approach to vision building.

Roles of the Visionary Leader

One of the main ways God provides leadership in His kingdom is through fathers. Father leadership involves the same heart attitude displayed in raising children (see 1 Thess. 2:11; Heb. 12:7-11). I have had the privilege of working with a very young leadership team composed of both single and married people.

Taking a father leadership approach is much different from a boss approach. As a father, I speak into their lives with abundant encouragement, communication, availability and love. God is, of course, the ultimate Father. He says, "I will be a Father to you, and you shall be My sons and daughters" (2 Cor. 6:18). We also see in 1 Corinthians 4:15-16 that we are to be fathers: "For though you might have ten thousand instructors in Christ, yet you do not have many fathers; for in Christ Jesus I [Paul] have begotten you through the gospel. Therefore I urge you, imitate me."

The visionary leader fulfills the role of a father in the sense that he or she brings security as his or her love is shown. This leader brings an atmosphere of warmth to the church. A good father also imparts his spirit and his mantle. This is done through training emerging leaders and passing on the lessons learned and the anointing that is in the mantle. A good father is an unwavering rock, stable in all situations. That does not mean that you don't show emotion or sensitivity, but it does mean that you stick to your principles in every situation. These characteristics of a father culminate in a final attribute: authority. A father must command authority, not only in a humble and gracious way, but also in such a way as to let the people know that he or she is leading the way on the road to the vision. Just as a referee blows a whistle, so too the leader should have the authority to make decisions that will steer the ship in the right direction.

The other role of a visionary leader is that of a coach. One coach I greatly respect is Mike Krzyzewski of the Duke men's basketball team. He has led teams to several championships and is the winningest coach in college basketball. He builds winning teams because he can instruct clearly and clarify the basics. He motivates people toward a goal and a vision, gains the respect of the team, deals with team members' different personalities and produces a sense of community in team members. He's a coach. A coach also knows how to tap momentum, and Krzyzewski has a game plan for every game. I remember sitting in on a few pregame meetings and watching how the team prepped for the game. The coaches went up to the front of the room and wrote a game plan on a whiteboard. They considered the opponent—who held the point guard position, who played post, who rebounded the best—and then they planned their attack: Start with man-on-man defense, full court press, force the guard to dribble with his left, and so on. Each game is different, so each requires a different game plan. A coach prepares for every game and has a specific strategy for that particular game. So does a visionary leader.

The visionary leader sees untapped opportunities in hidden and obscure things. Some might call this characteristic optimism. Optimism does not necessarily mean that you think everything is going to turn around, but that you see an opportunity in the seemingly routine or mundane and do something with it. Visionaries are dissatisfied with the status quo and are willing to change things in order to expand the vision. Think big. Set aside some time to imagine what could be done differently or what could be transformed to reach more. Then be contagiously enthusiastic. A visionary is so charismatic and passionate about the goal that he or she gets others excited about it and motivates them to work for it.

A visionary is able to articulate the details of the vision. He or she can see the big picture and also the little steps needed to get there, and he or she is able to put the vision and strategy into words and formulate a cohesive plan. A visionary also knows that the key to vision success is credibility. Solid integrity must be at the hub of the decision-making wheel. People will not follow a leader who they do not trust to take them where they need to go. Establish credibility with wise decisions and proven character. These are the vision basics.

VISION REALITIES

There are several facts that need to be realized about vision.

VISION DEMANDS CHANGE

Everybody is in favor of progress. It's change we hate! We get into a rhythm of doing things, and everything is running just fine; it's comfortable. But at the back of our minds, we know that something needs to change if we want to reach more, do more, be more.

I had the privilege of studying at Oral Roberts University for my master's and doctorate degrees. It is a world-class school that impacts thousands of people globally. Its founder, Oral Roberts, was a visionary. He wanted to reach millions of people with the gospel message. But it was the 1950s, and even the thought of reaching that many people was fairly outlandish. At the time, the most popular way of evangelizing large audiences was tent meetings. These meetings brought hundreds of people to Christ, but Roberts wanted to see more. In 1954, he started to film the meetings and then air them on television and radio during primetime. Immediately, letters poured in from the many people who heard the gospel and accepted Christ.

By 1957, Roberts's ministry headquarters was taking in every day a thousand letters with stories of salvation and healing. In that same year, they counted over one million salvation decisions made through their ministry. Roberts made a profound impact on the nation because he had a vision and was willing to change the way things were normally done in order to see that vision become reality. Don't be afraid to change. You won't go anywhere new if you don't adjust your course.

Vision Takes Risk

Vision usually makes some people uncomfortable. It takes a measure of risk. The respected missionary Hudson Taylor wrote, "Unless there is an element of risk in our exploits for God, there is no need for faith."[5] God expects us to take risks and trust that the enormous vision He has given us can happen when we partner with Him and take a giant leap. Vision always requires faith. In fact, vision usually requires more faith than we are comfortable with. As pastor and author Andrew Murray once said, "We have a God who delights in impossibilities."[6]

One of the biggest risks I took in ministry was moving to Eugene (Oregon) along with 18 other people to start a church. I was teaching at a Bible college and on staff at a church, and then I was stirred to leave that place of comfort, take a risk and plant a church. We left with one month's salary and a $4,000 offering. With no building, no salary and no savings, we spent the $4,000 on sound equipment and communion trays. We then became officially broke.

We met in a Holiday Inn in a small room that seated 40 people. The room was right next to the swimming pool, separated only by a large glass window facing the pool. It was all a risk. I felt like George Washington crossing the Delaware on Christmas Eve, telling his troops it was victory or death. But the risk of faith paid off and we took in $516 in our first offering. Our bills were paid. We were officially out of the boat and on the water.

Those who accomplish great things take great risks. You can't live under an umbrella of comfort and expect that it will stretch to your community without you doing anything. Throw aside your security blanket and make some gutsy moves. Life is really more fun when you take risks than when you play it safe all the time.

Vision Requires Hard Work and Sacrificial Giving

Another fact about vision that we need to understand is that vision always requires hard work and sacrificial giving. It's the duck philosophy: While it looks smooth on the top, the feet are paddling like crazy underneath the water. But when people join to do the work, so much can be accomplished.

Nehemiah led the Israelites in building an entire wall in 52 days, because "the people had a mind to work" (Neh. 4:6). Both hard work and sacrificial giving went into seeing that the vision was accomplished.

Moses' tabernacle was not an overnight project either. It required lots of hard work and sacrificial giving. But the people did it and the tabernacle was built. In fact, the people gave so much that they "were restrained from bringing, for the material they had was sufficient for all the work to be done—indeed too much" (Exod. 36:6-7)! How would you like that kind of response? Too much money, too many volunteers, too many souls saved! That is my prayer for the church!

What happened with Moses' tabernacle was indeed a miracle. Everyone was mobilized to work and sacrifice for the vision. But we must also recognize the reality that not everyone will embrace the vision at the same time. Some jump on board the moment you finish casting the vision, and some take a little while to warm up to the idea. Still others never embrace it (see Judg. 7:3). One reason for this is that vision usually unfolds progressively. Sometimes it comes "precept upon precept, line upon line" (Isa. 28:13). As the vision opens little by little, some misinterpret and misunderstand how the pieces will eventually fit together. It takes time for all the pieces of the puzzle to be fitted together to complete the picture. This is unfortunate, but it is usually how vision unfolds.

Vision Attracts Attack

Vision that is grand and God-inspired provokes the enemy to attack before the vision can become a reality. In the desert, the Israelites encountered many attacks before reaching the Promised Land. They were pursued by the Egyptians, attacked by enemies in the wilderness, deceived by the devil to construct false idols, and more. Vision has a way of drawing out the enemy. But our assurance is that Christ is with us and "no one will attack you to hurt you" (Acts 18:10).

Vision Needs Faith and Prayer

Vision can provoke an attack, but it also drives everyone to a new level of prayer. As clergyman and author E. M. Bounds wrote, "Prayer is a wonderful power placed by Almighty God in the hands of His saints, which may be used to accomplish great purposes and to achieve unusual results."[7] Our struggle is not in the flesh but in the spirit. Thus we need supernatural weapons to achieve supernatural results, "for the weapons of our warfare

are not carnal but mighty in God for pulling down strongholds" (2 Cor. 10:4). Historically, every major tragedy has been followed by an epidemic of people turning to God and bonding together in prayer. When the vision is attacked, pray. When you don't see a way to achieve the vision, pray. When you are doing well and are on pace with the vision, pray. Contend for the vision continually, and rise to a new level of prayer.

VISION REQUIRES UNITY

Vision is fulfilled by a visionary leadership who has the heart and unity of a visionary people. Unified people can do things that we have never imagined. That is why Paul pleads with the Corinthians to "speak the same thing, and that there be no divisions among [them], but that [they] be perfectly joined together in the same mind and in the same judgment" (1 Cor. 1:10). Unity takes all the individual efforts and talents and channels them to one cause that generates strong force. As Helen Keller once said, "Alone we can do so little; together we can do so much."

Let's return to the example of the Hebrews bringing their gifts to build the tabernacle. Note that "*all* the men and women whose hearts were willing" brought material to build the house (Exod. 35:29, emphasis added). Everyone participated. The result: "the people were restrained from bringing, for the material they had was *sufficient for all* the work to be done" (Exod. 36:6-7, emphasis added). When we pursue vision and the people are motivated to give to it, we need to trust in the supernatural provision of God and believe that everything we need is within our grasp as we reach out to Him in faith.

VISION TAKES SUPERNATURAL PROVISION

The vision demands change, takes risk, requires hard work and sacrificial giving, needs faith and prayer, and requires unity; and it also takes supernatural provision that only God can provide for the supernatural-sized dream.

VISION ABSOLUTES

The Lord Jesus is the builder of His church, and you as a leader are a very important absolute for Jesus to build with. The Lord desires to appear to you in a personal and powerful way. He has a vision for you to fulfill—a vision that will capture your heart.

GOD THOUGHTS

As the Lord opens your heart to His intentions and designs, He will bring you the God thought that will become your "now" word for this "now" time. "How precious also are Your thoughts to me, O God! How great is the sum of them!" says the psalmist (Ps. 139:17). God thoughts coming your way will be numerous, and they will lift you out of your own natural realm of thinking so that you can begin to think God thoughts, which will be different from your own. As God says, "My thoughts are not your thoughts, nor are your ways My ways. . . . For as the heavens are higher than the earth, so are My ways higher than your ways" (Isa. 55:8-9).

Even as you read this, God's thoughts are aimed at you like arrows zeroed in on a mark. These thoughts are in motion now and when they hit you, they will enlarge your vision capacity. I call these pivotal prophetic moments, turning points that set in motion a series of events that shape a person's future. Eyes are opened. Everything is seen differently. It's a John 9:6-7 experience: After Jesus anointed the eyes of a blind man and the man washed in the pool of Siloam, he was able to see. Jesus desires to anoint our eyes to see differently. He wants to open our eyes like He did for Paul: "Immediately there fell from his eyes something like scales, and he received his sight at once; and he arose and was baptized" (Acts 9:18).

Believe with me that the scales over your eyes are being removed, and you will see vision exactly how God wants you to see. See the vision for the now time: a vision to raise biblical churches that make biblical disciples who impact cities and regions for Christ. Have vision to see the nations God has for you and your church to connect with so that nations can be impacted for Christ. Grasp the now word to see new leaders who are already in your midst ready to be raised up, ready to join the team. Catch the now word coming to you to see your city as a place where God desires to do great and mighty things through you, the vision leader, and through the church and churches of your region. John Sculley, former CEO of Pepsi, said, "The future belongs to those who see possibilities before they become obvious." Perceive the now word to see the now generation God is moving upon to become a generation that shakes the world with the gospel.

A PERSONAL VISION

God has a vision for you to fulfill that is both biblically based and personally fitted to your gifting and the church where God has placed you. Believe Jeremiah 29:11: "For I know the thoughts that I think toward you, says the LORD, thoughts of peace and not of evil, to give you a future and a hope." You are a vision leader, one who sees the future as if the future were already here. One who is not content to live within the natural realm but determined to live in the supernatural realm. One who has ideas or concerns that others see as impossible; but you see and say, yes, it is to be (see Num. 14:6-10; Matt. 19:26). You, the vision leader, determine to overcome all obstacles and do all that is necessary to finish the vision, "being fully convinced that what He had promised He was also able to perform" (Rom. 4:21). Here is a great verse from 1 Chronicles 28:20 to believe, declare, pray and take for your life and ministry:

> Be strong and of good courage, and do it; do not fear nor be dismayed, for the LORD God—my God—will be with you. He will not leave you nor forsake you, until you have finished all the work for the service of the house of the Lord.
>
> Take charge! Take heart! Don't be anxious or get discouraged. God, my God is with you in this; he won't walk off and leave you in the lurch. He's at your side until every last detail is completed for conducting the worship of God (*THE MESSAGE*).
>
> Be strong and brave! Do it! Don't be afraid and don't panic! For the LORD God, my God, is with you. He will not leave you or abandon you before all the work for the service of the LORD's temple is finished (*NET*).

You have got to rely on the God who will not let you go. He does not relax, He won't abandon you, and He will not leave you when you are in need. E. Stanley Jones, a missionary and theologian, said, "Faith is not merely you holding on to God—it is God holding on to you." He will not let you go! You can be strong and walk confidently into your future because your God will not give you up and His face will not be turned away from you—ever (see Gen. 28:15; Deut. 31:6; Josh. 1:5; Ezra 9:9; Ps. 71:9)!

Holding the Vision

Take hold, be strong and unafraid, you must get a firm grip on the vision. To be strong and take hold is to be determined and unafraid to do what is needed to be done—to seize it and not let go (see 1 Chron. 22:13; 2 Chron. 32:7; Isa. 41:10; Hag. 2:4; Zech. 8:9). The strength to take hold of is the power of the Holy Spirit, not the might of humankind. Gideon had a word from God to go against the Midianites, but to possess the reality of that word, he had to take hold of the men God had given him. He had to determine what needed to be done and be firm in his commitment to do it. Those following him then *took hold* of what God had placed in their hands, and they finished the battle without lifting a sword (see Judg. 7:8-20).

Taking hold does not mean having superior forces but having faith in what God has given you. Taking hold does not mean superior skills but obedience to do what God has called you to do. It is " 'Not by might nor by power, but by My Spirit,' says the LORD of hosts. 'Who are you, O great mountain? Before Zerubbabel you shall become a plain! And he shall bring forth the capstone with shouts of "Grace, grace to it!" ' " (Zech. 4:6-7). The "not by might" refers to the influence we have in our hands, things that already exist. They are visible things; but to win, we will need more than what is in our hands. We will need what's in God's hands. "Not by power" means we are stretched to the limit like a bowstring. We desire to shoot arrows at far targets, but the bow is stretched to the limit. It is at that moment that the Spirit of the Lord takes over. He takes our hands and pulls the bowstring of vision back as far as it will go, to its limit, and then lets the arrow fly to hit a higher mark—a God mark—a God vision.

REGAIN STRENGTH AND TAKE AGGRESSIVE ACTION

The counsel of David to Solomon in 1 Chronicles 28:20 was to "be strong and of good courage"—to take heart and be brave—in order to take hold of the vision to build the Temple. The vision leader needs a stout heart filled with bold courage to make the entire vision a reality. Reject fear, don't panic, and trust that God is in control. The Bible is full of commands to be strong, courageous and unafraid (in addition to those mentioned above, see Pss. 3:6; 23:4; 118:6; Isa. 41:13-14; 43:1,5; 44:2). By the grace of God, the leader grows stronger and stronger and faces all challenges with an attitude to win and fulfill all the vision (see Job 17:9). "Be of good courage, and He shall strengthen your heart, all you who hope in the LORD" (Ps. 31:24; see also Pss. 27:4; 35:2). Regain your strength by hearing the voice of God; hear these words in your ear: "Only be strong and very courageous, that you may observe to do according to all the law which Moses [God's] servant commanded you; do not turn from it to the right hand or to the left, that you may prosper wherever you go" (Josh. 1:7). Be overtaken with a holy stubbornness, a righteous obstinate attitude! Be aggressive.

The opposite of aggression is passivity. A passive attitude is a dismayed one. It is demoralized, beaten down and broken because it has been so overwhelmed by obstacles that it has lost the ability to stand. When your heart is dismayed, your faith becomes like a glass that has been thrown against the ground and shattered into a million pieces. Don't be dismayed. Why? God is with you, God is fighting for you, and you will possess the land (see Josh. 1:9; 10:25). It's times like these when you need to remember who your partner is. Your partner is Yahweh, the God who is personal and with you at all times in every experience. He is with you to build you up, not to tear you down. He will be all that is necessary for your situation as the need arises (see Exod. 3:13-14). Know who your God is. The prophet Daniel wrote, "The people who know their God shall be strong, and carry out great exploits" (Dan. 11:32).

The evangelist George Müller was headed to Quebec on a boat when a dense fog moved in and delayed his journey. Müller told the captain that he must get to Quebec on time, and he started praying that God would get him there. The captain looked at Müller in disbelief and asked, "Do you realize how dense this fog is?" Müller replied, "No, my eye is not on the density of the fog but on the living God who controls every circumstance of my life."

Who is the God you are looking to? Is it the almighty Jehovah-Jireh, your provider? No mountain is insurmountable with a God of courage, a God touch that creates a new mindset of "yes, we can do this—this mountain shall be moved!" Take up your weapons of warfare and take your city; take more ground.

Live in the Faith Zone, Not the Safe Zone

The 1 Chronicles 28:20 word to vision leaders is "do it." I live in and around the kingdom of Nike sports king Phil Knight. Knight was inspired to name his company Nike after the Greek goddess of victory. According to Greek mythology, Nike led the chariots of Zeus, ruler of the Olympic pantheon in Olympus. She flew over battlefields in her gold chariot and rewarded victors with fame. When the Greeks went to battle, it was customary to say "Nike" when they won. The Nike athletic franchise was hatched with the idea to create footwear that would "lift the world's greatest athletes to new levels of mastery and achievement."[8] It was the Nike company that made the phrase "Just do it" a one-line hit all over the world. It became a call to reach for greatness and go beyond.

For spiritual leaders, "Just do it" is a God word made famous by King David's counsel to young Solomon who was faced with a vision way beyond his years and his leadership maturity. Vision must include action. Do it, execute it, and implement it. Get it out of your head and into action. This is living in the faith zone, not the safe zone. Step out, step over, and get out of the boat. The safe zones rob us of our greatest moments and memories. In their book *Great by Choice*, Jim Collins and Morten Hansen say that the greatest companies "accept, without complaint, that they face forces beyond their control, that they cannot accurately predict events, and that nothing is certain; yet they utterly reject the idea that luck, chaos, or any other external factor will determine whether they succeed or fail. . . . [They] display extreme consistency of action—consistency with values, goals, performance standards, and methods."[9]

What great companies have in common is that they act. They do it. They move into action in the face of all the stuff that stops other companies. As someone once said, "Upon the plains of hesitation are the bleached bones of countless millions, who on the threshold of victory, sat down to wait, and in waiting they died." Procrastination is not part of the strategic leader's makeup, and it doesn't build strategic churches. It is the counterproductive deterrent of actions or intentionally delaying tasks for a later time.

Vision leader, just do it! Finish what God started in your heart and keep working until the plan you designed is complete. Find a point you want to reach, move toward it, and keep moving until all the work necessary is done (see Exod. 40:33; 1 Kings 6:9-14). Put away perfectionism and tear up the overwhelming to-do list you never do. The greatest visions are yet to be. What would have happened if Michelangelo said, "I don't do ceilings," or Noah, "I don't do boats," or Moses, "I don't do rivers," or David, "I don't do giants," or Mary, "I don't do virgin births," or Paul, "I don't do letters"? Do all that God says (see Acts 13:22). Take action with the vision—today!

Strategic Church Growth

It was a dream fulfilled for me to be on the Fuller Theological Seminary campus in April 1987. I had decided to start working on my master's degree and was drawn to Fuller's program because they had excellent one-week and two-week-long intensive courses on a variety of subjects. When I arrived at the campus and busily went about finishing my last leg of registration for the first intensive on church growth, I quickly found out that I needed help getting ready for class. A perfect gentleman named Peter saw that I was having trouble doing college orientation on my own, trying to find out what to do, where to go and who to see. He kindly took me on and walked me through the whole process. He also took me to my first class, which was church growth. It was then that I realized I was with Dr. C. Peter Wagner! I was both humbled and amused.

My time at Fuller was life changing for me as a church-planting pastor. My wife and I had planted a church in Eugene, Oregon, with a team of 18 young marrieds and singles in 1981. From 1981 to 1986, we experienced slow yet steady growth. During those five years, we grew from a congregation of 18 people to 80 people, then to 120, 260, 330, and then 460 church participants. We built a new building and moved in, seeing sudden growth from 560 to 720 people in one week and from 720 to 920 people in one month. At that point, I realized that we had entered into a new realm of church, and I wasn't equipped to do church the way it needed to be done.

The classes at Fuller were my mentoring classes for this season of church growth. I read over 50 books for Church Growth I and II and countless more books for courses on leadership, partnering, and planting churches. The books and instruction helped me become a better leader and a better pastor who desired to grow a healthy church. I remember having certain pivotal breakthroughs in conceptual thought that needed to happen in order for me to lead more effectively. The first concept was that the pastor must want to grow the church and also plan to grow it if the church is to grow. I hadn't planned for growth in a real, strategic manner.

Another important principle I realized was that the pressure of taking care of the internal tasks of the church—budgets, staff, building programs, education programs, training leaders, and trouble-shooting—can dull any desire to grow the church because it causes a priority shift. Guilty! I was 100 percent guilty of this one at that time. I had become a pastor with more building, more staff, more needs and more questions, and I was being consumed. I knew I had to change or else we were doomed to plateau and be another quick-growth/quick-plateau story. As I learned from my coursework at Fuller Seminary and from several other pastors in my classes and others outside the class with whom I had developed relationships, I needed to make many adjustments.

The indispensible condition for a growing church is that it wants to grow and it is willing to pay the price for growth. I believe the price paid for growth is not nearly as expensive as the price paid for failing to grow or for leading a stagnant church. The price of growth is easily embraced when we keep in perspective the worth of a soul and the powerful influence of a growing church modeled after the New Testament in today's world. Our faith for growth is in direct proportion to vision and strategy for growth.

My experience as a church planter who had to grow, who did grow and who planted other growing churches is part of this chapter. My experience of leaving my church plant after 12 years and returning to take the lead pastor role of my sending church, which at that time was 41 years old, is also embedded in this chapter. I have worked with a young and new church and an old and mature church. I have worked with my own team chosen and trained by me, and I have also inherited someone else's team that was not chosen by me and was trained by someone else. In both situations, we needed to grow and keep growing in order to fulfill the supreme task of the great commission: Make disciples of all people and see effective multiplication of churches in receptive societies of the earth. Fulfilling this command is the ultimate purpose of every church. It should guide a church's entire mission, establish its priorities and coordinate all its attitudes.

This mandate has been my guiding star for all I do as a leader and as a pastor who is committed to grow a dynamic, healthy, Christ-exalting church. Non-growth is not an option for me. It's something I will never accept. If you will decide in your heart that a growing church is God's will and that God will grace you to grow the church as a lead pastor or part of the church leadership team, then it will grow.

In 1954, Roger Bannister made history when he was the first to run a mile in under four minutes. His record is particularly interesting because the scientists and the sports physiologists of the day said it could not be done. They said that the human body was not made to go that fast and that the runner's heart would explode. Bannister determined that he could run a mile in under four minutes and he did so, to the disbelief of many in the scientific community. What is perhaps even more remarkable is that during the year following Bannister's record, 33 people broke the four-minute mile. The next year, over 200 people did it! What happened was that people determined and made a choice that it was possible to break a record—to do what scientists said was physically impossible—and they did it.

It is possible to see record-breaking growth! But you need to have a conviction that growth is biblical and the determination to see it happen. I lead a multisite, multicultural and multigenerational church with a team of leaders who desire to grow this church and multiply our growth in the metro area and beyond. We have a vision and we have seen this vision fulfilled. However, there is still more to do and more records to break.

SEVEN CONVICTIONS OF MINISTRY

I have determined to build a culture of growth into the leaders I work with and the congregation I lead. I have settled on several ministry convictions that help us to lead with clarity and consistency. I urge you as leader to establish these convictions for strategic church growth of your own:

1. We will give our lives to starting churches, growing churches and multiplying growing churches nationally and internationally.
2. God wants His church to grow, He wants the church we lead to grow, and no growth is unacceptable.
3. Building a culture of church growth is a God-pleasing and God-ordained attitude.
4. Leading a growing church is a decision, a conviction and a commitment to break through all necessary obstacles with hard work, prayer and strategy.

5. As leaders, we will deal with all seasons of church growth—planned growth, surprising growth, thriving growth, warfare growth and plateaus and declines in growth.
6. Declining or dying churches can be revived and can experience a turnaround season.
7. God has opened a door of opportunity for a great season of church growth.

The seventh conviction is especially important, and it *is* biblical. First Corinthians 16:9 in *THE MESSAGE* describes it this way: "A huge door of opportunity for good work has opened up here." God has set an open door in front of us. Revelation 3:8 declares, "See, I [God] have set before you an open door, and no one can shut it." Mark it, pay special attention to it, and enter that door of opportunity—God has opened it.

Deciding to Believe for Growth

The decision to believe that growth is God's will both for you and your church is a vital first step. God desires that we be fruitful. When Isaac blessed Jacob, he said, "May God Almighty bless you, and make you fruitful and multiply you, that you may be an assembly of peoples" (Gen. 28:3). Fruitfulness is a sign of life and a source of deep satisfaction. When a gardener plants a seed, he or she expects to grow a vineyard. God has called us to watch over His vineyard, the church, and it is to be fruitful.

In the first chapter of Genesis, God the Almighty One, by His omnipotent power and through His spoken word and the moving of the Holy Spirit, made creation happen. Creation was not formed out of preexisting materials but made out of nothing. "The earth was without form, and void"—it was in a state of confusion and emptiness (Gen. 1:2). Then the Spirit of God moved, hovering over the waters. Then God said, willed, decreed, appointed, and there was an immediate result. He said let there be, and it was so. God can do the same for your church right now. He can speak and move, even if the church is without form and void, and He can make it fruitful.

On the third day of creation, God said, "Let the earth bring forth" (Gen. 1:11). This is not the same as Genesis 1:1-10 when God calls creation forth. Now God says, "Earth bring forth." He didn't call greenery into existence; He made it grow. He established a process of gradual and responsible growth. The divine principle was set in place—the principle of growth: the seed, the fruit, the reproduction after its own kind and, finally, a beautiful and fruitful garden. God can call growth forth with a miraculous move of the Holy Spirit, or He can grace us to bring it forth by a gradual process of seeding, watering, weeding and patience. We can pray for the miracle, but we should work for the gradual growth. You don't need to grow something exotic or a designer fruit or some sort of super tree that produces something only a few select, special people can grow. You do however need to be fruitful.

RESPONSIBLE GROWTH

The growth that God desires for us is, first, fruit that remains, is lasting and will endure from generation to generation. Every leader's vision should be to plant a spiritual legacy, a fruit tree that perpetually bears fruit. Fruit that remains is fruit grown from a healthy tree that is the product of planning, pruning, wisdom and forethought. Jesus clearly tells us that we are commissioned to be and grow healthy lives: "You have not chosen Me, but I have chosen you and I have appointed you [I have planted you], that you might go and bear fruit and keep on bearing, and that your fruit may be lasting [that it may remain, abide], so that whatever you ask the Father in My Name [as presenting all that I AM], He may give it to you" (John 15:16, *AMP*). Our church—our vineyard—can and should be of the highest quality.

Growth that continues to grow is a growth that is made possible because the leader is alive in Christ, filled with Holy Spirit virtue, has integrity of motivation and leads righteously. It requires all the ingredients of a healthy, growing church: a dynamic biblical vision, a pipeline of leaders, thinking strategically, discipling believers, receiving abundant resources, making wise decisions, practicing deep prayer, worshiping with sincerity, and reaching the city. All these are important ingredients that make up growth that remains.

The leader may face a *no-fruit church,* one that is disconnected from the divine source. It is a striving, comparing and tired church. This is the church described by Jesus in a parable: "A certain man had a fig tree planted in his vineyard, and he came seeking fruit on it and found none. Then he said to the keeper of his vineyard, 'Look, for three years I have come seeking fruit on this fig tree and find none. Cut it down; why does it use up the ground?' " (Luke 13:6-7). This tree had zero fruit. It missed its divine purpose, which was to be fruitful and multiply. This is not God's plan for our churches.

You might face a *bad-fruit church,* one that is producing fruit, but the fruit is not usable or healthy. An example of this type of church comes from Jesus' teaching: "For a good tree does not bear bad fruit, nor does a bad tree bear good fruit. For every tree is known by its own fruit. For men do not gather figs from thorns, nor do they gather grapes from a bramble bush" (Luke 6:43-44). Compromised principles, destroyed values, a breakdown of spiritual virtues, and something lost can all contribute to production of bad fruit.

The leader can also face a *some-fruit church,* one that has some life and some fruit but that is not making an impact and is not where you want it to be. It's trapped with some old paradigms, some barriers, a ceiling or a lid of resistance that is limiting its fruit bearing. The apostle Paul mentions this fruit-producing tendency, saying to the Romans that he "often planned to come to [them] (but was hindered until now), that [he] might have some fruit among [them] also, just as among the other Gentiles" (Rom. 1:13). He intended to visit that church for the express purpose of bearing fruit there, but he was hindered. There was some cap that limited his ability to get there and produce fruit. They were trapped in a some-fruit stage.

There is also the *more-fruit church,* one that has been through some seasons of pruning of the dead wood and is now in a new season of growth. As leaders, we should desire our more-fruit churches to become much-more-fruit churches by a new grace for multiplication that lifts the lid off our growth. Believe for this growth! Have a renewed heart of faith and vision. We can believe the Mark 4:20 principle that those who hear the Word accept it and bear fruit, "some thirtyfold, some sixty, and some a hundred." At whatever stage you are, believe for increase and new growth, both by the power of the supernatural and the power of gradual growth.

GROWTH IS GOD'S PLAN

Every church can and should grow. The church does not exist for itself but for the world. It should be a place of growth, power and excitement, a place God ordained to become a force in the earth. Every church should see its region impacted, evidenced by thousands of people coming to Christ to do great things for God that influence thousands more toward God. One author describes church growth this way:

> Growth is the characteristic of the churches of the New Testament. Churches in the first century grew in all kinds of circumstances: in times of great revival and renewal (Acts 2:41), in periods of tension and persecution (Acts 4:4), in periods of inner church problems (Acts 5:14; 6:1,7), in times of civil and religious peace (Acts 9:31), as a result of spontaneous witnessing (Acts 11:19-21), as a consequence of organized teaching (Acts 11:22-26), when the church is built up strong (Acts 16:5), and as a result of planned efforts (Acts 19:10,20).[1]

Some churches explode in size like the New Testament church did, while others go through a more gradual growth process. It's important to remember that regardless of the growth rate, Christ builds the church. As one of the greatest church builders points out, the church is "built on the foundation of the apostles and prophets, Jesus Christ Himself being the chief cornerstone, in whom the whole building, being fitted together, *grows into* a holy temple in the Lord" (Eph. 2:20-21, emphasis added). Some churches are not ready for sudden, exponential growth. They need the right organization and infrastructure in order to be able to meet the needs of a great influx of people. Just like a baby is not born one day and then becomes a full-grown adult the next day, a church needs time to put a good structure in place, develop leaders and learn from mistakes so that they can be ready for the growth when it comes.

Different Kinds of Growth

Numerical Growth

A church with numerical growth experiences increases of people by addition and by multiplication—by all means of people growth: biological, transfer and conversion. *Biological growth* happens when current members of the church encourage other family members to join the church. Some believers come to the church from another church. This is considered *transfer growth*. Then there is *conversion growth*. This is one of the most exciting types of growth because it encourages the church's mission of seeing people turn their lives over to Christ. Only 5 percent of all churches in America are growing at all, and their primary growth is coming through new converts. A church will always have all three types of growth, but we must contend for conversion growth.

Organic Growth

Organic growth concerns the internal structure of relationships within the local congregation. It is shown in the people's movement toward maturity, transformation and discipleship. As the congregation grows, new leaders emerge and begin entering the leadership pipeline, thus contributing to organizational growth, which is the natural development of organization in a church to perform its ministry and fulfill its mission. A church that is growing organically serves its people well because it is growing leaders who have passion and vision to meet the needs of the church; and those leaders then design ways, or structures, that will help satisfy the needs of the congregation.

Influence Growth

The expansion of the church as seen by its effects on its environment, cities, nations and the world indicates enlargement in its influence. Through outreaches, church plants and training more converts, the congregation extends into another community yet remains as one church. It eventually reaches to world growth, activating new congregations among all nations around the world. Increased influence is the result of numerical and organic growth. The lost are found, saved and discipled in the local church. As believers develop as leaders and grow spiritually, they catch the vision and heart to serve the community at large, find ways to meet the needs they see and then go outside the church building to reach more people. This is a fascinating and exciting growth process for any church, and it is a definite characteristic of the SC.

Google Growth

One of the most influential companies in the world today is Google. Chances are, you are using a Google product to read this book or you used a Google search engine to find some reviews or information about it. The company started with a couple of students who had an idea to optimize search engines in a truly innovative way. They went from 3 employees in a friend's garage to over 20,000 employees who get to work in a massive "Googleplex" in California, in a 311,000-square-foot building in

New York City, and in other offices around the world. That is certainly numerical growth.

Although Google employs thousands of people, it is as concerned about the health of each individual as it is about the company's stock portfolio, and it understands that individual development is vitally important to the success and growth of the whole company. Each employee must spend 20 percent of his or her time doing innovative thinking. They stop all other projects and just explore their own interests, sometimes finding ways of doing things better or faster. Gmail, Google News, and AdSense are just a few of the results from these thinking sessions. The Googleplex is set up for employee-to-employee interaction: There is a massive recreation center where employees can play all sorts of team sports. There's a snack room in just about every building and plenty of room for creative stimulation.

From its humble beginnings, Google has become a worldwide enterprise that puts its products in countless hands. In May 2011, Google tracked its one-billionth unique visitor to the site. Billions of people worldwide use the wide-ranging products offered by Google—from Gmail to Blogger to Picasa photo sharing to the Google+ social network. "Google" is even an official entry in the *Merriam-Webster Dictionary*! What a story of numerical growth, organic growth and influence growth. Certainly the leaders who built this company had vision and the work ethic to make it happen. How much more growth can we, with God on our side, see?

SEASONS OF NON-GROWTH

Although we all want to see church growth, the fact is that the church goes through all kinds of imaginable seasons. As a leader, you walk through those seasons with the church, and you may be tempted to get discouraged when you face seasons that challenge growth. But once you know about the non-growth seasons in the life of a church, you should be ready to confront them:

- *A season of plateau*—A church may hit a plateau, a stage at which no progress is apparent. The church attains a certain level of success, but then it levels off and stagnation sets in. Sadly, most pastors today live at this stage: Eighty percent of churches are at a plateau or are declining. Fifty percent of churches in the United

States will not add one new convert in the next two years.[2] Trade-offs have been made: spiritual passions for empty rituals, spiritual power for clever methods, spiritual life for carnal complacency, and spiritual principles for carnal creativity.

- *A season of decline*—Decline is a stage of downward progression. This is a gradual falling off from a better state. Decline is probable but not inevitable. There is a natural decline that is not bad as long as you understand it. Programs grow old and ministry systems need to change. If you don't respond properly, you will end up in stagnation.

- *A season of a dying church*—A dying church is one that is slowly fading away, eventually coming to an end. Such a church has sold out spiritual life for cultural confusion, spiritual power for counterfeit strength, truth for lies, and eternal souls for cultural comfort.

- *A season of a city demographic adjustment that affects growth*—People change geographic locations due to work, school or other life choices. Senior pastor Tim Keller wrote that "the density of the city creates the possibility of strong minority communities. Density creates diversity."[3] When demographics shift, we should see it as an opportunity to expand and reach the new group that is on its way.

- *A season of a spiritually unhealthy atmosphere, an atmosphere of division that attacks unity*—Division destroys church unity. It is forbidden in the church (see 1 Cor. 1:10); condemned in the Bible (see 1 Cor. 1:11-13,18); contrary to the desire of Christ (see John 17:21-23); and proof of a carnal spirit (see 1 Cor. 3:3).

Going through any of these seasons can be tough and can put a significant strain on leaders. Even Jesus, when He was touched by the woman with a chronic blood disease, said He felt power and virtue go out from Him (see Luke 8:46). As you continuously give and pour out your heart to the church, you might come to a place where you are spiritually drained by having to grapple with church issues. Spiritually drained leaders are emptied leaders.

SYMPTOMS OF EMPTY SPIRIT SYNDROME

Empty leaders have given everything until nothing is left and they are drained of all resources. They have reached the point of exhaustion and therefore lack the ability and strength to produce anything that brings satisfaction or fruitfulness. Some personal signs of being spiritually drained are lack of joyful anticipation for life and ministry, lack of freshness in personal prayer and worship, being quickly irritated with little things, and making negative comments from a negative attitude. Spiritually drained leaders also feel weary. They lack motivation or desire, and they don't take time to appreciate those around them on the team. Sufferers of an empty spirit know something is wrong but do not know what that something is.

These are some more symptoms of Empty Spirit Syndrome:

- *Overloaded*–You feel as if you are carrying a heavy load with a weak spirit.
- *Overtaxed*–You feel fatigue without a way to re-energize.
- *Overburdened*–You feel overburdened without the grace to cover the burdens.
- *Overworked*–You feel overworked without knowing which pieces to take away.
- *Overwhelmed*–You isolate problems only to find that they are growing faster and bigger.
- *Overcommitted*–You feel that you must solve the world's problems, but you can't even solve local problems.

When you lose your virtue or you feel that it is running low, you need to set all things aside and get it back. When I feel as if my meter is getting low, I shut myself in my study, turn on praise music, and sing and pray in my spiritual language until I am recharged and again ready to fire on all cylinders. What do you do when your gauge is nearing the empty mark?

When you signed up for ministry, if you thought that it was always going to be easy and that your church would never go through rough seasons, you might want to reconsider your perspective. Look at Paul's description of ministry:

> We've been surrounded and battered by troubles, but we're not demoralized; we're not sure what to do, but we know that God knows

> what to do; we've been spiritually terrorized, but God hasn't left our side; we've been thrown down, but we haven't broken. What they did to Jesus, they do to us—trial and torture, mockery and murder; what Jesus did among them, he does in us—he lives! Our lives are at constant risk for Jesus' sake, which makes Jesus' life all the more evident in us. While we're going through the worst, you're getting in on the best! (2 Cor. 4:8-9, *THE MESSAGE*).

The apostle's picture of ministry contrasts human helplessness with divine enablement. We are pressed on every side, meaning in every aspect, both from inward and outward pressures; we are surrounded with no way out but God! If you don't allow God to work through you and you try to lead with your own knowledge and skill, you will run out of steam fast.

I read a story a few weeks ago about a man who set out to rob a gas station. Having already hit two stations in one evening, he headed to the third target in his SUV. There were no workers or customers in the convenience store, so he rammed his SUV through the glass doors of the store's front. Grabbing a few cases of cigarettes and scratch-off lottery tickets, the thief hopped back into his car and got a few miles down the road until the car sputtered to a stop. It had run out of gas! The thief had visited three gas stations but had not thought to fill his gas tank so that he could continue his robbing spree. The local authorities found him running away from his vehicle and arrested him.[4]

You can't run on an empty tank. Ministry is tough. Church life is bumpy. If you are not daily filling up your heart and life with the presence of God and Holy Spirit power, you will get frustrated and discouraged and be tempted to quit. Your heart must be full of virtue, and it must be committed if you are to build the SC. An empty vessel doing the right thing is the wrong thing. If you lose your spirit, you must know how to get it back so that you can minister from a heart that is full of supernatural faith and vision that sees growth.

Empowerment for Breakthrough Growth

If you suffer from Empty Spirit Syndrome, you *can* regain your spirit and lead and empower your team for breakthrough growth. It is possible to not lose heart (see 2 Cor. 4:1). If you are drained of your spirit, it's time to break through into a new season of growth.

Breaking into Surplus Anointing

God desires His leaders to be empowered to break through the Empty Spirit Syndrome into a new season of surplus anointing. Surplus anointing means having so many more resources than are required that they spill over the top. It means having a cup that runs over with the anointing oil (see Ps. 23:5). People living with overflowing anointing are characterized by the word "beyond." They are divinely enabled to operate beyond their capacity, beyond their strength and beyond their vision of the future.

Surplus anointing comes as a transfer from the Holy Spirit. He puts on you authority, power and honor that totally saturate who you are, what you say and what you would do in service to the Lord. With the Holy Spirit's power, you have the authority to break the force of spiritual bondage.

Once you have broken into surplus anointing, you need to keep pressing and increasing in anointing. That is done through using your spiritual language. A spiritual language is a spiritual resource that every believer can and should use. It is scriptural, predicted by Jesus and practiced by the New Testament church. There are several powerful benefits of using this language.

First, using spiritual language puts in mind that we are part of one international body and that we must take the gospel to all nations. There are over 6,000 different languages spoken on the planet and there is one heavenly angelic tongue. When you pray with your spiritual language, you confirm that you are part of the worldwide fellowship of believers.

Second, using spiritual language causes growth in understanding spiritual matters. Paul writes that "he who speaks in a tongue does not speak to men but to God, for no one understands him; however, in the spirit he speaks mysteries" (1 Cor. 14:2). A mystery is that which is outside the range of unassisted natural apprehension. It can be made known only by divine revelation. Praying in the spirit allows the Holy Spirit to reveal truth and things to our minds and spirits that were otherwise unknown.

Third, using spiritual language makes the inner man stronger: "He who speaks in a tongue edifies himself, but he who prophesies edifies the church" (1 Cor. 14:4). Edification is the act of building and promoting spiritual growth. Edifying the church is Paul's desire, but he is not negating edifying yourself. Praying in private to build up your spirit and soul is comparable to praying in church to build up the church. To break into surplus anointing and grow the anointing, we must use all the gifts given to us, including our spiritual language.

God has established us in Christ and given us the Holy Spirit as a seal and guarantee that He will be with us at all times and in every season (see 2 Cor. 1:21-22; Eph. 1:13). Our response to the anointing is to abide in it and seek to increase it (see 1 John 2:27).

Breaking into Supernatural Growth

Strategic leaders are empowered to break out of a season of plateau, where stagnation has begun, and break into new supernatural growth. In the plateau stage, no progress is apparent because you simply replace what you have lost. When you are in a season of plateau, you are called to "break forth in singing, and cry aloud. . . . Enlarge the place of your tent, and let them stretch out the curtains of your dwellings. . . . For you shall expand to the right and to the left, and your descendants will inherit the nations" (Isa. 54:1-3). Break out of maintenance mode and push your borders a little farther.

A bonsai tree is a common house or office decoration. It usually sits in a small pot that is no bigger than the breadth of your palm. The tree begins life like any ordinary tree, but drastic pruning quickly limits its growth. The gardener cuts the roots back, limiting the bonsai's ability to draw nutrients from its environment. Then the tree is planted in a small container, further restricting it to a small existence. The bonsai went from being a dynamic, life-filled tree to being a miniature decoration, confined by the size of its container. Its environment defined its potential.

To get off the plateau and start seeing growth, you have to make room for growth. Stretch out, push your borders farther, and open some space for the harvest. Numerical, organic and influence types of growth are supernatural growths that require supernatural responses. When it doesn't make sense in the natural, stretch out in faith, trusting that God—who is faithful—will break through the stagnant season and bring you into healthy, supernatural growth.

Breaking into Multiplication Growth

Strategic leaders are given power to break into a new level of multiplication growth that surpasses anything in the past. Multiplication growth is explosive. It increases mightily, resulting in abundance. A multiplying congregation will enlarge, expand and extend its reach, superseding past achievements and accomplishments. Our inheritance and mandate as children of God is to be fruitful and multiply so that we may be "an assembly of peoples" (Gen. 28:3).

The key to multiplication is preaching the Word of God. Throughout the New Testament, when the Word of God was preached or spread, "the number of disciples multiplied greatly" (Acts 6:7). There are many temptations to preach other things, but this would result in neglecting the primacy of preaching the powerful, living Word of God. Preaching the Word can be unpopular in an entertainment-oriented, short-attention-span generation. But preaching the Word is a must if we are to break into multiplication growth. The greatest power ever known is the spoken Word of God. It has called worlds into being, toppled empires, healed and comforted the sick, shaken the proud and resurrected the dead.

The Bible is the authoritative Word of God. When the Bible speaks, God speaks. Ray Stedman, the noted pastor and biblical expositor, wrote:

> The authority of Scripture is the authority of Jesus Christ. They are indivisible. To attempt to distinguish the two is like asking which blade of a pair of scissors is more important, or which leg of a pair of pants is more necessary. We know Christ through the Bible, and we understand the Bible through the knowledge of Christ. The two cannot be separated. That is why Paul calls it "the word of Christ."[5]

God is the ultimate author of Scripture. His words "are life" (John 6:63). Therefore, when we preach His words, He breathes life on the hearers and draws them to Him. When the Word of God was preached in Asia, the believers "were multiplied" (Acts 9:31). The same can happen today when we share the gospel. Strategic leaders position the church to move into a new level of multiplication: new converts in the local church, new church plants established, and new missionaries and international ministries sent. This is multiplication.

BREAKING INTO THE MARKETPLACE

It is a fact that people spend more time working than any other social activity. To many, work is a toilsome necessity that must be done to survive but carries little of their hearts. The marketplace is, however, God's workplace, and we as leaders must believe and have a vision for marketplace impact. Of the 52 parables Jesus taught, 45 were set in the context of the marketplace. Of the 40 miracles in the book of Acts, 39 were done in the marketplace. Jesus was a worker for almost His entire adult life. God has called people to the marketplace to be Kingdom minded, to prosper and be successful, to learn skills of stewardship and financial accountability, and to break the spirit of lack and poverty.

Believers have the capacity to establish and expand the kingdom of God. This Kingdom has no barriers or limitations, and it is most definitely in the marketplace as believers work and build the Kingdom within the frame of their jobs or careers. Workers must see their placements as God-placements intended to advance the cause of Christ and advance His kingdom. Our work is sacred and our call is from God (see Ps. 1:1; Prov. 3:5; 1 Cor. 10:31). God is present and active in the workplace and is empowering people by the Holy Spirit to work skillfully with their anointed gifts and to be successes in every way.

Building a pathway into the marketplace is a strategic move because marketplace people are positioned in a place of great tactical advantage. According to God's providence, business controls the supply of fuel—the materials needed to do business and ministry. The cause of the Kingdom needs financing. Institutions with ungodly worldviews have been well funded while the Kingdom church is underfunded. Marketplace people with a biblical worldview about resources and how God can use them are great assets to the cause of the Kingdom. They understand that increase is biblical and that it is God who gives us the "power to get wealth, that He may establish His covenant" with us, which is prosperity, peace and favor as long as we stay obedient to His commands (Deut. 8:18; also see Deut. 28:11; 2 Chron. 20:20; 3 John 2).

For many years, we have had a group of business leaders called Business with a Purpose (BWAP) who minister to the businesspeople in our congregation. These are key leaders who model marketplace ministry by how they do business and how they see business as a God tool to expand God's kingdom. Their mission is to evangelize in the workplace, mentor and equip leaders, foster networks and relationships, and prosper for the Kingdom. They are driven by the vision to help people fulfill their workplace callings. We believe that the workplace should be used for evangelism, that Christians should exemplify integrity and excellence in the workplace, and that Christians should be a positive influence in the workplace and community. God desires to confirm His covenant by enabling His people to prosper.

We have several ways of helping businesspeople fulfill their workplace callings. People can sign up for Email Inspirations, which are frequent emails with inspiring and challenging ideas that relate Scriptures to everyday work situations and subjects. We have a website that keeps people up to date on ministry activities in the church and offers a job finder for those looking for a job and those wanting to hire. Users can also receive free advertising for their businesses with the business directory on the site.

The BWAP team also offers free business counseling for those needing help in starting a new business, expanding an existing business or facing a challenge. An on-line prayer link is available on the website for users to take advantage of as the need arises. Prayer requests go to our BWAP prayer team, which also organizes teams for on-sight prayer at businesses. We also organize several small groups for women, young business leaders, couples and single businesspeople. Through these groups, and through quarterly meetings and the array of resources already mentioned, the community of people in the marketplace are charged to lead the way in the workplace through evangelism and prosperity with a purpose.

The marketplace person can be used to break the spirit of poverty, lack, and bondages of unbelief. We should not and cannot accept a spirit of poverty, which is really expecting lack. When Jesus came to earth, He declared that an anointing was on Him "to preach the gospel to the poor . . . to heal the brokenhearted, to proclaim liberty to the captives and recovery of sight to the blind, to set at liberty those who are oppressed" (Luke 4:18). The spirit of poverty is a bondage that can be broken. The marketplace person has an anointing to break that bondage by being a conduit to release resources in "good measure, pressed down, shaken together, and running over" (Luke 6:38).

The anointing on the businessperson is also present to break the attitude of greed. Greed is an excessive desire for more material things. It drives people to build bigger and bigger storehouses to hold accumulated possessions that are not going to be used but could benefit someone else. Greedy people never have enough, and their attitude results in stinginess that in turn prevents giving any finances or resources.

To combat the spirits of poverty and greed, the marketplace person with a purpose must have a few particular qualities. First, he or she needs to be filled with the power of the Spirit. This comes by continually digesting and declaring the Word of God. The one who delights in the law of the Lord and ponders it day and night "shall be like a tree planted by the rivers of water," immovable, unshakable and a bearer of much fruit that is used for the Kingdom (Ps. 1:3). This position will result in being set apart in the marketplace as one who works with unquestionable integrity and godly character. A person such as this will reconcile with bosses and will reconcile bosses with employees. This person will not let issues continue unresolved. A worker with integrity forgives people who have hurt, offended or taken advantage of him or her. This person doesn't steal from the company in any way and doesn't gripe. Instead, he or she is an atmosphere changer who is fair, kind and caring. This person is free and lives pure, resisting extramarital attractions toward workers. No gossip, no undermining, no holding on when they need to let go.

Second, the marketplace person must activate faith with a positive mindset by praying over his or her job and business. In tough times and good times, the marketplace person must hang on to and believe by faith Romans 8:28-30:

> And we know that all things work together for good to those who love God, to those who are the called according to His purpose. For whom He foreknew, He also predestined to be conformed to the image of His Son, that He might be the firstborn among many brethren. Moreover whom He predestined, these He also called; whom He called, these He also justified; and whom He justified, these He also glorified.

Whatever the circumstance, we must believe God is at work in us and for us. Trust. God is working through it all: loss of job, loss of business, loss of growth, financial loss. God is not finished. He is refining and getting us ready to break off the spirit of poverty and lack and break into open heavens and increasing prosperity. The effective marketplace person who is rooted and immovable is filled with the Spirit and exercises faith in all situations.

Breaking into the Next Generation

One of the church's greatest needs today is to break into the next generation and reap a great harvest. The next generation is searching for something that impacts their lives and something that will build them into better people. As the generation faces numerous reasons to be negative—global problems, wars, wrecked economies, disease and hopelessness, among others—it is seeking for ways to define itself other than vocationally. Altruism is on the rise in America today because this generation does not want to be defined by a job title but by its impact on the world. They are searching for hope, something intrinsic, something that lasts long past the 9-to-5 workday.

On a trip to Argentina in 2006, an American named Blake Mycoskie found that the children where he was traveling had no shoes. Out of his desire to help, he created TOMS Shoes and started the One for One movement. For every pair of shoes purchased, the company gave a pair to a child in need. In just the first year, Blake and a group of family, friends and staff brought 10,000 pairs of shoes to children in Argentina. He saw a need and wanted to make a difference. His company is still making a difference.

A young girl named Alex was diagnosed with cancer just before her first birthday. At the age of four, she told her parents she wanted to help doctors find a cure for cancer. Her fundraising vehicle was a lemonade stand set up in her front yard. The first day, Alex's Lemonade Stand made $2,000. She set up new stands every year while bravely fighting her own cancer. As news of this extraordinary girl and her cause spread, people everywhere were inspired to start their own lemonade stands and donate the proceeds to finding a cure. In 2004, Alex passed away at the age of eight. During the four years she ran lemonade stands, she raised over $1 million toward finding a cure for cancer. Her parents carried on the work and started Alex's Lemonade Stand Foundation, which has now raised more than $50 million.

This is the generation of altruistic innovators that we must reach and harvest with the message of hope and life in Christ. Imagine what will happen when God taps into their hearts and they launch ministries and businesses that will raise thousands and impact millions! I believe the Holy Spirit will fall upon every leader who will open his or her life and heart for a fresh anointing. I believe we as leaders will break off all that has entangled us, break open all that is hindering a new future, and break into new realms of supernatural growth—dramatic growth, multiplication growth.

Strategic Dynamic Atmosphere

The struggle I have as a builder of the local church and as someone trying to assist pastor-leaders to do the same is my ability to trust the simplicity of Scripture. I seem to feel the need to do something more with the church model I read in the book of Acts and see explained in the Epistles. I don't always simply rest with the biblical model—I wrestle with it. I see various successful growing churches doing things that are much more relevant, cool and inspiring, and I think, *They must have a better idea of what church should be.*

But when you dig a little deeper into different church models in today's world, you might be surprised—and even a little shocked—at what you find lies beneath. The surface looks inspiring, but underneath, where are the disciples? Where are the true converts, the fruit of Christianity, those who are to impact the city and the nations? Where is the prayer; the true, Spirit-driven worship; the evangelism; the purity of lifestyle; Bible knowledge; and personal devotion to Christ? If a chosen church model does not produce biblical Christianity, then it's time to go back to the blueprint.

In 2008, Brad Waggoner wrote an insightful book called *The Shape of Faith to Come*. In it, he gives several staggering statistics about the Body of Christ today. His findings are the result of a survey of 2,500 Protestants. One question Waggoner asked was, "How much do you agree/disagree: I desire to please and honor Jesus in all that I do?" Fifty-four percent responded with "agree strongly," and 29 percent chose "agree somewhat."[1] That means a little less than half of the group desired to honor Jesus. Pretty alarming. Another question Waggoner asked was, "How often do you read the Bible?/Study the Bible (more in-depth than just reading it)?" Sixteen percent said they read their Bible every day; twenty percent reported reading "a few times a week"; and 12 percent said they read it "weekly." That amounts to about 48 percent of churchgoers reading the Bible at least once per week.[2] How are people supposed to grow into spiritually healthy individuals without reading and meditating on the Word of God?

The discouraging news continues. "In the past six months, about how many times have you, personally, done the following: made a decision to obey or follow God with an awareness that choosing His way might be costly to you in some way?" Thirty-six percent could not recall even once in the past six months when they chose to obey God and knew that their choice might be costly. Twenty percent said they could recall one such decision, and 44 percent said they had done so at least twice or more.[3]

The responses to Waggoner's questions about evangelism are just as interesting: "How much do you agree/disagree: It is every Christian's responsibility to share the gospel with non-Christians." Forty-six percent said they "agreed strongly," and another 26 percent said they "agreed somewhat." A little less than half of the respondents felt strongly that sharing the gospel was a personal responsibility.[4] Personally, I think everyone in the church should see evangelism as his or her mandate! Here is another one about spiritual formation: "How often do you do the following: Pray for the spiritual status of people I know who are not professing Christianity." Twenty percent said they included unsaved people in their prayers every day; 20 percent included the unsaved a few times a week; 12 percent included the unsaved once a week; 9 percent included the unsaved once a month.[5]

It looks as if there are some things we could do better in church today. People may not be discipled and taught how to read and study the Word. Being relevant is absolutely important. Connecting to today's culture and communicating in ways people can understand is absolutely necessary. But when we construct the communications bridge to our world, we must be certain we have something meaningful and eternal to carry over that bridge. The content of the message we carry is just as important as the communication techniques we use to connect. Hunger for relevance may drive the leader to prioritize what people want and will respond to before fully considering what the Scriptures have established as the basic and nonnegotiable ingredients that make up the church.

THE ATMOSPHERE OF THE FIRST CHURCH

Now that we have some background on strategic leadership and the importance of vision, let's delve into a few of the prominent characteristics of the SC in the New Testament. There is something significant about the first church built by the master builder, Christ, and His Holy Spirit-filled leaders (see Acts 2:40-47; 1 Cor. 3:9). Look at what happens when the church is first getting started:

> And with many other words [Peter] testified and exhorted them, saying, "Be saved from this perverse generation." Then those who gladly received his word were baptized; and that day about three thousand souls were added to them. And they continued steadfastly in the apostles' doctrine and fellowship, in the breaking of bread, and in prayers. Then fear came upon every soul, and many wonders and signs were done through the apostles. Now all who believed were together, and had all things in common, and sold their possessions and goods, and divided them among all, as anyone had need. So continuing daily with one accord in the temple, and breaking bread from house to house, they ate their food with gladness and simplicity of heart, praising God and having favor with all the people. And the Lord added to the church daily those who were being saved (Acts 2:40-47).

The first characteristic of this SC that you can feel when you read this passage is the dynamic atmosphere in and around this church:

- *Salvations*—The fellowship of believers started with 120 people in an upper room, and in a matter of days, nearly 8,000 more people were added (see Acts 2:41; 4:4).
- *Miracles happened*—Every person in Jerusalem at Pentecost heard the gospel message spoken in his or her native tongue. One hundred twenty people were speaking the same truth in different languages and the crowds could not only hear but also understand what was said.
- *Restoration was manifest*—A man destined to sit outside the temple gates and beg for his welfare was instantaneously restored to full health and he leapt and ran on strong legs (see Acts 3:1-10).

- *Abundant supply*—Everyone sacrificed and gave to each other so that no one had a need that went unmet. Extraordinary unity saturated their church environment. All the believers "were together, and had all things in common" (Acts 2:44).

Wouldn't you like that kind of atmosphere? Atmosphere is the pervading or surrounding influence, a general mood and an environment that can be felt. Every place has an atmosphere of some kind, a "felt atmosphere." You may not be able to put your finger on exactly what the atmosphere is, but it is there. You may love it, like it, hate it, find it interesting or find it annoying; but it is real.

Think about the last time you went shopping at the mall. Every shop is designed to give you a particular feeling from the moment you step in the door. My wife loves the Williams-Sonoma store. They have all the latest cooking, baking and grilling tools, along with all those kitchen accessories the "serious chef" just can't do without. When you step through the open French double doors, you are warmly greeted by a friendly worker dressed in a crisp white shirt, nice slacks and a Williams-Sonoma apron. The soft light bouncing off an elegant hazelnut-colored wood floor along with soft jazz music immediately puts you at ease. An aroma of savory spices and a fresh-cooked meal for sampling tantalizes your taste buds. As you move to the demo kitchen and sip some hot apple cider, you feel a surrounding presence of warmth and comfort. Now you can shop in a relaxed mindset, browse the cookbooks and the other wares with no salespeople hovering over your shoulder. It's just you, the kitchen merchandise and a warm, cozy feeling.

You see what that store did? It created a certain atmosphere that put you in a somewhat nostalgic mood and probably made you more open to buying their products. Now, imagine walking a few doors down to the latest skater outfitter; and the blaring rock music, bright lights and grunge-style décor will throw you into a completely different mood. That is the power of atmosphere.

Every person carries an atmosphere. It may be an atmosphere of anger, pride, argumentation, sensuality, faith, generosity, approachability and kindness. Every home has an atmosphere that can be negative or positive. It can be a place of contention and strife, or it can be a place of warmth, hospitality and grace. Likewise, the SC also has a definite felt atmosphere—an air of excitement, laughter, joy, expectancy, faith, generosity, prayer—the list of positive possibilities is innumerable.

The atmosphere to which people submit themselves has the power to actually change and shape their lives, because atmosphere can be magnetic. As long as people are in or under a particular atmosphere, they become a certain kind of people. In an atmosphere of excitement, people are mobilized to volunteer for an outreach, lead an evangelism initiative and tell their neighbors about church, because there is an air of anticipation and enthusiasm about what is happening at church. The strategic leader knows the profound importance of a right atmosphere and works hard to build a dynamic one.

At City Bible Church, we use the fall season to build lots of momentum and really raise faith and love for the church and the community. People are just getting back from summer vacation, school is about to start, and it is a perfect time of year for transition and movement toward the community. Last year's theme was "Live.Love." Our purpose was to empower a movement of people who are devoted to making a difference in society by living lives beyond themselves and being committed to reaching out to people in need throughout our community. Thousands of people made a difference by gathering in small groups and on community projects as well as by serving in a variety of community partnerships.

The weekend this movement began, we held a special service called Super Sunday Night (SSN). We have these services about four times every year, and they are great momentum builders. Every campus and international fellowship that meets at CBC gathers in one location for a dynamic service of prayer, worship, preaching and other special presentations (we also end it with a dessert buffet!). This SSN, we introduced the various Live.Love. projects that each campus and small group was going to do. We handed out touch cards, interceded over what was going to happen in the following weeks, and believed together that something powerful was stirring. There was definitely a feeling of excitement in the air!

Over the following four months, the awesome people of CBC volunteered more than 10,000 hours to do projects that ranged from home renovation to health clinics, from hosting mini-soccer tournaments for underprivileged kids to delivering hygiene bags to the homeless. We have served in over 30 community organizations and conducted over 100 small-group projects, and the impact is still being felt by thousands of people in our community. On one Sunday, over 270 people volunteered to purchase and help hand out gifts to children and families in the community who had nowhere to go for Christmas and no money to afford presents. That is what happens when there is an atmosphere of excitement and passion to live like Jesus and share His love! People sacrificially give their time and resources to build the church and help the community because they are energized to do it.

The first church as seen in the New Testament had a specific, overarching atmosphere. The atmosphere, the pervading surrounding influence was electric with the powerful moving of the Holy Spirit, the anointed preaching of Peter, the unity of heart amongst all the leaders, the expectation of faith in the air, the hunger of people to respond, and the believers' response to the Word. It exploded with salvations, baptisms, prayers, worship, people being filled with the Spirit—all while building community, showing unbelievable generosity and reaching out with heart to others. This is an atmosphere we all would love to see in all churches—and it is possible!

Lessons from the Earth's Atmosphere

Atmosphere is layered, and each layer becomes a significant part of the whole atmosphere. There are five principle layers in the earth's atmosphere.

First there is the troposphere. This level starts at ground level and goes about 9 miles high. This is where our weather happens. You might experience sunshine and clear skies; or if you live in the Northwest like me, you get mostly clouds, rain and hail. Next is the stratosphere, starting just above the troposphere and stretching about 31 miles above the surface of the earth. This layer serves as a protective blanket for the earth by absorbing harmful ultraviolet radiation. The third level is the mesosphere, which rises about 55 miles above the earth's surface and has extremely low temperatures (as low as -184 degrees Fahrenheit). The fourth level is the thermosphere. Starting from about 74 miles up and rising to about 372 miles high, this is the level where space shuttles fly. Finally, there is the exosphere, which extends from the top of the thermosphere until it hits outer space. Each of these layers serves a specific purpose. You and I may not understand all the layers or even appreciate what they do, but they are all working together to make up a felt atmosphere where we live, affecting how we do life.

Similar to the layers of the earth's atmosphere are the layers of the atmosphere in a church, where the substance of atmosphere consists of right attitudes, perceptions, vision and core biblical values. We as strategic leaders build an atmospheric layer that affects the one atmosphere we feel when we gather for our church services. The dynamic atmosphere of an SC is not built by the lighting, sound, décor, seating arrangements, size of buildings or anything else we might think is the source of our atmosphere. Do these things affect felt atmosphere? Yes. Do they make up the felt atmosphere? Yes and no. All the natural, practical things we pay attention to are important. The sound, temperature in the room, lighting, platform presentation–everything must work in order to do church services. But we must understand that these elements do not make up the layers of dynamic atmosphere.

Atmosphere is built by the layers of spiritual DNA as seen in Scripture and applied in our meeting place. If you change your platform, your music, your lighting, service length or communion style, will your spiritual atmosphere that shapes people's lives change? No. Atmosphere as seen in Acts 2 (and throughout the rest of Acts) was not in the buildings, the music or the styles of worship. Atmosphere was first of all a spiritual power released from practicing spiritual principles that released spiritual power into the ugly rooms with no lights, no sound or no décor! The atmosphere was in the kingdom-of-God DNA. The physical elements can add or subtract from an atmosphere, but they are not the source, nor do they create even one of the layers.

Spiritual Layers of a Dynamic Atmosphere

The atmosphere described in Acts 2 and beyond can be built by strategic leaders who see the layers that need to be built: the Word of God and the Spirit working together, powerful prayer, supernatural expectancy, the powerful presence of God, leaders working in unity, and vision to reach people and cities. Vision has already been discussed (see chapter 2), but the other layers are part of the chapters we'll develop throughout the rest of this book. In the meantime, let me give you some overarching spiritual layers of atmosphere that can create a dynamic spiritual atmosphere in any local church.

1. Atmosphere of Open Heavens

No spiritual hindrances are allowed in this place. The open heavens idea is a biblical one that speaks of spiritual flow and power being more easily received. Open heavens are gained by spiritual unity, prayer and fasting, and a fresh outpouring of the Holy Spirit. Our churches can be places where heaven and all its power and resources flow freely into our midst, just as the Holy Spirit flowed in the upper room of Acts 2 (see Lev. 26:19; Ezek. 1:1; Mark 1:10; Rev. 4:1).

Building this atmosphere starts with praying as the psalmist did, saying, "My soul thirsts for God, for the living God. When shall I come and appear before God?" (Ps. 42:2) and "God—you're my God! I can't get enough of you! I've worked up such hunger and thirst for God, traveling across dry and weary deserts. So here I am in the place of worship, eyes open, drinking in your strength and glory" (Ps. 63:1-2, *THE MESSAGE*). As leaders and churches, we can believe that God desires to release breakthrough upon us, push back the forces of darkness and crush the enemy's strongholds. God can open the windows of heaven and pour out His Spirit, hope and healing and bring salvation to many. Such an atmosphere is developed as you lead the way in the place of worship, praying for the heavens to open.

2. Atmosphere of Unified Expectancy and No Business-as-Usual Church Services

Unified expectancy is anticipating that the greatness of God's will and work will be done. God is "able to do exceedingly abundantly above all that we ask or think, according to the power that works in us" (Eph. 3:20).

When Jesus returned to His hometown, He was limited from doing many miracles "because of their unbelief" (Matt. 13:58). The people in His hometown were hindered with an attitude that said, "Jesus and His family lived with us; therefore, He cannot have all this wisdom and ability to do miracles." Their attitude predisposed them to expect nothing new from Jesus except maybe some tips on good carpentry. Our attitude should be the complete opposite, like the paralytic and his friends who cut a hole through a roof to get to Jesus (see Mark 2:1-4). Jesus Christ is the most exciting, inspiring, power-filled personality in the universe. When He shows up, no one sleeps in the pews, people bring their friends, things happen!

A study was conducted in Europe that asked the simple question, "What makes some people luckier than others?" The researchers assembled two groups of people. One group professed that they felt lucky and that good things happen to them. The other group felt they were unlucky and that nothing good ever happened to them. Each participant was told to go shopping at a certain mall, one at a time. They didn't know that there was a 100 Euro note on the ground by the door. Eighty percent of the "lucky" people noticed the note and picked it up. Seventy percent of the "unlucky" people did not even see the note, much less pick it up. I don't believe in luck, but I do believe that the people who expect something good to happen experience good things and blessings because they are constantly looking for them.

Building an atmosphere of unified expectancy starts with believing what God says in Jeremiah 33:3: "Call to Me, and I will answer you, and show you great and mighty things, which you do not know." God does not want your church services to be stale and be the same from week to week. He wants to reach into your gathering and show each person that He is greater than any circumstance, more powerful than any sickness and more forgiving than anything humanly possible. In His presence, great things happen. Approach each service with high expectancy for God to do something totally unexpected. Jesus promised to be in and with His people every time they gather, and our attitude and teaching should reflect this awesome faith.

3. Atmosphere of Supernatural Surprises

It's no common, ordinary God we serve. When I read the book of Acts, I am certainly inspired by the uncommon greatness of God working in the midst of those early disciples. Thousands were saved in one day, people were healed of all kinds of diseases and broken lives were mended in His presence and in community. God astonished them with supernatural surprises. That same power should be active with us today so that the attitude of expecting supernatural surprises shapes the way we do church. Hudson Taylor wrote, "Satan may build a hedge about us and fence us in and hinder our movements, but he cannot roof us in and prevent our looking up."[6] God has supernatural surprises in store for every church. We will pray larger prayers if we see God's greatness ready to move among us. Look up! See, believe, pray and get out of the boat. Build a thriving atmosphere by believing and proclaiming that miracles can and do happen and that today could be a miracle day. It changes a church to believe Jesus is in the house–and Jesus is the same yesterday, today and forever.

4. Atmosphere of Everyone Can Receive

Limitations are not allowed to be placed on any person at anytime. This atmosphere boldly proclaims that God is able to do something for you, no matter how impossible it seems. Jesus assures us that "everyone who asks receives, and he who seeks finds, and to him who knocks it will be opened" (Matt. 7:8). Everyone is important to God, and everyone can receive from God. No one can hide or be missed.

In 1998, a group of people in Britain set out to end "rough sleeping." Believing that every person is important and no one should be left sleeping on the streets, the people who started this initiative wanted to get homeless people off the streets, into sleeping charities and eventually into their own homes. The initiative was called "No One Left Out." In 10 years, the number of rough sleepers decreased by 67 percent, and the group aggressively pursued their goal to eliminate rough sleeping by the year 2012. They started programs that encouraged people to take control of their lives rather than succumbing to destitute living on the streets. They built low-income housing shelters right in the neighborhoods where many homeless people lived. Classes on various trades and skills (such as time management) were offered so that the homeless could get the experience and knowledge they needed to get a job.[7] The project organizers were convinced that everyone is important and that everyone should have a fair shot at sleeping in a warm bed at night and working at a meaningful place: No one left out.

The same atmosphere should be in our churches. No one is left out and no one is excluded! When we teach that God is near, willing and powerful and that everyone is within the reach of God's love, there comes an attitude that establishes a great atmosphere where everyone believes they can receive. Our message is "Behold, the LORD's hand is not shortened, that it cannot save; nor His ear heavy, that it cannot hear" (Isa. 59:1). As strategic leaders, we build this atmosphere with faith and victory and a positive outlook on life and the future that says God is ready to do great things for you. Such an attitude permeates the air and reaches all people of all races and backgrounds and the young and old in every season of life.

5. Atmosphere of People Are Important and No Person Is Undervalued

People are drawn to an atmosphere of love and acceptance. People are our inheritance, and valuing them is the essential message of the gospel. People come to church just like the rest of us: thorny and fragile and in desperate need. Rahab was a prostitute, yet she's included in Hebrews 11 as a champion of faith. Paul was vicious in his persecution of the church, but he brought the gospel to the Gentiles. King David committed adultery and murder, Mary Magdalene was filled with demons, and Gideon was a coward. There is no limit to what God can do with a life, and there is no room for condemnation and unbelief in God's kingdom. If God puts no limits on a person's life, then neither can we.

One of my heroes of the faith is Mother Teresa. Her life is an inspiration to anyone, whether they agree with what she stood for or not. One biographer describers her as "for the most part unremarkable, not particularly educated, not particularly intelligent. In fact it was for her ineptitude at lighting the candles for Benediction that some remember her best."[8] Yet this remarkable woman gave her life to helping the poor in the slums of Calcutta, India. Every day she got up at 4:30 A.M., washed in icy cold water, brushed her teeth with ashes from the kitchen stove, prayed for an hour and then went to the slums until 5 P.M. Mother Teresa had a strong conviction that everyone is important to God. Her peers had not singled her out as the one who would bring change and a message of hope to so many thousands in her lifetime, but God put no limits on her, and she put no limits on others.

Flowers come in all shapes and sizes. Some are soft and delicate; others are strong and thorny. Yet each one has a unique fragrance and beauty. People are God's garden. They are His bouquet and He loves variety. In fact, the Bible praises Jesus for "[redeeming] us to God by [His] blood out of every tribe and tongue and people and nation" (Rev. 5:9). Establishing an atmosphere that values people is done by the preaching, the prayers and the ministries we offer at the church and through the church. This is a layered atmosphere of unconditional love and grace that is in every leader's heart and every person's vocabulary.

6. Atmosphere of Victorious Living

We've all quoted the verses, "If God is for us, who can be against us" and "I can do all things through Christ" (Rom. 8:31; Phil. 4:13). Nothing–absolutely nothing–is impossible with God. A church secures this atmosphere when she no longer only listens to these verses but is charged with the power of these truths. Fear doesn't stand a chance. We can look adversity in the eye and know that God is powerfully working every detail to our advantage. This is genuine faith: confidence in a God who is for us, who did not spare His own Son, and who graciously gives us all things. That's an atmosphere that is contagious. It gives hope to the hopeless, makes a way where there is no way, causes darkness to flee in terror and releases the miraculous power of a God who knows no defeat. God is able to deliver anyone at anytime (see Rom. 8:31; 1 Cor. 15:57; Phil. 4:13).

When you lead with expectancy and faith that resists a defeatist spirit, you carry an atmosphere of victorious living that rubs off on others. Winston Churchill, widely regarded as the greatest statesman of the twentieth century, was a leader whose faith for victory inspired leaders, an army and a nation to fight for victory in World War II. Look at these words from his speech to the House of Commons on June 4, 1940:

> We shall go on to the end, we shall fight in France, we shall fight on the seas and oceans, we shall fight with growing confidence and growing strength in the air, we shall defend our Island, whatever the cost may be, we shall fight on the beaches, we shall fight on the landing grounds, we shall fight in the fields and in the streets, we shall fight in the hills; we shall never surrender.[9]

It's impossible to read Churchill's words and not feel inspired! Churchill's official biographer, Sir Martin Gilbert, wrote of Churchill, "It was Churchill's own opposition to all forms of defeatism that marked out the first six months of his war premiership and established the nature and pattern of his war leadership."[10] That is the kind of leader we must be if we are to develop an atmosphere of victorious living in our churches. Our faith and our hope are in Christ, the One who never fails. He conquered every imaginable opposition and, therefore, He can help you conquer the enemy in your path. Let your faith level rise so that your personal atmosphere of optimism lifts the church atmosphere to living life free and without hindrances.

7. Atmosphere of Communion, Where the Voice of God Is Heard Clearly

God's voice, though seldom discernable to the natural ear, is the most powerful sound there is. One word from Him and the most troubled heart is comforted. Confused circumstances are made clear and broken relationships are healed. These are exhilarating days for the church. There are fresh outpourings of the Spirit, growing churches, an increase of the miraculous, power encounters, and healings. But the factor that affects the lives of people most is hearing God. He is talking to His people. He's revealing His love one word at a time. Decade-long bondages are broken in a moment. Prayer is taking on an added dimension: listening. More can be said in silence than from the pulpit because it's Him—our very God—who is speaking.

Remember the story of Mary and Martha? Martha busily set the table and prepared the meal. Mary on the other hand seemingly ignored her responsibilities and sat idly with Jesus. Yet we are told that Mary chose what was the better (see Luke 10:42). In Western culture where activity is king and success is measured by the entries in our Blackberry, Mary would have put down her Smartphone, unplugged her Bluetooth and focused her attention on Jesus. I have been in countless services where there were things to do, announcements to make, people to greet and songs to sing; but there was just this sense that we needed to stop everything and listen to the still, small voice. Every time I listened to that inner prod to press in a little further, I was not disappointed or sorry that I had waited. In a world of dizzying busyness, let's not neglect what is better, and let's sit at Jesus' feet. Let's keep our ears ever tuned to His voice.

The SC is one with a dynamic atmosphere. There is life, hope, excitement and peace there. The collective church is "the eternal purpose" of God, a manifestation in time of God's eternal purpose (see Eph. 3:10-12). The church is God's final instrument to fulfill His plan of the ages, and it has the keys of the Kingdom in its hands (see Matt. 16:18-19). The church is divinely energized to the degree that it pursues that purpose. I believe these seven attitudes will transform your church atmosphere and charge your people to pursue its divine purpose.

Strategic Unique Culture

When Gallup structured a poll on the number of evangelicals in America, they had a hard time determining the defining criteria. They concluded that evangelicals are a subset of Christians who take their religion very seriously and might be highly involved in politics, especially in the Republican Party.[1] Did you see any mention about their belief system or anything about how evangelical Christians behave? Besides being active in a political party, there are not many obvious characteristics that easily distinguish Christians from the rest of the world. Whether evangelical, protestant, foursquare, Baptist or any other denomination of Christianity, we seem to be having a hard time living in the world without being conformed to its culture. We seem to be marching to the same cadence and defining morals and acceptable behavior by what contemporary culture dictates.

As strategic leaders, we are supposed to build a strategic church that has a dynamic atmosphere and also a unique and definable biblical-spiritual culture. We should march to the beat of a different drum. Cultures we live in influence our thinking, our values, the life we live and the way we filter truth and life experiences. "Culture" generally refers to a certain group's particular way of life. This includes moral beliefs and social meanings of various aspects of life such as race, ethnicity, language, religions, trends and styles. Every culture has stories about its origin and history that weave a cultural mythos, a way of thinking and making sense of the world by defining beliefs, values and appropriate behavior. And every culture has accepted biases—some good, some not so good.

Whatever values and social norms a culture holds, that culture deeply impacts people. The church is a culture within a culture and will be influenced by its surrounding society. The challenge is to know our own culture, understand how we are captive within its biases and discern what is a good influence, what is harmless and what violates the biblical principles that church must adhere to. The three cultures all leaders encounter and thus must understand are world culture, Kingdom culture and church culture.

World culture is the culture of the nation, state, province or city in which we live. It includes unique demographics, languages, customs, moral complexity, economic influences, friends, family, and the like. All world cultures are distinctly different and have influence upon the people in that culture and also upon the church in that culture. The world culture that accepts and promotes ideas that are anti-God, anti-Bible, immoral, humanistic, polytheistic and in other ways non-biblical is one that the church must resist and confront. The church should oppose the culture of immorality, prostitution, pornography and filth of any kind (see Rom. 12:1-2).

On the other hand, *Kingdom culture* is the culture of Christ's kingdom, which is transferable and definable in any world culture. Jesus is the savior of humankind, and He is the gateway—and the only way—into the kingdom of God. The kingdom of God exists wherever King Jesus is the ruler over His citizens of the kingdom who obey and live out Kingdom principles and Kingdom truth. Kingdom culture crosses the boundaries of race, color, socioeconomic status, background and nationality. We embrace a living relationship and allegiance to Jesus Christ, separate from and distinct from institutional Christianity, which can be driven by politics, money, power and other selfish realities.

Our Kingdom culture is all about authentic Jesus and His teachings and His principles. It is a culture that gives life to the poor, the needy, the broken and the searching. We hold to Kingdom values that produce righteousness and purity in our lifestyles, and behaviors that elevate Kingdom truth and standards. Those standards say we believe in absolutes as seen in the Word of God, including the sanctity of human life and the sanctity of marriage (see Lev. 18:21; 20:1-5; Deut. 19:16; Prov. 6:16-19; Ezek. 35:6; Mal. 2:11-16). A Kingdom culture can and should be established within any context (see Matt. 4:23; 9:35; 24:14; Mark 1:14; Luke 8:1).

Church culture, like *Kingdom culture,* is also a very real, definable culture within whatever world culture surrounds us and is part of the Kingdom culture we establish as our mandate. At its roots are the church's basic theology (doctrine of God), ecclesiology (doctrine of church) and pneumatology (doctrine of the Holy Spirit), along with a unique spiritual heritage coupled with the Holy Spirit's work with and in that church. Building on its unique history and heritage, church culture is usually shaped by a combination of the leaders who build the church, the vision, the values and a very real corporate grace. Corporate grace is the specific grace God gives each particular church that forms that church's destiny and overall spiritual impact upon its region and beyond. The church culture should reflect kingdom-of-God values and practices as clearly seen in the Scriptures. The church should be in the world today, connecting to the culture but not allowing the world to shape it, especially its core values, beliefs and behaviors. The need for relevant church is in high demand today, but relevance must not reshape the church into a place the world likes but Jesus struggles with. The church culture must be a culture that is consistent with Scripture.

Many leaders are asking the right questions about church in the culture and culture in the church. How far is too far? What should we reject, receive or redeem? Music, the arts, atmosphere, technology—what part of these aspects of world culture can we righteously use in our process of building a church culture? I have found that there are several obvious shapers of church culture and some not-so-obvious shapers of church culture; but before I discuss those, we must establish the main shaper of an unshakable and powerful church culture: the Word of God.

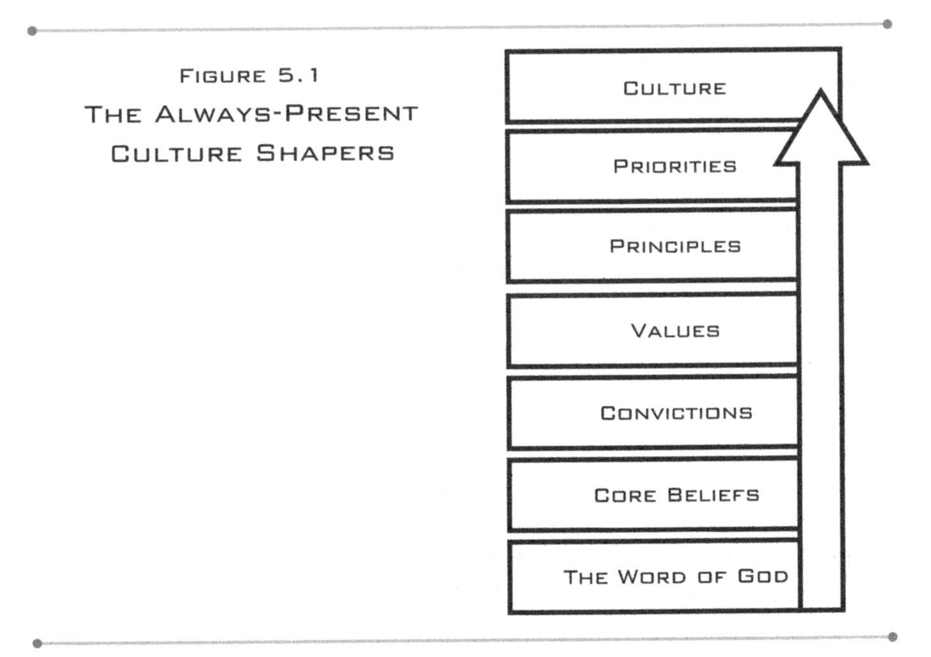

Figure 5.1
The Always-Present Culture Shapers

The Foundation of Church Culture

The Word of God

The foundation of church culture for the SC is the absolutely trustworthy Word of God. When a leader seeks to build a lasting, impacting, life-giving strategic church, the Word of God is the ultimate authority in vision, doctrine, values and principles. The Word of God is just that—God's Word. When the Bible speaks, God speaks. The Scriptures as a body were written by the Holy Spirit's inspiration and are thus the words of the living God and His infallible wisdom (see 2 Tim. 3:16-17). All that we seek to build begins and ends with the Word of God. The Bible is a supernatural book. Natural minds think it is foolishness because understanding comes only through the Spirit of God.

Core Beliefs

At the root of all you grow in ministry and the church you seek to build are your core beliefs. These beliefs inspire values that will become your convictions. Our core beliefs hold us steady during rough times, and they are always dependable as guides to help us see vision strategy clearly. Core beliefs about who God is, who Christ is, atonement, salvation, grace, the Holy Spirit, church, the local church, prayer, worship, evangelism and any other subject will greatly affect the church culture.

Convictions

Convictions arise from our core beliefs. Everyone holds to certain core beliefs that establish specific values, principles and, ultimately, behavior patterns. Convictions are more than personal opinions or preferences. Convictions are directly connected to how you see and read the Bible and to your core beliefs. You are convinced about certain things you see as right and, therefore, you are committed to those beliefs. A leader must have convictions about the kind of church he or she is building and must be committed to those convictions. Convictions build culture.

Values

Our values drive our choices and actions. To value something is to esteem it as something of worth or cultural importance. We may value the wrong things, like status, recognition, fame, riches, church popularity or church size. These things feed our ego. Right values are defined as consistent, passionate, biblical core beliefs that drive the core of our church. Values build culture because we intentionally choose our values to produce an intended result. What are your church values? We have 12 core values at CBC: the written Word of God, vision, local church, personal growth, presence-empowered worship, the power of God, stewardship, team leadership, family, relationships, purity, and reaching people.

PRINCIPLES

Principles are the concrete laws that build everything. They are never compromised. Our values form the essence of principle-centered ministry and principle-driven church. Principles are firm and deeply rooted and will not allow for conformity to something less. Principles of honesty, integrity, reliability, truthfulness, moral purity, faithfulness, a team spirit, a focus on the family, and loving people are just a few principles that build a specific culture. Principled leadership is exemplified by leading and building from a firm foundation of right beliefs and values.

PRIORITIES

Priorities are those things that take precedence. A list of priorities is established by ordering items by importance and urgency. Every leader has a written or unwritten set of leadership priorities that arise from his or her beliefs, convictions, values and principles. The church that we as leaders guide is directed by the priorities we set or allow to be given our time, resources and strength. The church culture we build will incorporate those things that we deem a priority and that must become reality. Great leaders unleash all the talents and gifts of their team toward the highest priorities of the vision being built.

CULTURE

The church you build and lead will have a church culture and, hopefully, a strategic culture that has been created out of the elements listed and defined above. Combining our core beliefs, convictions, values, principles and priorities, we begin to see how to build church culture. Add to the list the leadership gifting, the team's gifts and talents, demographics, and the ministry maturity and skill level of those shaping the culture. Each strategic leader and team must know what they believe, what are their convictions, values and priorities to live by. These are the obvious and always present elements that build church culture.

The Obvious Shapers of Church Culture

Vision

Church vision is the embodiment of a church's passion that unifies everyone to a common purpose. This set vision guides decision making and is the hidden force behind everything. A specific ministry philosophy and vision will cultivate a specific church culture.

Leadership

Church leadership is one of the most powerful shaping tools. What the leadership team reflects—how it leads, treats people and respects the identified values—tremendously contributes to the culture. Leadership can help create an environment that stimulates people to do their best and reach for the highest level of excellence with a servant spirit. Day by day, church leaders continually shape the culture.

Celebration

Celebrating is taking a purposeful pause in our church services and rejoicing in our values through prayer, testimony, worship and any other possible way that says that "we value this." Celebration reveals the church's heartbeat and what is esteemed. Celebrate who you are, what you value, your church victories, salvations, baptisms, ministry to your city and ministry to the poor and needy.

Demographics

The congregation's demographics will have some bearing on the overall church culture. A church with predominantly white members will have a different culture than a multi-ethnic one. I believe that a church should reflect the composition of the region where the church is. City Bible has a specific conviction that we should be multiethnic and multicultural. We have Laotians, Sudanese, Hispanics, Burmese, Russians and Romanians, among other ethnicities, in our congregation. Being multiethnic was part of our vision, so we went into the world to reach them and bring them into our church.

History and Heritage

Every church has a story, a journey, a beginning and a process of becoming the church God called it to be. That heritage is part of the DNA that gives the church its identity. We honor tradition, but we are not tied to just our past. We must build upon principles and truth, not just traditions and acceptable ways of doing things.

THE NOT-SO-OBVIOUS SHAPERS OF CULTURE

THE LEAD PASTOR

The lead pastor, along with the entire pastoral team, is a strong shaper of church culture. Leaders are positioned to profoundly influence church culture, because they can challenge people's underlying beliefs and assumptions and consequently affect their attitudes and practices. Standing at the helm, the leader has the potential to bend the culture in certain directions. He can point the church on a positive course by putting a high value on people, volunteers and staff, along with an attitude of humility, approachability and transparency and an open-door policy. Such an attitude and policy encourage creative ideas, changes and input that make for a welcome atmosphere among church staff and congregants. There is a noticeable effect on the environment when you give grace to those who are out of spiritual alignment and need to be restored or when you allow leaders to participate in their kids' sports or school activities when those activities conflict with church schedules.

My personal take on the latter is to give parents the grace to miss a church service or a meeting in order to honor their children and live their lives. One Sunday, my son's basketball team was scheduled to play in a basketball tournament. As a father and supporter of my children, I make it a point to not miss any event in the lives of my family. I made a video recording of my message for Sunday and went to the tournament to support my son. This act spoke not only to our congregants but also to the staff. It showed that I highly value family and that they should put family in front of work and ministry. That action shaped our culture in a very tangible and positive way.

The lead pastor can be a grace-filled person or a hard, unbending and even authoritarian leader. Either attitude shapes church behavior. Also recognize that the way a lead pastor is treated shapes church culture. The lead pastor who is shown grace and mercy is bound to reflect those attitudes in the way he or she pastors and treats people and staff.

Every leader has a certain inclination because of the particular gifting to build church culture that he or she has been given. This bias adds a particular flavor to the church culture. An administrative leader, for example, emphasizes structure, schedule, programs and methodology. In the mind of an administrator, church is to be run efficiently. The visionary leader, however, emphasizes developing new ministry initiatives, lifting faith attitudes and driving expectations. This attitude puts people as the highest priority and views ministry to people as the norm. The church then becomes a place that beats with a caring heart that reaches out to meet people's needs, to encourage each other and to expect the miraculous.

The bottom line is that someone shapes church culture, and the lead pastor and the leadership team are powerful shapers—both visibly and invisibly—of church behavior and culture.

THE CHURCH'S SPIRITUAL HEALTH

The healthy church has a spiritual and organizational culture that exhibits a sense of clear air, unity, joy and an overall pleasant atmosphere. You might have heard people comment that church simply feels like home. That feeling is a cultivated atmosphere in a healthy church.

Healthy churches build an immune system that resists diseases. It is much wiser to prevent an illness than to contract one and cure it. There are several signs that a church has allowed a disease to penetrate and cause an unhealthy culture:

- Continually discouraged pastors and leadership team
- Spiritual and doctrinal imbalance
- Heavy-handed authority
- Lack of spiritual sincerity or depth
- Little or no momentum
- Little or no conversion growth
- Emotionally unhealthy leaders
- Unresolved issues within the congregation
- Financial lack and pressures
- No new ideas or creativity
- Internal focus
- No community involvement

Another cause of an unhealthy church culture is dysfunctional organization. A church that is poorly structured, poorly administrated and/or poorly managed will hinder God's work in the church and in the people.

Problems with dysfunctional organization can be seen when there are unrealistic demands, blame shifting, intimidation, power struggles, dishonesty, an atmosphere of fear, unclear job descriptions, and people not adequately compensated. All these things make for a very unhealthy church culture that indeed hinders the church's growth and impact in that region.

The healthy church is a place where the leadership team has a positive vibe, an authentic atmosphere of unity and teamwork, and a faith atmosphere that sees the future and believes for great things to happen. This is a church culture where people belong and are relationally connected.

The Saturating Presence of the Holy Spirit

Church today should be a place where the Holy Spirit has a prominent expression and is honored in every way. The first church, recorded in the book of Acts, was a Spirit-filled, Spirit-formed and Spirit-empowered powerhouse. Blending Spirit-filled values into a relevant, vibrant church that connects with today's culture is always a challenge for any church. I see five Spirit-filled, Spirit-forming values that should be kept in high esteem when building church culture (see Zech. 4:6; Acts 1:4-8; 2:1-4; 2 Cor. 3:17; Eph. 6:18).

1. The Value of Prayer

Prayer culture is a spiritual life principle established by the leadership team. The kingdom of God is found in prayer, and prayer releases God's kingdom on our meeting places. Without prayer, the church is an empty organization, lifeless and powerless. A church that builds a powerful prayer culture is one that believes in Spirit-empowered praying. Every person is called to be a Spirit-empowered intercessor (see Isa. 58:12; Ezek. 22:30; 13:5; Matt. 16:18).

2. The Value of Worship

A worship service is convened to serve and please God with our praises and meet people's needs with God's sufficiency. Worship is an opportunity for us as God's worshiping people to invite His power and presence to move among us. It affects every person who attends church regularly *and* those who visit.

Cultivating a worship culture is of primary importance, as it impacts the overall atmosphere in a major way. It begins with honoring God's presence with sincere, wholehearted worship. It is then built on and expanded by the musicians, singers, worship leaders, and creative artists who feel the life flow and spiritual DNA of the church. Finally, the atmosphere is infused with the Holy Spirit, resulting in an environment where people regularly invite and expect God's presence in a service (see Pss. 9:1-2; 87:7; 111:1; 113:1; Eph. 3:14-17).

3. The Value of Prophetic Presence

The culture of prophetic presence in a local church is a somewhat subjective term and has even more of a subjective feel in the church culture. The idea I'm referring to is the presence of the God thought that covers our worship, prayer and preaching and that penetrates the hearts of God's people with a quickened Holy Spirit thought, idea, picture or feel. Receptivity to that presence opens us to the realm of God speaking today in our corporate worship and prayer. Our worship is an integral part of the prophetic culture. The lyrics of songs may have a prophetic spirit, and this prophetic unction brings a dimension—a divine quickening—to our worship (see 1 Cor. 12:31; 13:9; 14:3-4).

Valuing the prophetic presence recognizes the need for and significance of people receiving personal prophetic thoughts quickened by the Holy Spirit. We need words of encouragement (see Jer. 15:16), words of reviving (see Jer. 20:9), words that we sing back to God as spiritual songs (see 1 Chron. 25:1,7), words of life (see John 6:63), and words that make us adjust our behavior (see Ezek. 3:16-17).

A culture of prophetic presence begins with the belief that the prophetic spirit is still resting upon churches today and is a valid part of church culture. First Corinthians 14:26-33 says:

> How is it then, brethren? Whenever you come together, each of you has a psalm, has a teaching, has a tongue, has a revelation, has an interpretation. Let all things be done for edification. If anyone speaks in a tongue, let there be two or at the most three, each in turn, and let one interpret. But if there is no interpreter, let him keep silent in church, and let him speak to himself and to God. Let two or three prophets speak, and let the others judge. But if anything is revealed to another who sits by, let the first keep silent. For you can all prophesy one by one, that all may learn and all may be encouraged. And the spirits of the prophets are subject to the prophets. For God is not the author of confusion but of peace, as in all the churches of the saints.

Everyone can receive personalized, direct edification from the Holy Spirit in the worship environment of the local church (see Pss. 40:5; 139:17-18; Jer. 29:11).

4. The Value of Holy Spirit Gifts and Activity

Without the power and presence of the Holy Spirit alive and flowing in our church culture, we cannot fulfill our complete calling as a strategic church. The three chapters of 1 Corinthians 12–14 give us clear teaching on the gifts of the Spirit in a local church, that is, a church with a culture of spiritual gifts. These chapters in 1 Corinthians call for varied and multiple manifestations of the Spirit. Paul's teaching urged a general respect for the activity of spiritual gifts in an unselfish, others-centered, love-motivated culture. There was also an edifying, orderly and controlled manner in the way spiritual gifts were expressed.

The gifts culture in any church starts with a belief that all gifts are intended and available for today's church and, further, that they make the church a fully functioning, Holy Spirit-endowed church. The things of the Spirit are not limited to some spiritual elite or professional ministry. They are intended for every member in the Body of Christ (see Rom. 12:4-8; Eph. 4:11-12; 1 Pet. 2:5).

5. The Value of Supernatural Expectation

The culture of supernatural expectation is vital for a powerful atmosphere of faith and expectation. I believe God is the same yesterday, today and forever. The church that builds a culture that sees miracles, healings and the supernatural starts by developing a culture of faith based on a definite theological conviction that miracles and healings are for us today. God has something prepared for me that is good, miraculous and life changing. He is ready and willing to work miracles through any person who has a heart to believe in God's unlimited power and possibilities.

It is so important to have supernatural expectancy. In 1 Corinthians 2:9, Paul quotes Isaiah 64:4: "Eye has not seen, nor ear heard, nor have entered into the heart of man the things which God has prepared for those who love Him." Later, he goes on to explain that we "do not look at the things which are seen, but at the things which are not seen. For the things which are seen are temporary, but the things which are not seen are eternal" (2 Cor. 4:18). A culture of supernatural expectation encourages people to believe and express faith. Thus, faith and expectation become the very essence of church culture.

One of the killers of an expectation environment is being easily pleased. C. S. Lewis writes about this phenomenon:

> Indeed, if we consider the unblushing promises of reward and the staggering nature of the rewards promised in the Gospels, it would seem that Our Lord finds our desires not too strong, but too weak. We are half-hearted creatures, . . . like an ignorant child who wants to go on making mud pies in a slum because he cannot imagine what is meant by the offer of a holiday at the sea. We are far too easily pleased.[2]

We must encourage people to raise their expectation level by not being satisfied with the current level of Holy Spirit activity (or inactivity). We do that by having eyes of the Spirit to see the miracles God has done, is doing and will do. Church should be alive with a declaration that God has a storehouse of miracles for every believer. And the stock is full, abundant and ready to be released! A church that has this kind of atmosphere embedded in its culture breathes with an attitude that says God is able, God is willing, and nothing is impossible with God. Things happen!

The Church's Role as a Cultural Reformer

The SC not only has a unique church culture, but it also reforms the world culture where it resides. Much discussion centers on the ability of the world culture to influence the individual and pollute biblical church culture. It is certainly true that world culture is a powerful force of influence, but the church can also influence and reform the world culture by the power of a Kingdom culture! The Bible talks about the church and leaders who reform the world culture as people who raise a standard: "So shall they fear the name of the LORD from the west, and His glory from the rising of the sun; when the enemy comes in like a flood, the Spirit of the LORD will lift up a standard against him" (Isa. 59:19). A flood is a rising and overflowing of something, usually used of a body of water. It is overwhelming. Symbolically, a flood represents the tactics of our enemy used to overwhelm people, cities and nations with relentless evil. It twists truth in lies and destroys righteous foundations.

Floods We Face Today

The church today faces many floods seeking to demolish our faith. We face the flood of humanism, a religion that dethrones God as the centerpiece of life and enthrones man. We face the flood of atheism, a disbelief in the existence of God. Then there are the floods of amorality, immorality, pagan religions and devaluation of human life. In the year 2007, a total of 827,609 abortions were reported in the United States. "The abortion rate was 16.0 abortions per 1,000 women aged 15-44 years, and the abortion ratio was 231 abortions per 1,000 live births."[3] This is what happens when we allow the floods to overtake us. These floods put man outside the sphere to which moral judgments apply. But there must be absolutes if there are to be morals, and absolute moral laws will dictate a certain perimeter, or boundary line, for moral behavior.

Leaders Who Lift Up a Standard

When the floods threaten to overtake us, we have the assurance that the "Spirit of the Lord will lift up a standard" to stem the flood (Isa. 59:19). The Spirit will come and He will raise a standard! A standard is a rallying point, especially in time of battle. It is a cause that people can identify with and stand up for. In the Bible, a standard represented God's hedge of protection, His promised presence and His aid in leading His people in the execution of His will (see Num. 1:52; 2:2; Isa. 49:22; Jer. 4:6).

The Spirit comes upon leaders who raise a standard, and the Spirit empowers them to be leaders of a new reformation. A standard-raising leader must have a clear perspective on the mission of the church in society today as a voice, light, salt and truth: We "are the salt of the earth. . . . the light of the world" (Matt. 5:13-14); and we are to "[speak] the truth in love" (Eph. 4:15). To be that salt, a leader must have a firm grip on the message of the gospel and how the gospel is to be preached in today's culture. The gospel should include repentance resulting in life transformation (see Matt. 3:2; John 1:5,7-8; Acts 2:38). Peter preaching to the crowds in Jerusalem urged them to "repent therefore and be converted, that [their] sins may be blotted out, so that times of refreshing may come from the presence of the Lord" (Acts 3:19). God's Word is absolute truth. It is the final authority in our life and decisions. Absolute biblical values are necessary in developing enduring virtues.

Standard-raising leaders are committed to courageously defend their ground despite the odds, the cost or the intimidation of the enemy. They must not be seduced by the religious spirit and attitude of passivity and withdrawing from culture (see Acts 17:26-27; 18:3). Instead, they are committed to choosing life, truth, what is right, and getting involved with lifting a standard (see Deut. 30:19; Ezek. 22:30).

One man who got involved with raising a standard was William Wilberforce. This man stood his ground to end the slave trade in England despite incredible opposition from slave owners and even his own peers. When the political resolution to end slavery was passed in 1807, it took another 26 years for the slave trade to be formally abolished. The Slavery Abolition Act passed in 1833, just three days before Wilberforce died. He was known as the "man who stopped the most malignant evil of the British Empire: slavery; by his faith and persistence." He spent his life raising up a standard against the flood of slavery and he held that standard high, even when he was intimidated, when he was discouraged and when he was finally victorious.

Like Wilberforce, a standard-raising leader must be willing to become a standard-bearer, one who will be attacked first. You make yourself a target, a focus point of criticism and judgment by others (see John 3:19-21). Paul was such a standard bearer. He wrote to the church, "Now I go bound in the spirit to Jerusalem, not knowing the things that will happen to me there, except that the Holy Spirit testifies in every city, saying that chains and tribulations await me" (Acts 20:22-23). Paul knew he was targeted everywhere he went, but he willingly put himself at the front of the battle lines. Why? He made a commitment to the process of impacting culture. A standard-raising leader must make the same commitment to sowing seed, watering it, nurturing it and raising up a standard in all levels of society. A standard-raising leader must commit to relating to culture and creating culture. Being relevant is not about conformity; it is about clarity and connectedness, about speaking truth with credibility, reality and authenticity. The kingdom of God is not "eating and drinking, but righteousness and peace and joy in the Holy Spirit" (Rom. 14:17).

The church is both the foundation and pillar of truth in today's culture of disillusionment, confusion and compromise. We must march and sing our faith again in the public arena—in the streets and in the mass media. The church is the standard-bearer composed of true believers joined together by the Spirit of Christ. Standard-raising leaders are at the forefront of this reformation, and they are raising up another generation of leaders who have the tools and the faith to impact culture (see 2 Tim. 2:2).

We must penetrate every arena, and we shouldn't be afraid to use the marketplace as one of the tools to generate reform.

William Lloyd Garrison used journalism to fight slavery in the United States. Florence Nightingale used her profession as a nurse to reform hospitals and reshape professional education in nursing. In our present day, James Dobson is lifting a standard against the flood of destructive ideas that seek to destroy the moral values of our nation. He uses radio broadcasts, print materials, the Internet, and politics to reform culture. Today, we need standard-raising leaders in the marketplace of ideas to fight the floods of lies and worldliness and to reform the world culture into Kingdom culture. This is our time to take the church culture built on the Word of God and reform the world culture with the help of the Spirit. Let us raise a standard in our world today!

Strategic Team of Teams Culture

In our digital age, there are thousands of gadgets professing to boost your productivity. From the countless apps that help you organize your tasks to the dozens of gadgets claiming to help you finish your home improvement project in half the time, something more innovating always seems to be out there, some tool that maximizes your time and energy.

When building the strategic church, there is one tool that is proven and extremely effective, and that is the team. Not only can one team accomplish more with less time, but also a team of teams expands the leader's reach to every aspect of the church. As the leader develops a team and then trains those people to develop their own group of leaders, a network of people working together to achieve a common purpose—the vision of the church—is formed. That is what defines a team: a specific number of people with gifts, talents and skills engaging in collective interaction and accountability to achieve a common purpose. Teams multiply effectiveness and they are essential in any organization. It is not biblical to think of ministry alone.

Any leader—any individual, in fact—who always tries to complete a large project on his or her own often finds that trouble rather than perfection ensues. Consider, for example, this story a bricklayer described on an insurance claim form after he tried on his own to move a 500-pound load of bricks from the top floor of a building to the ground:

> It would have taken too long to carry all the bricks down by hand, so I decided to put them in a barrel and lower them by a pulley which I had fastened to the top of the building. After tying the rope securely at ground level, I then went up to the top of the

> building, I fastened the rope around the barrel, loaded it with bricks, and swung it over the sidewalk for the descent. Then I went down to the sidewalk and untied the rope, holding it securely to guide the barrel down slowly. But since I weigh only 140 pounds, the 500-pound load jerked me from the ground so fast that I didn't have time to think of letting go of the rope. As I passed between the second and third floors I met the barrel coming down. This accounts for the bruises and lacerations on my upper body.
>
> I held tightly to the rope until I reached the top where my hand became jammed in the pulley. This accounts for my broken thumb.
>
> At the same time, however, the barrel hit the sidewalk with a bang and the bottom fell out. With the weight of the bricks gone, the barrel weighed only about 40 pounds. Thus my 140-pound body began a swift descent, and I met the empty barrel coming up. This accounts for my broken ankle.
>
> Slowed only slightly, I continued the descent and landed on the pile of bricks. This accounts for my sprained back and broken collarbone.
>
> At this point I lost my presence of mind completely, and I let go of the rope and the empty barrel came crashing down on me. This accounts for my head injuries.
>
> And as for the last question on your insurance form, "What would I do if the same situation arose again?" Please be advised I am finished trying to do the job all by myself.[1]

We need each other! If not for our sake, at least for the sake of someone else struggling to do a big job on his or her own. The Bible is a history of men and women working side by side in ministry together. Paul worked with Barnabas, Silas, Timothy and John Mark. Jesus worked with a core team of 12 disciples. It is not biblical to do ministry alone. Since Jesus worked with a team, then we should too! In 1 Corinthians 1:10, Paul pleads that the church "speak[s] the same thing, and that there be no divisions among you, but that you be perfectly joined together in the same mind and in the same judgment." Committees discuss; teams do. Committees advise; teams accomplish. For a church to be all it can be, the team of teams factor must be a reality. The strategic church is made of a team of teams guided by the lead pastor who has the ability to impart the heart of the team, the skill to know how to build a team, and the principles to know what sustains a team. Let's look at each of these elements in more detail, starting with the need of the team leader to impart heart.

The Need to Impart Heart

The team leader, or what I am labeling as the "lead" or "senior pastor," is typically a person with a mix of the gifts described in Ephesians 4:11-12—apostle, prophet, evangelist, pastor and teacher. This leader has been set in that place of leadership and anointed to direct vision, steer the ship and feed the flock. Wise leadership involves leading leaders, building the church through leaders and strategizing an effective organizational structure that complements the spiritual aspects of the church.

Besides preaching from the pulpit, how does a pastor get a specific vision into the hearts of every person in the church? The leader can't spend exclusive time with each individual member and explain everything in his or her heart, but the leader can spend time with a team of leaders who can then pour the vision into their teams and so on, until every member is reached. That is how teams multiply effectiveness.

In larger churches, the team of teams ministry is especially useful. It is unrealistic to think that the lead pastor or the pastoral team can do all the work necessary for doing church. It takes teams of volunteers, greeters, sound technicians, musicians and so on to make a church service happen and to run the daily operations of church ministry. There's a team specifically suited for following up with visitors, making calls and answering questions about your church. Another team is made up of gifted organizers who can enter information in databases and help plan special events. Still others who like interacting with people form a team of greeters who wave at cars as they come into the parking lot and shake hands with people as they walk through the doors.

A team is not confined to a group of highly skilled people making decisions in a boardroom. It may happen that a meeting room is the place where the team leader imparts the heart of team ministry to the leaders who will share that heart with their teams and so on. The heart of team ministry, though, is what happens when individuals work together using their unique talents to achieve a common goal of loving people and reaching the lost; then their efforts are exponentially increased and the church's impact reaches farther than where the individual could reach by himself or herself.

Here is a fairly simple conceptual diagram of the team of teams culture concept:

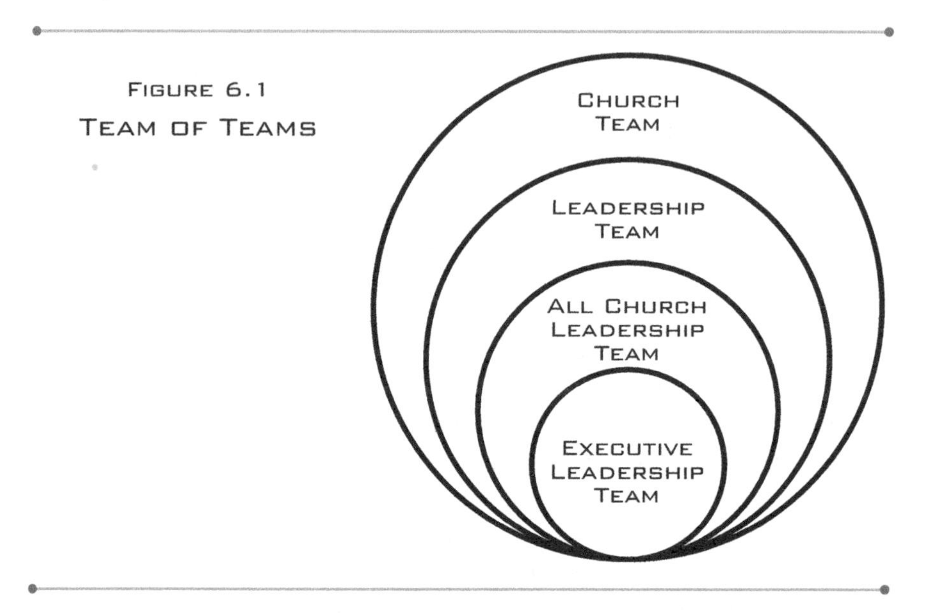

Figure 6.1
Team of Teams

Let's say that this church's vision is "Helping people encounter Christ." The lead pastor gets together with the Executive Leadership Team (ELT) made up of a few strong, cohesive leaders, and together they agree on the vision and come up with a strategy to get there. Part of that strategy is mobilizing small groups to do community projects. So the ELT meets with the All Church Leadership Team (ACLT) made up of leaders representing all departments in the church—from children's pastors to worship leaders to administrative staff. The ACLT gets excited about the community project idea and then meets with small-group leaders to talk about what projects they can do. Those small-group leaders are typically people in the marketplace or involved with a profession outside the church building. They get together with their groups and discuss that group's particular project; and everyone thinks it's a great idea, and they can't wait to start the project.

The vision of helping people encounter Christ was set by the lead pastor, agreed upon and strategized by the ELT, and then passed on so that every person in the church understood the vision and committed to do something to meet that vision. A team is not a team just because they work together or because they call themselves a team. A team is first a team in heart and commitment. Everyone is on the church team!

As a lead pastor, I regularly meet with several teams and together we lead our church. Here are those teams:

- *Eldership team*—This team is the legal and spiritual overseeing body of leaders. This is the official voting team that confirms changes and enlarges the vision.

- *Executive Leadership Team*—This is a small group where relationships, accountability and ministry discussions take place on a personal and ministry level. We focus on strategies that enhance vision implementation, including organizational function, staffing and aligning the budget with the vision.

- *Stewardship Committee*—This team is composed of appointed and confirmed elders specifically focused on all departmental and overall church budgets. They deal with policies, legal issues, properties and future needs.

- *Regional Campus Pastor Team*—This team is made up of the pastor of each of our campuses. Our church is a multisite church, meaning we have campuses throughout our region. Each regional campus has a pastor who is part of this team that meets with the lead pastor to discuss the overall functionality of the broader leadership team and the facility, programs and staffing of each campus.

- *Corporate Service Team*—This team prepares for the weekend service by reviewing all aspects of the service from opening to closing: prayer, worship, video announcements, lighting, and more. The team discusses how to use creative elements to set a certain mood in the church that is consistent with the vision.

- *Worship and Creative Arts Leadership Team*—This group structures, strategizes and discusses the vision and values of worship ministry, assuring that worship values are consistent and spiritually healthy.

- *Generation Unleashed Team*—This team leads our youth ministry, from junior high to high school to young adults. Each regional campus youth pastor meets with the regional campus pastor to assess the current way we engage with young people, how we can be more effective and what we are doing to identify and train emerging leaders. I as the lead pastor have input into this ministry regularly, along with the other executive pastors.

- *All Church Leadership Team*—This group consists of all pastoral teams, which include children's ministry, youth, worship and creative arts, international ministry, and more.

These are the teams that I as a lead pastor meet with regularly. Each church is different and will require different teams to serve their needs and fulfill their unique vision. The bottom line is that a team of teams culture will achieve far greater and better results than a culture where everyone is isolated.

As a lead pastor, I have encountered a few myths about church leaders that, if not dispelled, can get in the way of building an effective team of teams. While the lead pastor faces a unique set of challenges, there are some myths that should be disproved.

Myth #1: The Lead Pastor Determines Whether a Church Succeeds or Fails

Some people might look at a leader's skill set and think that he or she is the most gifted, most talented, best thinker and best of the best in regard to teaching; therefore, he or she is the lead pastor. While such a leader may be very gifted, he or she still cannot single-handedly be responsible for the success of the church. That is an unrealistic expectation. For a church to succeed, it must excel in the basics of team principles and values, with a clear purpose and mission. To that end, the leader focuses on setting a clear vision so that the team can pursue it and, in so doing, be successful. Once the team knows its mission, it can then focus on setting specific, attainable goals and approaches for which each member can be accountable. The purpose goes well beyond individual accomplishment. As I've heard it said, "Play for the name on the front of the shirt, not the one on the back." Play for team Jesus, not team me.

A team of teams ministry demonstrates that the lead pastor does not determine the church's success or failure. The leader may set the pace, but every church member is responsible for carrying out the vision. At times, leaders may need some nudging. People tend to get into an "electric fence mentality" rut where they know how far they can go before getting challenged and therefore operate within limited boundaries. Remind and encourage your leaders to go beyond fence lines, even pushing and/or pulling them over the border at times. Getting team leaders to take risks and enlist help distributes the workload and makes it evident that the church's success does not ultimately rest on the lead pastor's shoulders.

Myth #2: The Lead Pastor Has to Be in Charge at All Times

At times, a lead pastor must change the organizational structure, which in itself is not a doctrinal issue or even a spiritual issue but simply a wise management of people, resources and time. This may mean redesigning a faulty management process or restructuring the decision-making process. When the team is playing the same old game with the same old rules but not understanding that the game has changed, the team loses momentum. Complacency and comfort with leadership strategy and organizational approaches that worked well in the past will kill momentum and productivity. A well-functioning team creates new organizational plans that could better align decisions and actions with strategy and operational priorities. When the leader makes an occasional organizational shift, the action may be interpreted to mean that he or she is operating independently. While some key decisions need to be made without a team process, the reality is that important decisions are made as a team, some even without the lead pastor's involvement.

Recently, we restructured our strategy for sending missionaries. It was a major undertaking that needed to be done. Several meetings took place, policies were rewritten countless times, and every piece was carefully discussed. I was not involved in all these meetings that made major changes to the strategy. However, I *was* involved in the final approval as part of the Executive Leadership Team. But I was not directly involved in the overall process. Strong leaders on many different teams make great decisions all the time that never reach the attention of the lead pastor. That is why the lead pastor should seek to expand the capacity for leadership and independent initiative among team leaders. Peter Drucker, the authority on modern management, once said, "So much of what we call management is making it difficult for people to work." You don't have to micromanage. Let people make decisions.

At times, team performance is worth the extra time it takes to accomplish a task; however, there are other times when time is crucial. It's like working a good plow but in the wrong field. Using a team when the speed and efficiency of a single-leader decision makes better sense can be difficult. The lead pastor must know when to make a single-handed decision and when a matter needs full team discussion. The leaders of other teams must also know when this is the best for the church and the teams. Obviously, if you are going to build teams, single-handed decisions should be the exception, not the rule.

Myth #3: The Lead Pastor Is Always Right and Should Never Be Questioned

The philosophy that "the king can do no wrong" might arise from the necessity of the lead pastor to establish clear guidelines and boundaries in regard to which issues are in the team's domain and which issues remain the prerogative of the lead pastor. A leader may opt to give a lead responsibility to one of the team members on particular assignments, but the lead pastor is still the overall leader. Clarity of leadership allows the team more flexibility, not less. Leadership that communicates clear margins is necessary because, without it, the team becomes frustrated and views meetings as a waste of time and energy.

A successful lead pastor understands that he or she is fallible and is open to suggestions and change. The fact is that he or she is tasked with understanding the actual challenges and real problems that are inhibiting the church from fulfilling its mission or growing numerically or spiritually. In his book *The Go Point: When It's Time to Decide—Knowing What to Do and When to Do It*, Michael Useem writes that "ultimately, every decision comes down to a *go point*—that decisive moment when the essential information has been gathered, the pros and cons are weighed, and the time has come to get off the fence."[2] Don't be afraid of making a decision. If the team agrees on the causes of the problems or the best immediate strategy to move forward, then the lead pastor can successfully direct the team in dealing with urgent issues. An open and humble attitude will quickly dispel this myth that the lead pastor is always right.

The Skill to Build the Team

Along with imparting heart to the team leaders, who then pass on that heart to their teams, a lead pastor needs skill to build a dynamic team. A leader does not build a team by simply establishing a team environment or teaching team philosophy. A leader forms a team by actually working and making decisions with the whole team. Understanding team dynamics and effectiveness without having a disciplined application results in missed potential. When the team is free to have vital input and make impacting decisions, it becomes a more cohesive and, consequently, more effective unit.

One of my favorite times of the year is March Madness. There is nothing like a couple weeks of nonstop college basketball! I love watching how a coach is able to take so many talented individuals and organize them on a court so that each one lends his talent to the rest of the team and, together, they win games. In 2011, head coach Mike Krzyzewski ("Coach K") of the Duke Blue Devils became the winningest coach in college basketball history with over 903 wins. He also coached the US Olympic basketball team to the gold medal in 2008. Coach K has the ability to select and train individuals who become standout teams. In his book *The Gold Standard: Building a World-Class Team*, he writes, "You do not select a team, you select a group of people and then work together to develop into a team. In other words, teams don't instantaneously *become*, they *evolve*."[3] Forming teams takes a lot of work and time. Don't be discouraged when you do not see immediate cohesion in your team. Instead, commit to purposefully reinforcing team principles and purpose rather than individual agendas.

Adding Team Members

There are several circumstances that call for members being added to the team. Throughout Acts, we see that people were continually being added to the team because they had been changed. Three thousand souls became part of the church in one day (see Acts 2:41) and, beyond that, the Lord "added to the church daily those who were being saved" (Acts 2:47). These people became part of the collective team called the church.

As the church grew, people were also added to the team because they were needed. The 12 disciples found that they did not have enough time to study and teach the Scriptures and also police the daily business of the growing group of followers. So they chose seven men to help carry out the mission of serving the people in practical ways, like feeding the orphans and widows (see Acts 6:1-7). These seven leaders were added out of necessity.

Then there are times when a person is added because of God's sovereignty. Such was the case when Matthias was chosen to take the place of Judas Iscariot (see Acts 1:21-26). Think about Paul. He was present at Stephen's stoning and then was divinely called while traveling to Damascus (see Acts 7:58; 9:1-9). Ananias found Saul as the result of a supernatural vision God gave him to go to a street called Straight, lay hands on Saul and bring him the word of the Lord (see Acts 9:10-19). Barnabas found Saul in Jerusalem and stayed with him a whole year while they preached (see Acts 9:26-30). Saul, now Paul, then took on a trainee, bringing another great addition to the team (see Acts 16:1-5). Only God could have foreseen and engineered such a dynamic team. Teams are built with relationships, needs, seasons in life of a church, and the sovereign hand of God putting people together. I am the product of all these processes with the team I am on now.

Forming a team takes time, relationship, and commitment from each team player. The challenge of being a team player is keeping a right perspective when you have only partial knowledge of the whole picture. This is where we need to trust in the Holy Spirit, trust the integrity of leadership and trust in the biblical principles by which we function. Ultimately, the Lord builds the team and places His leaders in the place He chooses. The Holy Spirit orchestrates the gifts and talents. As the skilled leader, recognize the strong gifts within the individuals on the team and then challenge those individuals to work together. Legendary football coach Vince Lombardi said, "Build for your team a feeling of oneness, of dependence on one another and of strength to be derived by unity. . . . Individual commitment to a group effort—that is what makes a team work." The best teams capitalize on individual strengths as they compliment the collective dynamic.

Avoiding Obstacles

While it is easy and convenient to say "teams are effective and you should build them," it is another matter to build teams and then manage them. Several obstacles stand in the way of a team of teams culture. There is the lack-of-conviction obstacle where a person believes teams are good when you need them to accomplish something quickly, but as just a group of individuals, they do not perform well. Or a person may think the team concept is good but in reality finds that teams waste time in unproductive meetings and that too much discussion produces more work, more complaints and fewer results. Still others think teams are good for relationships but not for getting work done, nor for decisive action.

Another obstacle is the habit of quitting too soon. A team requires effective communication and constructive conflicts that deepen interpersonal skills and genuine relationships. However, the frustration of growing together causes some people to think that leaving the team or staying in the team but withdrawing emotionally and mentally is the right response to tension. On the other hand, some leaders have a hidden fear of working with a team. They may be loners, be really shy, or just like to work alone, doing it the way they want to do it without questions and interruptions. The idea of meeting and being vulnerable to other people, having discussions and maybe disagreeing with someone or, worse yet, having someone make them explain their perspective causes anxiety.

One of the hardest obstacles to overcome is the perception that there are greater and lesser leaders. As Casey Stengel used to say, "It's easy to get good players. Getting them to play together, that's the hard part." A leader might think that putting all of his or her time and effort into the hands of a group of people who he or she thinks is unfit for getting work done or for decisive action is a waste of time and will dilute his or her leadership aspirations. While there are some leaders who are not as fully developed as others, the perception that there are greater and lesser leaders is just that—perception. Team culture must be built to tolerate some failures and some goals not met on time and to accept the fact that every team member can develop if given time, mentoring and opportunity (see Ps. 71:21; Jer. 18:1-4). Give talent a chance to grow and fail. When people know that you support, love and accept them just the way they are, they will gradually invite you to help them stretch and grow to reach their full potential (see Josh. 17:17-18). Be an encourager, a builder and a maker of great team players.

The power of encouragement goes a long way in developing outstanding individuals who make a great team. Mary Lou Retton, an Olympic gymnast for the United States, said this about her journey to the Olympics:

> It takes talent, discipline, a very strong work ethic, and a love for your sport to be an Olympic champion. But that's only 50 percent of it. I wouldn't have become an Olympic champion without the other 50 percent that my coach, Bela Karolyi, gave me. He made me believe the unbelievable, that I could be an Olympic champion.[4]

Retton, who won gold, silver and bronze medals at the 1984 Olympics, was the first American woman to win the all-around title in gymnastics, receiving two perfect scores in two of the all-around events.

A team built with positive words and attitudes leaves less room for degenerating attitudes that result in negative thoughts being verbalized:

"This is a waste of time." "We have no clue why we meet." "Nobody is really into doing what we are doing." Such comments and personal attacks, usually made behind people's backs, assault team unity. As a leader, you can combat this destructive force by affirming your team and holding them accountable. You don't have to lie, but you do need to take time in your meetings to point out where the team succeeded and then challenge them to push each other so that each member is helping someone else grow. A sense of interdependency grows among a group when individuals are asked to help a teammate. The well-regarded Coach K wrote, "You can become others' teachers. In a team environment, the talent and expertise of the person next to you is not a threat, but an opportunity."[5] Everyone can learn from someone else's perspective. True teamwork happens in an open environment where all members are free to express opinions, offer constructive criticism and share workload, because they are committed to the mission.

When creating an open environment, it's important to withhold your personal opinion on the subject at hand. When we were in discussion about having women in the eldership, the team never knew what I personally thought for quite a long time. I purposefully did not express my personal view, and that allowed the team to express their true feelings and opinions on the subject without being swayed by my bias. It fostered real and open dialogue that enhanced our cohesiveness as a team.

Principles to Sustain the Team

Just like there are seasons in nature, there are seasons in the life of a team. The team starts as a bunch of disconnected yet talented individuals, perhaps within a department, who work together at a distance. They share information and ideas but not with a common purpose and intent of accomplishing the goal together—kind of like a pseudo-team that exists but isn't effective. The team then moves to the potential team phase. It gains traction and slowly starts to adhere as a unit. Some teams get close to this point but cannot overcome individualism and thus get stuck in this season. We live in a society where individual accomplishment as a measure of success has been ingrained in every mind. A strong individual leader may prefer to work alone or with very few people because it is faster, cleaner, gives more quality control and allows for his or her leadership gift to function without restraint. These leaders like the old saying, "If you want something done right, do it yourself." This is a hard mindset to overcome, but it can be changed as the individual commits to fulfilling the team mission.

Those who do move past individualism become a real team that has all the pieces in place. They are committed and have a passion to build a real, functioning team. After this group has weathered the storms, it emerges as a high-impact, great-achievement team that is deeply committed to each other's growth and success, along with the common purpose and vision of the church.

This powerful, dynamic team, however, is subject to human nature, and a variety of problems can arise and threaten team unity and effectiveness. To prevent this, there are six principles of team ministry that, if practiced by each member, will protect and preserve the team's success.

Principle #1: Recognition

Secure leaders are okay with sharing credit for an accomplishment, and they even compliment others on a job well done. Go ahead and point out someone in a team meeting and tell that individual what an awesome job he or she did spearheading that campaign or finding all those volunteers. This is the principle of "esteem[ing] others" that Paul talks about in Philippians 2:3. Our actions should not be motivated by our own secret agenda or desire for recognition; rather, we should value and respect others and their efforts (see Phil. 2:3-4). Team leaders who believe everyone can be great and is called to greatness build great teams. Such a leader reflects an Ephesians 2:10 attitude: "We are His workmanship, created in Christ Jesus for good works." To be such a leader, you need to recognize your team as people of potential greatness and unusual achievements, never letting them settle for the status quo (see 2 Chron. 27:6; Esther 2:13; 2 Tim. 2:21). You will never lack people for the team if they know you believe every person can be a world changer, a person of greatness and someone who will make a difference (see John 1:19-23; 3:26-31; Rom. 12:3-8; 1 Thess. 5:12-13).

Principle #2: Loyalty

Twice when Saul pursued David in the wilderness, David had the opportunity to kill Saul, but he was loyal to the office and anointing of the king (see 1 Sam. 24:1-10; 26:6-10). Uriah was similarly loyal to David, as was Ittai and the man who saw Absalom hanging from a tree (see 2 Sam.

11:9; 15:21; 18:12). Use adversity to prove your commitment. When you hear gossip about other team members, don't let the gossip continue. Refuse to give into the "we/they" syndrome that criticizes leaders who make decisions that affect your ministry. A loyal heart fights criticisms that threaten loyalty: "If this department is so important, why don't they give us more resources?" "They don't understand what we really do, so why should they make any decisions that affect us?" It is Christ's church we are helping to build and it is His anointed leader who is directing the team. Remember who you are serving. When you are placed on a team in any capacity, you should be joined with that team in heart and spirit. The glue that holds all things together is the divine partnership between loyalty and commitment (see Rom. 16:3; 2 Cor. 8:23).

Principle #3: Harmony

Unaligned leaders form *sub*cultures and create *sub*-vision within the vision. Subcultures cause confusion and low productivity. Teammates who are in step with each other and the leader know the vision, believe in the values and know how to utilize the team to build together. Think about Babel. Every person on earth agreed that they should build a tower that reached to heaven. Brick makers, architects, land surveyors—every citizen was mobilized to construct a giant building. Once their ability to communicate was disrupted, they scattered, forming smaller clusters of like-minded people who were no longer focused on the grand dream they started with. The vision was abandoned. Dissonance can be as damaging as harmony is effective. Preserve unity with effective communication (see Phil. 1:26; 2:1-2; 4:1-3).

Principle #4: Forgiveness

Unforgiveness can easily trip up a team. Perhaps one person fell short of a deadline or offended you with an upsetting remark. No matter the offense or shortcoming, it is more easily overcome through forgiveness and the resulting unity than by harboring anger and resentment and consequently causing disharmony in the group. Too often, we forget the vast number of mistakes for which we were forgiven, and we are stingy in showing the same grace that was so lavishly poured on us. Don't let unforgiveness tear apart your team's unity. Be quick to forgive. But remember that forgiveness is not the same as overlooking a fault. Inefficiency can be addressed and duties can be reevaluated, but a bitter heart is far more damaging than a few missed deadlines (see Matt. 18:21-35; Eph. 4:32).

PRINCIPLE #5: COMMUNICATION

How is a team expected to work together if they do not know the mission or the steps they need to take in order to reach the goal? Communication is an integral component to teamwork. First, the leader needs to communicate the vision and the steps he or she thinks need to be taken in order to get there. Then, each team member must commit to expressing his or her thoughts, concerns, strategies and ideas for implementing the proposed objective. Teams must commit to ongoing communication so that they can adjust responsibilities and components of the plan as they go. Let's return to our example of the tower of Babel. The Bible records God saying that He would "confuse their language, that they may not understand one another's speech" (Gen. 11:7). If one person could not understand what the other was saying, they could not build the tower. Communication was lost and the people scattered. If a team is going to be in agreement and work in harmony, it has to communicate so that they all know what they need to align with (see Prov. 11:13; 16:28; 17:10,17; Amos 3:3).

PRINCIPLE #6: PROPER ATTITUDE

Tying the first five principles together is the principle of a proper attitude characterized by humility, flexibility, teachability and servanthood. When the leader and every member of the team exhibits these attitudes, it is easier to work on a team because he or she is not easily offended. A leader's servant heart says, "I will take responsibility for this area because I want to see the vision become reality." Peter Drucker, the "Man Who Invented Management," found great success in building teams:

> The critical factor for success is accountability—holding *yourself* accountable. Everything else flows from that. The important thing is not that you have rank, but that you have responsibility. To be accountable, you must take the job seriously enough to recognize: *I've got to grow up to the job.* By focusing on accountability, people take a bigger view of themselves.[6]

A proper attitude takes ownership of the vision. That means you personally assimilate the vision into your spirit, soul and mind. You make the church or leader's vision your vision and commit your heart to have faith for the vision and impart it to others.

Imagine what would happen if every member of your church committed to put the vision in his or her heart and pursued it with the same passion that captured your spirit when God chose you and planted the vision in you. A unified church is capable of great things. Is your vision big? Build a team that matches the size of your vision.

Strategic Emerging-Leadership Culture

A carpenter worked with a home builder for several years. When the builder decided to retire, he asked the carpenter to help him with one last home. The carpenter agreed and went about his work building the frame, kitchen cabinets, a stairwell and other features. Like the rest of his work, he did a pretty slipshod job, cutting corners and putting in a fairly mediocre effort. When the house was finished, the builder called him into his office. Thanking him for the work he did over the years, the builder gave him the keys to the house. The carpenter just built his own sloppy house. The carpenter missed his opportunity to be the faithful worker with a right perspective on serving his boss. The boss also missed his opportunity to develop this person fully.

The tragedy of this story is not so much that a man built a terrible house for him to inhabit but that after so many years of working together, the builder did not invest the time, resources and training into his carpenter so that he would be an excellent worker. The carpenter may have started as someone full of potential, eager to learn his craft; but over time, he fell into a routine, was not challenged to be better or sharpen his skills and, as a result, did not grow.

Today we face the great challenge of not only building great churches but also growing great leaders to lead the church. All leaders are building the houses they will eventually live in, so, obviously, finding, developing and releasing qualified leaders into the local church is extremely important and should be the primary mission of the leadership team. I once heard a pastor say, "We don't do much to develop our people into leaders, but it seems to work." That does not sound like a very effective leadership philosophy. I don't want to be guilty of building a church and then leaving it without any leaders to carry on the vision and great work that was started. My philosophy is that every leader should be reproducing a leader at every level in the local church and that the local church is, by design, the most effective incubator of spiritual leaders. This conviction comes from 2 Timothy 2:2, which says, "The things that you have heard from me among many witnesses, commit these to faithful men who will be able to teach others also."

Leaders are keepers of the vision insofar as they learn the truth, identify people who are capable of teaching truth and then train those people to be leaders. All the leaders needed to fulfill the vision are in that church (see Gen. 14:14; Exod. 18:25-26; Num. 1:16). My passion is that in our lifetime all leaders will mentor, train and develop hundreds of leaders who will impact cities, nations and the world. In this chapter, my goal is to challenge you to strategically build an emerging-leadership culture that identifies, trains and releases leaders. Leaders are both born leaders and made into leaders. The potential for leadership is a God-given capacity that may or may not be developed.

GATHERING POTENTIAL LEADERS

The church today needs qualified leadership to lead her to the victories of tomorrow. Where does a pastor find qualified leaders? Should pastors raise up their own leaders or import them from a college or another life-natured church? If pastors do choose to train their own leaders, what methods are to be used? What qualifications should the leaders possess? We must look to the Bible, for the Bible is the source book for all pastors who are endeavoring to build a healthy local church and bring leaders to help that mission. Concepts and principles of raising up local leaders should be established upon biblical premise. A pastor has to have a vision for all the small areas of a church, not just the big overall vision. The pastor needs to juggle many aspects of the vision at the same time or the church becomes one-dimensional. Gathering and training leaders who are like-minded—which is a biblical principle—will help the church achieve the vision.

STICKLIKE, NOT SNAKELIKE

Gathering potential leaders is a risk. We may choose someone to be trained and work with us who turns out to be a snake, not a stick. This is what happened to Paul, as described in Acts: "But when Paul had gathered a bundle of sticks and laid them on the fire, a viper came out because of the heat, and fastened on his hand" (Acts 28:3). The heat exposed the true nature of the stick that was really a snake. We need the discerning eye of the Holy Spirit as we gather our potential leaders (see Isa. 11:13). Many want leadership, but not all are called.

Broken but Healed

Gathering untested leaders is a reality of finding the leaders we desire to train. They may have not proven themselves under the fire of testings, so we should gather untested leaders carefully and with the understanding that they will be tested, and we should be ready for that time. As Paul writes to the Corinthians, "Each one's work will become clear; for the Day will declare it, because it will be revealed by fire; and the fire will test each one's work, of what sort it is," we need to acknowledge that everyone will be tested (1 Cor. 3:13). Faith is proved genuine and "more precious than gold that perishes, though it is tested by fire, may be found to praise, honor, and glory at the revelation of Jesus Christ" (1 Pet. 1:7). Testing is inevitable, and it reveals what really lies beneath the surface. The leader who will benefit the church the most in the long run is the one who has embraced and has been changed by trials, disappointments, sufferings and the mysteries of life. Broken leaders are the best leaders, if they allow their brokenness to become healed and receive the grace of God.

Like-Minded

When choosing leaders, we also run the risk of gathering unstable or unfaithful people. James talks about the "double-minded man, unstable in all his ways" (Jas. 1:8). When you lean on these people for support, they buckle under pressure. They are not like-minded with you because they have two minds, two persuasions about things. Double-mindedness can also develop into disloyalty. As the person's mind is torn between the two perspectives, he can easily drift to the point where he no longer supports the leader's mission or leadership and starts spreading gossip or bad reports about the leader. Because they have not been tested and have not committed to faithfully building the church, they are easily dissuaded from their loyalty to God's appointed leader and leadership team.

Cooperative and Steady

Contentious leaders might also be in the bundle of emerging leaders you identify. These people are very opinionated and convinced that their perspective is not only right but also the best and only way. You want leaders who have an opinion and will voice it but who don't prefer to fight to get things done. They should be willing to give their input but then submit to the team's decision.

Also be careful of whirlwind leaders. They are always whipped into a frenzy and a lot of activity. This breeds insecurity in people, because such leaders tend to be impulsive and hasty in decisions and the way they deal with people. The people end up not knowing who to trust and not knowing if they can rely on the whirlwind leader. Yes, be quick and efficient, but don't sacrifice speed for quality that builds stability.

Birthing Kindred Leaders

You have the profile of an emerging-leadership culture and the factors that characterize it. Now it's time to start finding those emerging leaders! Before you begin, ask yourself and your team, what kind of leaders do we want to produce? What kind of leaders do we not want to produce? What Bible knowledge is necessary for leaders? There are some skills that can be taught and some that are more of a supernatural grace. You function as a teacher to teach them, a disciple to disciple them and a coach to train them.

Consider Different Backgrounds

By experience, people have various backgrounds that distinguish them from each other. When gathering potential leaders, it is important to consider their backgrounds.

- *Inherited Leadership:* A person gains this type of leadership experience by becoming the new pastor of an already existing church. Sometimes leaders with this background are good leaders, and sometimes they have great need. They have already been doing certain tasks and have formed certain concepts of the local church. They may become part of your team, or they may need to step off the team. They must be bonded to the vision you bring to the church and to your ministry.

- *Transplanted Leadership*: A person may gain this type of experience in a variety of different situations: Bible college, another church, etc. In the natural, when a doctor transplants a heart, liver, kidney or any other vital organ, he takes considerable care and exercises mature wisdom during the transplant. Even after many precautions, however, the body may turn on the foreign part and destroy the proper functioning of the whole body. A couple lessons should be realized here. First, be sure you know the person who has the transplanted leadership experience. Know his or her ministry philosophy and basic belief system as well as his or her integrity. On the other hand, when you join a leadership team, listen, observe and ask questions. Research the history of the church, identify with and bond with the church's history and vision. Then encourage the team members to have attitudes of learners, not changers. Again, take time to journey with these transplants because the principles, philosophy and vision of the church take time to learn, assimilate and own.

    If you follow the corporate culture of America and hire the best you can find, you may actually put the team and the church at risk. If the workers do not agree with the church's vision, those people may cause you much pain, aggravation, wasted time and loss of credibility. Hiring the wrong people to your staff without a proper process is a huge problem, but an even greater problem is firing those people. You may be afraid to fire them, or you may procrastinate so long that in the meantime, they find a place of influence and then releasing them is very hard indeed. If you keep them, they can make your life miserable and possibly affect others in a very negative way. It is costly in every way to place leaders as volunteers or staff people in the wrong positions.

- *Safe-Looking Leadership*: This type of leadership is the kind displayed by people who at first appear to be very safe to use or train. Traditional leaders may have excellent character qualities and be sincere in their willingness to work with you. The problem sometimes is their root ideas and concepts. If you begin to use them before you know their roots, then you will have great difficulty in protecting the church if they turn out to have faulty characters, flawed theology or just plain weird ideas.

- *Novice Leadership*: Novice leaders may be well equipped in fundamental knowledge and necessary character, but when the pressures and demands of the ministry mount, some are destroyed because they were used too soon. God will not entrust spiritual authority and leadership to those who have not been tested. Leadership is given to those who are not likely to be blinded by pride or jealousy, whose consecration has been proven, those with the touch of experience (see 1 Tim. 3:1-9; Titus 1:5-9; 1 Pet. 5:1-9). A tip to leaders with novice trainees: don't give them too much too quickly. Allow new leaders to function without giving them any authority, position or title. Let them minister but not be in authority. This allows a servant's heart to develop. It takes time to develop good leaders.

- *Team Leadership*: People from a team-leadership background are those who have worked with a team or have gone out with a team to establish a local church. For the most part, these people are stable, loyal and specifically marked people. Nevertheless, they too must be birthed into the house and the spiritual DNA of the church where they now seek to serve.

- *Home-Grown Leadership*: People gain this type of leadership experience when they have been planted in the local church at an early spiritual age. They have been filled with the ingredients that make up that particular local church, and they have been discipled and equipped.

Learn the Developmental Process

Leaders who are born in the house have the DNA, the spiritual genes, of that house. People are characterized by their places of birth or by the families in which they were born. We need leaders who are born in the house.

> "I [God] will make mention of Rahab and Babylon to those who know Me; behold, O Philistia and Tyre, with Ethipia: 'This one was born there.'" And of Zion it will be said, "This one and that one were born in her; and the Most High Himself shall establish her." The LORD will record, when He registers the peoples: "This one was born there" (Ps. 87:4-7).

Leaders who are birthed into the main elements of the local church have the vision of the house and its principles, philosophy, standards and doctrines engrained in their being. These elements are an integral part of the birthing process. All leaders should go through this developmental process that involves several stages.

The first stage of the developmental process is spiritual identification with the local church. For City Bible, this means belonging to the church and taking the church membership class. The person recognizes there is something significant about the local church. This plays into the next stage, which is spiritual illumination of the inner man. This is the comprehension stage where understanding of the vision of the house is achieved. Comprehension plays into spiritual inquiry with the local church. Is the emerging leader interested in what we are passionate about, or is he or she into other pursuits? The next step is spiritual inspiration to others. Are they excited about what God is doing in the church and exciting others with it? Do they invite people to church? Do they eagerly serve whenever and wherever they can? Do they participate in prayer and worship, and do they drink in the preaching of the Word? Finally we move into the spiritual integrity and spiritual intensity stage. Integrity is proven in the storm, and intensity is evidenced in faithfulness.

When a leader goes through this birthing process, he or she comes out with a full understanding of the church's history and heritage, its values, its principles and its vision. Armed with a clear picture of the vision, a passion to see it happen, and the integrity and intensity to stay the course, he or she marshals others in the church to fulfill the vision.

City Bible has several primary tracks all leaders-in-process take. We have Believe, which offers the basics of Christianity. Then there is Belong, which teaches the church vision and values. Then there is a leadership class, Leadership 101, which teaches the basics of what a leader is and how a leader functions in our church.

Diagnose Emerging Leaders

Finding those leaders who have the right base to build on is a skill of its own, but there are marks to look for. Here are four levels to consider when diagnosing emerging leaders:

1. *Knowledge level*—What do they know and who are they? Find out their philosophy, theology and types of judgments they

make. Are their judgments wise? On what values are their judgments based?

2. *Experience level*—What have they done? What are their people and ministry skills?
3. *Skill level*—What are they capable of doing? What have they proved they can do?
4. *Maturity level*—What do they need to work on? Find out what motivates them. Do they have sound characters, relationships and lifestyles?

Emerging leaders can be recognized by these positive signs:

- Faithfulness in all areas
- Humility when corrected or adjusted
- Willingness to serve in menial areas
- High level of personal integrity
- Responsiveness to preaching and teaching
- Genuine love for people
- Sensitivity to the needs of others
- Continual personal growth
- Successful relationships on personal, family and occupational levels
- Strong hunger for the Lord and the Word of God

Here are some negative signs that can also help us distinguish potential kindred leaders:

- Inability to keep confidences
- Decisions made in haste
- Constant displays of poor judgment (even after instruction)
- Aggressiveness and domineeringness exhibited in relationships
- Emotional instability
- Pushing for promotion and recognition
- Choices constantly made on the wrong side of decisions
- Continual conflicts with those under their charge
- Continual justifying and blame-shifting

Finding emerging leaders and training them is difficult work, but it needs to be carefully done if we are to see lasting growth in our churches.

Building an Emerging-Leadership Culture

As we saw in chapter 5, culture is an integral part of the individual because it involves beliefs, values, attitudes and expectations of people. The way we see people builds a specific culture that either hinders or encourages new leaders. The lead pastor and leadership team's attitudes and actions toward all people affect how emerging leaders will respond to development and how they will interact with each other. The ways we love, forgive, believe in and handle the failures and flaws of potential leaders all set the culture of leadership.

The culture in which good leaders emerge is one of acceptance, encouragement and affirmation. It is a place where there is plenty of faith to believe in people and encourage and equip them to grow to their fullest potential. Jesus chose a few faithful, available, teachable people. They were not scholars or people with special talents. They were ordinary people He could shape into leaders. An emerging-leadership culture is strategically and carefully built.

Culture of Inclusiveness and Grace

An emerging-leadership culture is one of inclusiveness and grace. It is all about recognizing that all people from all backgrounds and with all personality types can become great servant-leaders in God's kingdom. Excluding some people from participating or shutting out or limiting people will not only hinder those individual people but it will also hinder your church and deprive it of the contributions of those people (see 1 Chron. 12:8). You must have the ability to see, not just what a person is, but also what that person can become.

Barnabas was a leader who looked at a charismatic, emerging leader named Paul—who was rejected from a leadership team—and saw that this guy had the potential to lead thousands to Christ, preach the gospel to world leaders and make a lasting impact on the Church. He accepted Paul just as he was, took him under his wing and stood up for him in front of the apostles (see Acts 9:26-27). Barnabas's spirit was a mentor's spirit (see Acts 4:36; 11:22-24,30; 12:25; 13:1-2). This same spirit should characterize our churches. Rather than turning people away, we insist on believing the best of others and never hold anyone's past against him or her.

Build up your people with encouraging words that say, "When I look at you, I see someone who has great leadership capacity. I see someone whom God is using and will use to do incredible things. I am so blessed to be a part of your journey." We give them the Jeremiah 29:11 promise: "For I know the thoughts that I think toward you, says the LORD, thoughts of peace and not of evil, to give you a future and a hope." A church that carries this spirit will step up to the plate and lead, because people will see that you believe in them and are willing to help them become the leaders God intends them to be (see Deut. 3:28; Acts 14:21-22). We take the Deuteronomy 1:38 attitude toward people: "Joshua the son of Nun, who stands before you, he shall go in there. Encourage him, for he shall cause Israel to inherit it."

Culture of Hope for Change

Have you watched any of the *Extreme Makeover: Home Edition* episodes on TV? Some extreme makeovers range from unbelievable to miraculous. No matter how low, base, useless or unprofitable the original structure is, the builders can convert the space into something useful and almost unbelievable.

So it is with a culture of hope for change for all people. No matter how sinfully ugly, derelict, crippled or diseased—unattractive in their souls, so to speak—and no matter how unapproachable and distasteful people may appear to be, the culture of hope says people can change. People can go from useless to useful in the kingdom of God. Paul, writing to the slave master, says of the former slave that he "once was unprofitable to you, but now is profitable to you and to me" (Philem. 11). The name "Onesimus" means "profitable." Onesimus was a Phrygian slave from a group that was known for being unreliable and unfaithful. But after a God encounter—a pivotal life-change encounter with the apostle Paul who had a ministry philosophy that everyone can change and that everyone is important—Onesimus became profitable.

A culture of hope for change says, "I know you have had problems in the past, and I know your failures, but I choose to love and develop you. You may have been useless and disqualified, but you will become useful and valuable." This is the attitude that Jesus spoke of when He said, "The Spirit of the LORD is upon Me, because He has anointed Me to preach the gospel to the poor; He has sent Me to heal the brokenhearted, to proclaim liberty to the captives and recovery of sight to the blind, to set at liberty those who are oppressed; to proclaim the acceptable year of the LORD" (Luke 4:18-19).

We build a culture that does not turn away a leper but says that the leper can be cleansed, just as Jesus did: "Now a leper came to Him, imploring Him, kneeling down to Him and saying to Him, 'If You are willing, You can make me clean.' Then Jesus, moved with compassion, stretched out His hand and touched him, and said to him, 'I am willing; be cleansed' " (Mark 1:40-41). We believe Jesus restores the broken, heals the lepers and gives hope to the hopeless. He is the one who "redeems your life from destruction, who crowns you with lovingkindness and tender mercies" (Ps. 103:4). This is the powerful culture of building hope for change for everyone and anyone. Jesus' grace rules in this culture.

People do not follow leaders who are negative about other people (see Prov. 18:21). They follow leaders who are optimistic and have high expectations for others. Believe in the people and let them know that you believe there is more in them than what you see today (see Job 4:14). Stretch and challenge people; let them make mistakes, but hold them to a high standard of excellence. Coach McCartney once said, "The four most powerful words in the English language are 'I believe in you.' " Believe people can change, and show your belief with your actions and attitude.

Culture of Servant Leadership

Growing a leadership base necessitates growing a servant base to match the vision and structure. Every leader should commit to doing all that is in his or her power to ensure the success of the team, even when it is inconvenient to serve someone, because the ultimate aim is the success of Christ's church. A servant heart is one that is filled with the grace of Christ and is being shaped and transformed into feeling what Christ feels and thinking like Christ thinks. The foremost characteristic of the life of Jesus was and is His servant heart. We are most like Jesus when we serve as He served. Your ultimate purpose in life is to go beyond yourself. Going beyond is serving others beyond your position and title, beyond praise, pedestals, ego or fear of being the lesser. Martin Luther King once said, "Everybody can be great. Because everybody can serve. You don't have to have a college degree to serve. You don't have to make your subject and your verb agree to serve. . . . You only need a heart full of grace. A soul generated by love."[1]

Jesus said that "whoever desires to become great among you shall be your servant. And whoever of you desires to be first shall be slave of all. For even the Son of Man did not come to be served, but to serve, and to give His life a ransom for many" (Mark 10:43-45). Jesus used the word "servant" as a synonym for greatness, contrary to popular opinion today. He taught that a leader's greatness is measured by a total commitment to serve others. Jesus lived with an "I serve" attitude, as opposed to an "I lead" attitude. It is the act of serving that leads other people to be what they are capable of becoming (see Rom. 12:1; Phil. 2:22; Col. 4:7; 1 Pet. 5:2).

A servant puts other people's needs, aspirations and interests above his or her own. Service-focused leadership asks, "What can I do to make you successful in the kingdom of God? How can I serve you to greatness?" When you start seeing that people are not an interruption to your life or ministry but an addition, your perspective shifts so that you invest more time in people than in buildings. As Paul points out in Ephesians 4, we are all part of the team that is building God's house. No position or ministry stands separate from the rest of the team, neither is any position or ministry more or less important or valuable than the rest of the team (see 1 Cor. 3:6-10).

> Exemplary leaders are interested more in others' success than their own. The greatest achievements are the triumphs of those they serve. Knowing they have made a difference in others' lives is what motivates their own, giving leaders the strength to endure the hardships, struggles, and inevitable sacrifices required to achieve great things. Leaders who see their role as serving others leave the most lasting legacies.[2]

Servant leadership does not discriminate. Equal enthusiasm goes into serving those above and below in position and those who are struggling or overachieving. A servant attitude will attract and develop more leaders than a condescending attitude that excludes the unlovely or difficult person or is irritated with seemingly petty matters that are below his or her station. Serving is authority *with* people rather than power *over* people. It is having the respect of the people you serve so that everyone can do what is needed. The SC that builds its leaders from a service base will never lack for help with an outreach, volunteers for a kids program or funds for a project, because the leaders have developed a servant leadership mindset that permeates the church culture.

Culture that Resists the Hometown Limitation Put on People

According to Mark 6:1-6, Jesus tried to do ministry in His hometown but was greatly limited by the people who knew Him. They saw Him, not as the

Son of God and a miracle worker from heaven itself, but as a carpenter, a hometown boy who was a normal, everyday, regular Joe who pounded nails into wood. He crafted homes with His skills and sweat, ate lunch at the local town café and had brothers and a family. The townspeople probably wondered what the big deal was about a guy who was normal just like them. They didn't see why everyone else was so taken with this normal package of a person. This is the hometown attitude that resists and puts limitations on people because we know them: The more information we have about someone, the less we sometimes see them as special or as great people.

After being in His hometown, Jesus remarked, "A prophet is not without honor except in his own country, among his own relatives, and in his own house" (Mark 6:4). We see this same attitude in the Old Testament:

> Now Eliab his oldest brother heard when he spoke to the men; and Eliab's anger was aroused against David, and he said, "Why did you come down here? And with whom have you left those few sheep in the wilderness? I know your pride and the insolence of your heart, for you have come down to see the battle" (1 Sam. 17:28).

This same attitude can be a problem in our own houses—our own local churches. We know the family. Their kids grew up in the church. Now we're looking for a youth pastor, a children's pastor, a worship leader, so surely the only way to find someone great is to look outside the house. Sound familiar? This culture requires a radical change in our attitude. We should take this attitude: "I will respect and develop you and not let familiarity with you cause me to see you as wrong for the position or to limit your future. My unbelief because of knowing you so well is an obstacle that I will remove. I will not let the hometown attitude hinder your full development!"

Now this is a culture that inspires potential emerging leaders all around you, and they will rise to new levels. All people, all races, all backgrounds of life—everybody can become great in this culture. No one is left out—male or female, young or old, strong or weak—all can become all they are called to become (see 2 Sam. 5:10; Ps. 71:21; Eph. 2:10).

Culture of Empowered to Fulfill Great Dreams

A distinguishing mark of great leaders is charisma. Charisma is that unusually appealing quality of a personality that is able to attract followers and excite people to action. A strategic, charismatic leader pushes people to believe that the greatest things God placed in their hearts can happen. God said to Solomon, "Ask! What shall I give you?" (1 Kings 3:5). Ask what you want, because God desires to do great things in and through your life. Prepare your heart for a visitation from God. A divine encounter is coming to you. This is the culture of faith in other people's dreams, a culture that inspires faith, vision and dreams, that imagines the best, and that believes for the greatest things God has for everyone.

This culture builds dreamers. People who see what can be, not what is, and live by seeing the future as if it is already here. This is a Jabez-prayer culture: " 'Oh, that You would bless me indeed, and enlarge my territory, that Your hand would be with me, and that You would keep me from evil, that I may not cause pain!' So God granted him what he requested" (1 Chron. 4:10; see also Joel 2:28; Matt. 7:7-8; 1 Cor. 2:9-10). The SC develops this culture of teaching people to believe they have the capacity to dream, to empty out the old and receive something new. A personal trainer who tells his or her client, "I see the natural athlete in you," motivates the client to work harder, to do those last five reps. An emerging-leadership culture pushes people to go after their dreams, saying, "Let's destroy the limitations on your life and see you fulfill the great dreams of God." Take the weights off the runner, and let the runner run hard toward the dream. People follow leaders who encourage them to pursue their goals, because they don't feel threatened or afraid that following that leader requires giving up their calling or God-given dreams (see Gen. 37:5-6; 2 Kings 2:9).

Cultivating an Emerging-Leadership Culture

Cultivating a culture of leadership growth takes a variety of approaches or models. Generally, a mixture of the one-on-one discipling and mentoring model and the leader-to-team model is used. I see the leadership development culture as a pipeline that connects a pool of leaders at one end to the destination at the other end. The leader's job is to get people from that pool into the pipeline and to the destination, which is mature leadership serving in ministry. Emerging-leadership development, then, is not just a pipeline, but also a pool of people who can fulfill multiple ministries and serve in multiple positions. This model helps the church find multiple emerging leaders with the potential skills, gifts and talents that can be developed in groups. Potential leaders are recognized, trained and released. As Peter Drucker once said, "The best way to a great future is to create it."

Leadership development starts with you the leader using your time to train potential leaders and discern those who can do and those who can lead. This is where the leader has to think beyond his or her function and exercise the skill of getting work done through others rather than on his or her own. The inability to delegate increasingly blocks the pipeline of leadership growth. Understand that great leaders work through other leaders who work through others, thus multiplying their efforts, which multiplies results.

Like any culture, there are certain distinguishing traits, or elements, that characterize it. Here are eight characteristics that should distinguish you as the leader of an emerging-leadership culture:

- *Discerning eye*—Find emerging leaders in every ministry area and function of the church. Don't limit yourself to a specific age, background or gender.

- *Character reward*—Recognize and reward the right character qualities, being careful of self-assured and self-confident people who are not teachable.

- *Shared ministry*—Pass ministry on to emerging leaders without controlling or micromanaging them. The less you do, the more others can do.

- *No assumptions*—Give everything for leadership development with no exceptions; and treat everyone equally, even those who appear to be especially charming, persuasive and gifted.

- *Total person*—Encourage all emerging leaders to develop their heads, hearts and hands. Peter Drucker wrote that "the person with the most responsibility for an individual's development is the person himself—not the boss. The first priority for one's own development is to *strive for excellence*."[3]

- *Transfer of responsibilities*—Oversee the shifting of responsibilities of an emerging leader to a new ministry job that has a specified description of duties but maintain authority over the new leader.

- *Retention*—Communicate to emerging leaders that they have a future in the church and they are "keepers," highly valued potential leaders.

- *Team of teams*—Develop team leaders to lead teams that empower others and model the team value (see a more detailed discussion of this in chapter 6).

Training emerging leaders is one of the most vital parts of the SC. A lasting church has a well-established and well-oiled pipeline of leaders being identified, trained and released for ministry in the local church and the world at large.

Strategic Life-Changing Worship

I believe worship is one of the most dynamic shapers of the atmosphere in the local church. The great search of the human heart is the search to discover the One who is worthy of our worship. Worship is surely the most meaningful and delightful occupation of all humanity, especially the redeemed of the Lord. Everyone will worship something or someone. Whatever we value most, whatever captivates the deepest passions of our hearts, will also earn our worship (see Matt. 6:21; Luke 2:34). When we the redeemed worship, we are loving the person of the Lord Jesus Christ, the One whom we meet as we praise Him and proclaim Him as Lord of all.

A corporate worship service, or church service, is convened to serve and please God with our praises and to serve and meet people's needs with God's sufficiency. When the SC gathers, it is not for a concert or a performance. It is a piece of time intentionally set aside to tune in to what God is saying and to respond to His voice with our whole hearts. True worship has no room for spectating hearts. At its foundation, worship is participatory. Darlene Zschech, author of several well-loved worship songs, writes:

> To worship is to be full of adoration. . . . to bow down to Him, to revere Him, and to hold in awe His beauty. . . . a kiss toward heaven. Worship is a verb, . . . It is an active expression. . . . Worship involves the giving of ourselves. . . . It is a movement of our hearts, our thoughts, and our wills.[1]

"Worship" is a verb, an action word. It is not something done to us or for us but by us. Actively participating in worship is the biblical norm for the redeemed person. A. W. Tozer said, "But this I know: when the Holy Spirit of God comes among us with His anointing, we become a worshipping people."[2] Worship is the opportunity for us as God's worshiping people to invite God's power and presence to move in and do something as we worship. God's presence is the target. That is why it is common to start a service with prayer and singing. Praise has a way of positioning us to receive from God and open our hearts to invite His presence into our gathering.

Wholehearted congregational worship is free flowing, spontaneous and Spirit inspired. It provides the spiritual vitality of a local church by its meaningful and dynamic expression of worship. Pastor and songwriter Louie Giglio wrote, "True worship is a whole-life response to God's greatness and glory. A response that taps our mind, our soul, our heart or passion and all our strength."[3] The worship experience is an integral part of the life force of the heart of the congregation. The corporate expression of worship is a fountain that springs from a pool of water within the congregation. The health of the pool determines how healthy the fountain will be and how deep the well goes. A deep well is dug when the congregation is taught the principles of personal relationship with Jesus, a disciplined devotional prayer life, the principles of living above the impurities of our culture, Holy Spirit power, and living in and by the Word of God. Corporate worship is not just the sound, lighting and great bands who sing great songs. Corporate worship is worship given by worshipers, the people, the congregation that worships with all their hearts.

Styles of Worship

The styles of worship are various and many among the many different churches in the world. Styles vary—and should vary—but the biblical principle of worship should be the defining value of the worshiping church. In the United States, new styles of worship were introduced in the 1990s. For the first time, we heard concert-quality music with full bands and watched videos projected onto large screens. Praise music was backed by the prominence of electric guitars and rock-style drums. It was a new and different sound, certainly different from the traditional organ, piano and robed choir. This modern worship movement swept from the West Coast to the East Coast and became widely accepted in churches throughout the world. Research indicates that today, one in four congregations now use electric guitars and drums in worship, and these instruments and this type of sound are seen in both young contemporary churches and mainline evangelical churches.

Any music style—be it contemporary or traditional—is just that, a style. It is the heart that has to be directed toward God and touched by Him. The whole soul of the worshiper—the spirit, mind, will and emotions—must be invaded by the presence and power of God. "Bless the Lord, O my soul; and all that is within me, bless His holy name!" is the wholehearted response (Ps. 103:1). Worship leader and songwriter Matt Redman wrote, "When we face up to the glory of God, we soon find ourselves facedown in worship. To worship facedown is the ultimate outward sign of inner reverence."[4]

Styles and trends will change with culture and innovation and the availability of more creative technology for our worship services. Our challenge is to learn how to keep a powerful sense of the presence of God and keep people actively participating in worship rather than standing as spectators at a concert. Modern worship is a great bridge for the culture we live in. It helps draw people to church and brings a level of enjoyment to services that are creative, excellent in presentation and culturally tasteful. This is certainly a plus for the church and provides an added opportunity for evangelism and growth. It is also a source of continuing challenge to make sure our worship is biblically based and is not driven by culture. We use the latest technology, modern décor, signage, building shapes and sizes, but we don't build our church on cutting-edge things without the presence and power of God.

Regardless of the style, worship should create an atmosphere where God moves in with His presence and power, drawing people to be touched, healed, forgiven and redeemed. Excellent and creative musical compositions and performances cannot create hearts for worship, but they can give worship expression an articulation unlike any language known to man.

Worship is the soul crying out as the psalmist did: "I will bless the Lord at all times; His praise shall continually be in my mouth. My soul shall make its boast in the Lord; the humble shall hear of it and be glad. Oh, magnify the Lord with me, and let us exalt His name together" (Ps. 34:1-3). Worship is the person worshiping. It's the "I will" attitude of Psalm 61:8: "So I will sing praise to Your name forever, that I may daily perform my vows." It's the appeal of the psalmist who says, "Let my mouth be filled with Your praise and with Your glory all the day" (Ps. 71:8). True worship is done by a true worshiper.

Characteristics of Worshipers

Worshipers are first of all believers. They have accepted Christ as their personal savior and have committed their lives to Christ. The first church in Acts describes such people as "believers" (Acts 1:15, among many other instances). According to the biblical profile of believers, they are people who hear and believe the Word (see Acts 4:4), are "of one heart and soul . . . [having] everything . . . in common" (Acts 4:32, *AMP*), and increasingly add even more believers to the church (see Acts 5:14). Those believers are true worshipers.

Worshipers are followers of God, people who pursue God with all their hearts, souls, minds and strength. "As the deer pants for the water brooks, so pants my soul for You, O God. My soul thirsts for God, for the living God. When shall I come and appear before God?" is the deepest cry of worshipers (Ps. 42:1-2). They are lovers of God, placing all their affections, passions and emotions on loving God, unashamedly pouring out their love to Him. This is the greatest commandment of all: "You shall love the LORD your God with all your heart, with all your soul, with all your mind, and with all your strength" (Mark 12:30; see also Deut. 6:5).

Worshipers are responders, worshiping God with a fervent heart and voice along with actions that at times are expressed extravagantly. Worshipers freely pour out praise and worship to express their deep love for God. Their attitude is like David's: "I will praise You, O LORD, with my whole heart; I will tell of all Your marvelous works. I will be glad and rejoice in You; I will sing praise to Your name, O Most High" (Ps. 9:1-2). To give a wholehearted effort is to use all one's energy, enthusiasm and strength. It is giving the entire being–complete, undivided, total, heartfelt, holding nothing back affection. The SC teaches and nurtures people into wholehearted worshipers who give worship with all styles and expressions. Ranging from grand, declarative, jubilant statements to deeply personal, devotional love and appreciation, the church rejoices in God, using appropriate physical and vocal expressions. The church glorifies the Father through the name and person of the Lord Jesus Christ.

Worshipers are soul stretchers and transformers. No experience in life so broadens people's horizons or so stretches hearts and souls as this experience of true dynamic worship. When I think of the soul being stretched, I am reminded of the remarkable woman Joni Eareckson Tada. This beautiful woman suffered a traumatic diving accident at the age of 17, leaving her a quadriplegic. While attending a convention sometime after her accident, Tada sat in an audience and listened as the speaker closed his message by inviting everyone to kneel on their knees in prayer. Not being able to walk or have any feeling in her legs, she was the only one there who could not kneel. She recalls that in that moment, she prayed, "Lord Jesus, I can't wait for the day when I will rise up on resurrected legs. The first thing I will then do is to drop on grateful, glorified knees."[5] Tada may not be able to kneel physically, but she can kneel in her spirit and worship with her whole being. True worshipers transform the mundane into meaningful acts of service and reverence for the Lord that engage the whole person—spirit, soul, mind and body. That is the kind of worshiper God looks for.

Hindrances to Worship

Since we have been forgiven of so much and we serve a God who is so great, we should passionately bring true worship to God. Unfortunately, our corporate gatherings sometimes lack that excitement and energetic vibe. There are some things that can hinder a church from worshiping wholeheartedly—things that may be done by both the leader and the worshipers he or she is leading.

Hindrance #1: A Wrong Attitude About Worship

The immediate killer of worship is a wrong attitude. Some may look at expressions of worship and respond like Michal did when she saw David dancing in the streets: "she despised him in her heart" (2 Sam. 6:16). Responding to worship expressions with a negative attitude hinders worship.

Maybe you have heard this remark: "Some people just *need* a lot of exuberance. Others of us don't." The implication here is that mature people don't need to be outwardly expressive. Maybe you've heard this comment: "It's all a matter of a person's cultural background. You and I are culturally reserved." This reflects a wrong attitude because it suggests that "reserved" is socially superior or culturally advanced. There is nothing elegant about hanging on a cross in a public square. Yet that is exactly what Jesus did for us as His service and worship to the Father. If your heart is bursting to jump and shout praise to the Lord and you are in an appropriate setting (a worship service or your personal devotions), then do it!

The heart issue is another matter that is often used as an excuse to respond in a worship service without enthusiasm. The excuse might sound like this: "I believe that everyone should worship God in his own way and according to his own beliefs. After all, to do otherwise is, well, uncivil. Don't you believe that?" Or, "I wouldn't let it worry me. After all, what difference can it make? God looks on the heart anyway. All this activity doesn't add a thing!" There is some truth in this last comment. God does see the worshiper's heart (see 1 Sam. 16:7). It is from the heart that the body responds with outward actions such as lifting the hands, singing, clapping, etc. Just as "with the heart one believes unto righteousness, and with the mouth confession is made unto salvation," so too we confess or sing our praise to God from hearts that believe in His goodness, faithfulness, mercy and grace and that believe He is worthy of all praise (Rom. 10:10). What is in your heart must come out in your actions. The attitude you come in with determines the depth you go out with.

Hindrance #2: Limited or No Biblical Knowledge About Worship

Not having a biblical connection to the importance and prominence of worship limits a person's worship. The believer will best practice praise as he or she learns the biblical truth about it from both the pulpit and the personal study of Scripture. That is why it is so important for pastors and leaders to teach the Bible and teach about worship. If you don't know what the Bible says about God's faithfulness, how can you fully praise His character? If you don't know the Bible's instructions about praise, how will you know to praise continually? It is in the Scriptures that we learn to fill our mouths daily with praise and glory to God all day long (see Pss. 34:1; 71:8).

In Scripture, we learn that praise is a spiritual weapon to be used against the enemy. There is strength in our praises: "Out of the mouth of babes and nursing infants [God has] ordained strength . . . that [He] may silence the enemy and the avenger" (Ps. 8:2; see also Ps. 149:4-9). The Bible is "the sword of the Spirit" with which we defend ourselves from the enemy's attack and also attack him (Eph. 6:17). Know the Word of God so that you can use it in your praise.

Not having enough biblical knowledge about worship is just as dangerous as having wrong teachings or rigid church traditions in worship. Wrong teaching can quench the spirit of worship. If worshipers have been taught to never lift their hands, then they are stifled from fully expressing their praise to God because they have to work hard at keeping their hands at their sides and their demeanor reserved. Worship has never been intended by God to be an occasion for proving one's expertise in religion but for satisfying one's hunger and thirst for God.

HINDRANCE #3: LIMITED EXPERIENCES WITH BIBLICAL CHURCH WORSHIP

Worship experiences in a church can be a damper to your spirit if those experiences were less than biblical worship. Those substandard experiences may have taught you to be a spectator and to be quiet, reserved, dignified or religious. True church worship experiences should be dynamic, exciting, fulfilling and anointed—a spiritual encounter with the presence of God.

The difference between limited and full worship is kind of like the difference between a black-and-white movie-viewing experience and a high-definition movie-viewing experience. Those who watched films or looked at photos only captured in black-and-white never knew about the ability to capture moments in crystal-clear, even three-dimensional, color. The average disposable camera gives a better picture than the old accordion-style cameras accompanied by a poof of smoke after the flash. But before we were exposed to color television or Blu-ray, all we ever knew was good old black-and-white, a limited viewing experience.

Worship is a full, whole-hearted, high-definition expression for God's pleasure. Anything less than that falls short of the biblical norm. Matt Redman wrote, "Worship thrives on wonder. We can admire, appreciate and perhaps even adore someone without a sense of wonder. But we cannot worship without wonder. For worship to be worship, it must contain something of the otherness of God."[6] A full, unlimited worship service creates an atmosphere of wonder at the greatness and goodness of God.

HINDRANCE #4: LIVING IN A GODLESS CULTURE

For most of us, life in the twenty-first century consists of dizzying busyness. Our minds are filled with so many other things that we have no time to prepare or wait. It's a fast-food culture. "Everything must happen now or within the next two minutes; otherwise, I'm gone. God, if You don't show up by the end of the next chorus, I'm checking out." We easily lose track of our focus in worship because our minds are trained to jump to other responsibilities. Finances, building projects, new programs and so many other pressures push on our minds, attempting to disrupt our focus on God. In God's presence, there is peace and refuge from the questions swirling in your mind and from the pressures squeezing you on every side. You've got to move out of a godless culture and into God's presence.

Worship Encounters the Presence of God

The purpose of worship is to encounter God's life-changing presence. An unhindered worshiping church has a deep hunger for the presence of God to be revealed in each and every worship service. The desire of the SC leader is to position the church to have a fresh encounter with the powerful, personal, life-changing presence of God. Our request is the same as Moses' plea in Exodus 33:15-16: "If Your Presence does not go with us, do not bring us up from here. For how then will it be known that Your people and I have found grace in Your sight, except You go with us? So we shall be separate, Your people and I, from all the people who are upon the face of the earth."

The personal presence of God is not merely some "force" or "influence" that we seek but a real life-changing presence of a living God who abides in us and dwells among us. Moses understood that God's presence was a sign of God's pleasure in His people, and it would distinguish them from all others. The worshiping church has a passion for the presence of God, not just for great music or great songs. The presence of God as described in Scripture suggests the idea of God's face being turned toward us in acceptance, blessing and favor. His presence fills up, pervades, permeates and overspreads us as a thick cloud on a stormy day.

Characteristics of the Presence

There are different aspects, or characteristics, of God's presence that we see in Scripture. There is the omnipresence of God, meaning that His presence is everywhere, in every place—He is present in the whole of creation (see Ps. 139:6-8; Isa. 66:1; Jer. 23:24). We also see what is called God's manifested sovereign presence—God revealing Himself sovereignly at times of His own choosing (see Gen. 3:8; 4:16; 2 Chron. 5:1-14). At times, this strange sense of God may penetrate a building, a community or a region, affecting those who come within God's power. The great American preacher Jonathan Edwards visited a town on one of his preaching circuits and when he got there, he remarked that "the town seemed to be full of the presence of God." This is the manifested sovereign presence.

The manifested sovereign presence is a vivid, personal presence of God that is felt in a real and individual way. It's the omnipresence becoming the manifested personalized presence of God. This is what the psalmist is talking about when he says, "You will show me the path of life; in Your presence is fullness of joy; at Your right hand are pleasures forevermore" (Ps. 16:11) and "You shall hide them in the secret place of Your presence from the plots of man; You shall keep them secretly in a pavilion from the strife of tongues" (Ps. 31:20). King David in Psalm 51:11 prays, "Do not cast me away from Your presence." The presence mentioned here is the felt-realized personal presence of God. God wills that we should push into His presence and live our whole life there. It is more than a doctrine to be held; it is life to be enjoyed. "He who dwells in the secret place of the Most High shall abide under the shadow of the Almighty" (Ps. 91:1) and "the righteous shall give thanks to [His] name; the upright shall dwell in [His] presence" (Ps. 140:13).

The strategic leader teaches and leads the individual into a passion for God's presence, and the strategic leader positions the church to encounter God's presence during every corporate worship service. These are some characteristics of His presence that will help move the church closer to understanding what wholehearted, true worship is.

Position and Experience

The place of worshipers in relation to God's presence is not just a positional standing in God's presence but also the experience of His presence both personally and powerfully. It is living in communion with God with a continual awareness of His presence. In *The Practice of the Presence of God*, Brother Lawrence, a seventeenth-century monk, expressed it this way: "To practice the presence of God is to live in the conscious awareness of Our Father, engaging in quiet and continuous conversation with Him. It means we live an inner life of unceasing prayer and we strive for all we think, say, and do to be an outward reflection of what is pleasing to God."[7] The presence of God is a place where things happen.

God's presence is a place of covenant and blessing. In Genesis, the Lord tells Abram that if he walks blameless in God's presence, God will make a covenant with him to multiply his descendants and personal wealth (see Gen. 17:1-2). As long as Abram stayed in God's presence, he would receive the blessing. Believers who carry God's presence and abide in it will live in a place of blessing.

God's presence is also a place of intercession. David, hiding in a cave, said, "When [God] said, 'Seek My face,' my heart said to [God], 'Your face, LORD, I will seek'" (Ps. 27:8). When he was in trouble, David got into God's presence and interceded for his life.

God's presence is also a place of brokenness. We are made willing to depart from what has been holding us back and pushing us down, and we are able to move into a new softness, willingness and dependence on God. Something in us dies so that new life can begin (see Gen. 32:28-30; Jer. 18:2-6). Those who are satisfied with what they have rarely look to God to supply them with what they truly need.

Mercy and Relationship

In God's presence we find a place of mercy and communion. During Israel's journey through the wilderness, the Israelites built a tabernacle by following God's instructions. The tent was designed to be a meeting place with God. A major element of the tabernacle was the Ark of the Covenant, which symbolized God's presence. At the top of the Ark was the place called the mercy seat. It is from that seat that God promises to meet with us, speak to us and give commandments to us (see Exod. 25:22). His presence then is a place of mercy—mercy for your health, mind, spirit and church. It is also mercy for your relationships because it is a place of relationship.

When God spoke with Moses on Mount Sinai, He spoke "face to face, as a man speaks to his friend," and He wants to speak to us the same way—as a friend (Exod. 33:11). He wants to transform us so that we are more like Him, so that our desires line up with His will. God wants to set our goals. God wants to be our success in life. As long as we insist on writing our own stories, God cannot write His story. We need to let God transform us as we spend time in His presence (see 2 Cor. 3:17-18).

Brother Lawrence wrote a very simple yet profound statement about what it means to spend time in God's presence: "I make it my priority to persevere in His holy presence, wherein I maintain a simple attention and a fond regard for God, which I may call an actual presence of God. Or, to put it another way, it is an habitual, silent, and private conversation of the soul with God."[8] When you are in an ongoing conversation with someone, you pick up on that person's habits, on favorite phrases and on favorite places the person likes to go. Having an unbroken conversation with God develops a similar relationship, and you become so familiar with Him that you start to anticipate His next move. You know Him so well that you are comfortable sharing your dreams and even letting Him tweak those dreams. Your soul is refreshed in His presence (see Acts 3:19) and in the joy that comes from leaving your worries at His feet and taking up a garment of praise (see Ps. 16:11). His presence is a place where impossible situations melt: "The mountains melt like wax at the presence of the LORD" (Ps. 97:5). Your mountain is conquerable with God. Nothing is impossible with Him (see Luke 1:37-38; 18:27).

Finally, God's presence is a place of worship. We are invited to "come before His presence with thanksgiving; . . . shout joyfully to Him with psalms" (Ps. 95:2). Our praises create a dwelling place, a throne, for God to sit on and govern His people by His presence. Psalm 22:3 gives us a beautiful and bold image of God: He sits "enthroned in the praises of Israel." The original Hebrew description of a person enthroned denotes the presence of a king who is seated on his throne, which is a place that has been made ready. The reward of worship is God's enthroned presence, and it is His presence that will make our worship services exciting and life changing.

Biblical Ingredients of Life-Changing Worship

When we come into a worship service, we are preparing our hearts to hear God's words to us, not just sing words on a screen. We are preparing to commune with God and be inspired, comforted, healed, anointed, refreshed, refilled, refueled. We are talking about a living, powerful encounter with the presence of God! We must have a place for God's presence in each and every worship service, and our worship service should have several basic ingredients that are definable and measurable.

Centered on God

We worship God. Our desire is to please Him. Why do we worship if not for God? "He is your Lord, worship Him" (Ps. 45:11). "Give unto the LORD the glory due to His name" (Ps. 29:2). Worship Him in His house, worship Him in your room, and worship Him in your car. Every place you go can be turned into a place of worship to God alone.

Spiritual

The presence of God is the driving force of worship. Since God is Spirit, "those who worship Him must worship in spirit and truth" as the Holy Spirit flows in and through the believer and the worship team (John 4:24).

CONTEMPORARY

Contemporary means belonging to the same period of time—of the same age, current, up to date, relatable to the present day. Worship music should be contemporary and made powerful by the Holy Spirit. Music is a tool of influence. God made us with a capacity to feel deeply. Music can invoke an emotional response that, when turned to God, results in heartfelt worship.

SINCERE

It is with the heart focused on God, not on performance, that we worship. Sincerity is the quality of being genuine, honest, pure-hearted, free of hypocrisy, and devoted without reservation or depth of fear. Our instruction is to "serve [God] in sincerity and in truth, and put away the gods" that earlier generations and the world culture served (Josh. 24:14). Don't let the serpent corrupt your mind "from the simplicity that is in Christ" (2 Cor. 11:3).

PARTICIPATIVE

Worship is not a spectator event. To participate is to take part in something, to share and engage in it. Participation is the opposite of observation. Observers withdraw, so they can look on the event from the comfort of their armchairs. Participators get off the sidelines and join the celebration (see 2 Sam. 6:12-16)! Look at John Wesley's comments about participating in worship:

> Sing lustily and with good courage. Beware of singing as if you were half dead, or half asleep; but lift up your voice with strength. Be no more afraid of your voice now, nor more ashamed of its being heard, than when you sung the songs of Satan. . . . Above all sing spiritually. Have an eye to God in every word you sing. Aim at pleasing him more than yourself, or any other creature.[9]

Worship involves expressions such as kneeling, clapping, lifting hands, shouting and singing. These expressions might be the closest thing to an out-of-body experience for some, but it is biblical: "Serve the LORD with gladness; come before His presence with singing. . . . Enter into His gates with thanksgiving, and into His courts with praise. Be thankful to Him, and bless His name" (Ps. 100:2-4). Singing and praising are outward acts of expression. These are norms, according to the Bible.

ALIVE

Worship is alive with the Spirit of God! Alive is having life—not being dead. People who are alive are full of power, energy and activity. Their atmosphere is electric! Imagine what happened in the early beginnings of the church when the Holy Spirit came and mobilized the believers to preach. The blind were able to see, the deaf heard sounds, and the lame stood up, "walking, leaping, and praising God" (Acts 3:8). That atmosphere was not dead. The people were not halfhearted in their praise. No, they were set free from a lifestyle of bondage, from illnesses they could not change with their own strength, from a confined future and doomed to sitting outside a gate and begging for money to scrape together a decent meal and suitable clothing. In response to their freedom, they worshiped God with every cell in their bodies, with every thought, with every action they could think of doing to give praise and glory to God! That is what our worship should be!

RESPONSIVE

The fountain of worship rises out of a pool of believers who are experiencing and responding to God. We are touched by His presence, love, forgiveness and power. This stirring creates a response in us. We become hungry for Him. We are eager to know Him and serve Him. As we worship and spend more time in His presence, we crave it more and more. God responds to our response.

BIBLICAL

Our book of instruction is the Word of God. What do the Scriptures say and how can we honor the Scriptures? Ephesians 5:19 says that we should "[speak] to one another in psalms and hymns and spiritual songs, singing and making melody in [our hearts] to the Lord." Singing to the Lord is a clear mandate from Scripture. When we come into worship, we are preparing to meet with God, not with man. Contemporary bands, right sound, great lighting, awesome songs—yes, absolutely. But with all those elements, please let us not forget that the driving force is the presence of God.

EXPRESSIONS OF PRESENCE-FILLED WORSHIP

Among the ingredients mentioned above as being part of life-changing worship are psalms, hymns and spiritual songs. These three aspects of singing are not options for the church to choose from but are all to be operating in our worship today. Many churches sing hymns, and many sing parts of whole psalms, but spiritual songs may be pieces rarely included.

The command in Ephesians 5:18-19 starts with a direct exhortation to "be filled with the Spirit," or practice Spirit-filled worship (v. 18). This command is a key to healthy spirit-empowered presence-driven worship. The Greek verb translated as "be filled" is in the present tense, implying that being filled with the Spirit is a continuous process. The evidence of being a Spirit-filled community of believers is worship made with psalms, hymns and spiritual songs. In these expressions of praise, three purposes are fulfilled: the edification of self (see Eph. 5:9), the edification of others (see Col. 3:16), and the exaltation of God (see Phil. 2:9-11). Let's define these musical expressions so that we have a clear target to shoot at when we evaluate the depth of our worship in our corporate gatherings.

Psalms

Psalms are songs of praise from Scripture or songs in the character, spirit or manner of Old Testament psalms that are directed to God. We declare His Word in song. We learn and rehearse the eternal, unchanging word of His revealed truth in the Scriptures.

Hymns

One of the most beloved forms of praise, hymns are songs of praise written by people on Christian themes. Hymns are directed to people as a testimony and are a sound theological tradition. We announce God's works in song and we praise Him and review His attributes, testifying to His goodness as experienced over the centuries. One way to think about hymns is to spell it "H-i-m-s"—songs about the Lord. Every generation writes its own songs about and to the Lord. The hymns written in 2012 might sound different from the hymns written in 1712, but they all are written to the Lord.

Professor and author Tony Campolo was asked if worship songs should necessarily teach doctrines of faith. This was his response:

> I don't think hymns have to be sermons set to music. It is about time that we recognized the legitimate role of emotion. Pouring out one's heart and soul with passionate intensity is what worship is about at its best. When lovers finish talking to each other, I am not convinced that they have communicated theologies and

philosophies. I believe they have exchanged the deepest feelings of their hearts and minds. So, I believe that worship is a time of loving Jesus. Sometimes feelings cannot be put into words.[10]

Spiritual Songs

Spiritual songs are of a spontaneous or unpremeditated nature sung with unrehearsed melodies under the unction of the Holy Spirit. We welcome His will in song, giving place to the Holy Spirit's refilling and making a place for His Word to dwell richly within us. The Holy Spirit is the source of inspiration for this type of song. Like Paul, we are to "sing with the spirit, and . . . sing with the understanding" (1 Cor. 14:15).

A *song of praise* to God is our personal song of praise given freely unto God by lifting our hands and singing spontaneous praise. You must become a singer of praise with your own heart, voice and conviction. It must break forth in you first before it breaks out of you (see Pss. 34:4; 47:6; 98:4; 145:2; Isa. 54:1). Expressions of love and adoration to God–singing about His mercy, goodness and love–should be bursting from your heart so strongly that you cannot help but express them to Him in song. David, the great worshiper, sang these words: "The Lord is my strength and my shield; my heart trusted in Him, and I am helped; therefore my heart greatly rejoices, and with my song I will praise Him" (Ps. 28:7). David's heart could not contain the gratitude he felt, so he poured out a song to God.

This brings up another element of songs of praise–blessing God. One Greek word for praise is "eulogy," which means something written or said to honor, or extol, someone. A presence-filled worship time is a time to sing a song of honor. As we speak well of our God, we bless Him! We bless His greatness, power, goodness and character as the ruler of all things. We should be "continually in the temple praising and blessing God" (Luke 24:53).

A *sacrifice of praise,* another type of spiritual song, is a *tehillah* song. *Tehillah* is a Hebrew word that comes from Psalm 147:1: "Praise the Lord! For it is good to sing praises to our God; for it is pleasant, and praise is beautiful." This type of praise, taught less often than songs of praise, is done when every person moves past entertainment and spectator worship and is activated as the worshiper assumes the role of a New Testament priest to worship God with a personal sacrifice of praise. First Peter 2:9 says that we "are a chosen generation, a royal priesthood, a holy nation, His own special people, that [we] may proclaim the praises of Him who called [us] out of darkness into His marvelous light." Today, we in the church are the royal priesthood offering spiritual sacrifices with our worship unto God. Every person in this priesthood brings a sacrifice.

According to Hebrews 13:15, a sacrifice of praise should be continually brought to God's presence:

> Therefore by Him let us continually offer the sacrifice of praise to God, that is, the fruit of *our* lips, giving thanks to His name.
>
> Through Him, therefore, let us constantly and at all times offer up to God a sacrifice of praise, which is the fruit of lips that thankfully acknowledge and confess and glorify His name (*AMP*).
>
> Let's take our place outside with Jesus, no longer pouring out the sacrificial blood of animals but pouring out sacrificial praises from our lips to God in Jesus' name (*THE MESSAGE*).

Our sacrifices of praise are given at all times and in all seasons of our spiritual lives. The SC encourages and leads the people into a response to the presence of God by singing sacrifices of praise. Our sacrifices are given when there is a challenge beyond our strength and resources (see 2 Chron. 20:15,19-22), when discouraging circumstances do not change (see 2 Sam. 12:15-23), when the dealings of God are heavy upon us (see Jon. 2), when we experience a fiery trial of our faith (see Acts 16:23-26), when we experience God's amazing favor (see 1 Sam. 2:1-2), and when the Lord has given and taken away (see Job 1:21). We sing our *tehillah* song—we bring a sacrifice of our lips! We sing by faith unto God with outstretched arms and a heart filled with the Holy Spirit. Our sacrifice is a song of faith, a spontaneous new song, an unleashed song not written by man but written in the heart—a song of praise, a song of faith, a song of salvation and a song about the goodness of God. Church is meant to be a place where the people worship and give sacrifices wholeheartedly, unashamedly and passionately.

Strategic Powerful Praying

Every church has its own atmosphere that is built over time. The SC has a strategic atmosphere of Holy Spirit-empowered, powerful prayer that permeates every aspect of the church. This is the vital force in the SC: powerful, anointed, supernatural, earth-shaking, heaven-opening prayer. Jesus Himself said His house will be "a house of prayer" (Matt. 21:13). As such, every person in the SC must own the vision of a praying church. Every person must also recognize that this type of praying consists of more than one-dimensional, one-way, petition-centered prayers. SC people pray multileveled and multifaceted prayers. During both devotion times and all-church prayer times, SC people pray strong prayers of intercession, supplication, warfare, travail and agreement.

The New Testament church described in Acts was a praying church. In fact, the churches recorded in Acts were militant prayer churches. They loved life on their knees. They prayed for everything and anything all the time, at anytime (see Acts 1:13-14; 3:1; 10:4,36). Everywhere you turned, there were the Christians praying. They prayed in the Upper Room, in the Temple, in people's houses, in the village streets—everywhere! It was like what happens in this country in November during an election year: Everywhere you look there are people posting campaign stickers and signs, people calling you and knocking on your door, people running ads that ask for your vote, and every TV station is running some story about a candidate. You can't escape it!

The first church's consistent prayers worked in a particularly potent way and were the foundation for the witnessing and supernatural power that followed them. That power was so dynamic because behind it all, there was prevailing prayer, conquering prayer and prayer that got heaven's attention (see Acts 1:12-14; 2:1-4; 4:23-31; 12:1-2). That is why a more accurate name of the book of Acts would be "The Acts of the Holy Spirit Through the Apostles." The Holy Spirit showed His power through the apostles as they prayed and made room for Him to work.

Pastor and author Andrew Murray makes an interesting assessment of the way God governs the universe. He writes, "God rules the world and His Church through the prayers of His people. That God should have made the expansion of His Kingdom to such a large extent dependent on the faithfulness of His people in prayer is a stupendous mystery and yet an absolute certainty."[1] We can, therefore, determine the extent of our reach and impact in our communities and cities. The power to build the Kingdom and expand the church is in our hands through prayer. That is why prayer is so critical to success.

Prayer Responsibilities of a Strategic Leader

To be a powerful and life-changing church, you as the strategic leader must be committed to prayer. Not only must you spend personal time communicating with God, but also you must inspire others to pray. Teaching people how to pray and teaching them the value of prayer is a strategic, spiritual success principle for the church. It is the responsibility of the strategic leader to develop prayer in the local church that is both proactive and reactive to all the needs that arise in the life of that church. Prayer is the fuel that runs the church. It releases the hand of God to move and sustain the life flow of the Spirit. Jesus desires to make every church an instrument of intercession. He called His church "a house of prayer" (Matt. 21:13). Prayer is the most-resisted activity on the planet because of the powerful dynamic it releases! Without prayer, we literally function with no fuel and are left powerless to move the church forward. Prayer releases the power of God to prevail in any and every situation the SC faces. There is nothing impossible with God!

Biblical instruction on prayer includes teaching people how to commune with God and how to ask Him for the impossible. People must be guided to stand in the gap, build a hedge, cry out to God and expect Him to unleash unlimited power and resources. The strategic leader encourages an atmosphere of spiritual dependence on God. Such an atmosphere develops spiritual hunger and moves people to crave God's voice, make petitions with faith-filled prayers and then hear God's response.

E. M. Bounds, the great prayer master, said, "Praying saints are God's agents for carrying on His saving and providential works on earth. If His agents fail Him, neglecting to pray, then His work fails. Praying agents of the Most High are always forerunners of spiritual prosperity."[2] Prayer for the SC is of highest priority. The lead pastor, the leadership team, lay leaders and the entire congregation must all engage in this powerful practice.

Prayer is the primary habit and ingredient for the church and its leaders. The apostles determined to "give [them]selves continually to prayer" (Acts 6:4). When the church gives itself to prayer, it is in a state of constant communion with God. It is as if the channel between heaven and earth is perpetually open. Church is energized through earnest praying and frequent filling of the Holy Spirit. This atmosphere is the SC atmosphere—full of powerful, continual and fervent Holy Spirit prayer (see Acts 9:5-11; 22:8-18; 26:12-19).

Different Types of Prayer

When Baskin Robbins opened its first ice cream shop, it had the unique distinction of offering 31 flavors. Customers could get a classic flavor like chocolate or vanilla, or they could get something more specific like dark-chocolate-covered raspberry-cinnamon swirl. The ice cream shop had something for everyone. Because of its variety and also its deliciousness, Baskin Robbins ice cream attracted people from all over.

Although prayer is not an ice cream shop, it does have lots of variety. Prayer can be a general communion with God where we ask for something, believe in faith that we will receive it, and pursue God until we get the answer (see Matt. 21:22; Luke 6:12; Acts 3:1; 6:4; 10:31; Rom. 1:9). Supplication prayers are more specific prayers focused on a petition for a specific need—a material supply, an emotional breakthrough, or salvation for a loved one. Ephesians 6:18 encourages us to pray "always with all prayer and supplication in the Spirit, being watchful to this end with all perseverance and supplication for all the saints." As needs arise, prayer rises higher. The key to supplication is in specificity. Dial into the specific request and then stick with it until your request is answered.

There is also prayer that offers thanks to God. This praying saturates the church atmosphere with gratefulness, thankfulness and expressions of gratitude to God. We are encouraged to "continue earnestly in prayer, being vigilant in it with thanksgiving" (Col. 4:2). Every prayer should include words and postures that show gratitude for God, for salvation and for the innumerable blessings He has showered on us. Thanksgiving shifts your focus from what might be a dire situation and forces you to look for the positive in everything.

Another kind of prayer that is a powerful expression of the praying church is intercessory prayer. This type of prayer is a set time to meet with God to fight on behalf of others. Intercessors stand in the gap and build a hedge around others (see Ezek. 22:30; Rom. 8:27,34; Heb. 7:25). They pray with faith declarations, pray the Word of God, and pray with and in the Spirit. Throughout Scripture, the Holy Spirit lies very close to the practice of prayer (see Rom. 8:26-27; 1 Cor. 14:2,4; Jude 20).

Intercessory prayer is the spear in our hands, a focus with authority on the desired circumstance or event, person, city or nation. In ancient times, leaders in a battle used their spear to direct the army's attack. Joshua did the same in battle: "Then the LORD said to Joshua, 'Stretch out the spear that is in your hand toward Ai, for I will give it into your hand.' And Joshua stretched out the spear that was in his hand toward the city" (Josh. 8:18). Intercessory prayer strategically targets someone or something specific, just like an army attacks a certain objective. It does not give up easily.

In the New Testament, prayer is demonstrated as a matter of steadfastness and devotion. As people gave themselves daily to continual, earnest and importunate intercession, they consistently saw supernatural results. Intercessory prayer is focused and it is relentless. As E. M. Bounds wrote, "Importunate prayer is a mighty movement of the soul toward God. It is a stirring of the deepest forces of the soul, toward the throne of heavenly grace. It is the ability to hold on, press on, and wait. . . . It is not an incident . . . but a passion of soul."[3] This is intercession. (My book *Seasons of Intercession* deals more fully with this topic.)

Just as there are different types of prayer, there are different settings where prayer can happen and different ways to express prayer. The SC prays like Paul exhorts: "Pray at all times (on every occasion, in every season) in the Spirit, with all [manner of] prayer and entreaty. To that end keep alert and watch with strong purpose and perseverance, interceding in behalf of all the saints (God's consecrated people)" (Eph. 6:18, *AMP*). Whether personal prayer, group prayer, all-church agreement prayer, Scripture prayer, waiting-on-God prayer or proclamation prayer, we must pray at all times. The SC's prayer breaks the bondage of silence by praying fervently, lifting their voices, crying aloud and speaking forcefully all by the power of the Holy Spirit (see Pss. 32:3; 94:17; 115:17).

PRAYER THAT "SHAKES" EVERYTHING

The spiritual history of a church is written in its prayer life. "Pray" or "prayer" is mentioned more than 30 times in the book of Acts. It precedes every significant event and provides the link between power and the person of the Holy Spirit. In the Early Church's beginnings, the people prayed for God to stretch out His hand "to heal, and that signs and wonders may be done through the name of [His] holy Servant Jesus. And when they had prayed, the place where they were assembled together was shaken; and they were all filled with the Holy Spirit, and they spoke the word of God with boldness" (Acts 4:30-31).

Notice how the place where they were meeting "was shaken." "Shaken" means to move something by force or power, to remove obstacles and to shake off unwanted things. It arouses someone or something to action. There are several areas where the Holy Spirit shakes obstacles off of us. He shakes off spiritual dullness (see Matt. 13:19), shakes off prayerlessness (see 1 Sam. 12:23; Heb. 4:16), and shakes the mountains of resistance (see Isa. 37:14; 40:4).

WARFARE PRAYER

The enemy will not give up his strongholds without strong resistance and spiritual battle. God has ordained to dislodge and defeat Satan by the prayers of His people. Prayer makes the church a sharp, threshing instrument, like the one described in Isaiah: "Behold, [God] will make you into a new threshing sledge with sharp teeth; you shall thresh the mountains and beat them small, and make the hills like chaff" (Isa. 41:15). We fight the enemy's attack and get on the offense by using our prayers to slash through his territory.

Sun Tzu, who authored the classic book on military strategy, wrote about strong points and weak points and how to position an army for victory. One essential for winning is this: "Whoever is first in the field and awaits the coming of the enemy, will be fresh for the fight; whoever is second in the field and has to hasten to battle will arrive exhausted."[4] In spiritual warfare, we cannot afford to be caught off guard by a surprise attack. We must stake out the battle lines and then hold the lines through prayer. Then, with the Holy Spirit on our side, we will be fresh for the fight.

That is how we shake the enemy's stronghold. His weakness is that he is subject to the prayers of God's people. We have authority over him in Jesus' name. Jesus, the One who defeated Satan and took the keys to hell, has authorized and empowered us to live free from Satan's devices. So when a person is bound by one of Satan's traps—be it discouragement, pride or something else—the weapon we have to fight with is prayer in Jesus' name, which is authority over Satan. He is a defeated foe. Prayer shakes people free from Satan's hold.

Our prayers can shake the bonds of limitation off any and all people. The SC prayer atmosphere shakes people loose, shakes strongholds from the minds of people and opens up new doors of supernatural power (see Job 30:25; Isa. 23:11; Mark 9:29; 11:24; 2 Cor. 10:4). Thus the SC becomes the place where God shakes things.

SHAKEN PLACES

The special places shaken by prayer are spaces and/or atmospheres—such as areas of life or physical locations—that are defined by specific activities and purposes. For instance, a person may have a workplace, a business place or a financial place. Powerful prayer creates a possibility that our place will encounter the dynamic power of the freshness of the Holy Spirit that releases something supernatural and wonderful. This is a positive shaking, a supernatural visitation of God's power released into a place so that obstacles are removed and new pathways in the invisible realm are opened. The place where you do business is shaken so that creativity and new ideas spring up. The financial place is shaken so that resources from unrealized reservoirs gush out. There comes a new freedom when our place becomes a shaken place, a new place, a God place.

Prayer is the tool that opens the congregation to the shakings of God (see Acts 16:26). Prayer even opens the nations:

> For thus says the LORD of hosts: "Once more (it is a little while) I will shake heaven and earth, the sea and dry land; and I will shake all nations, and they shall come to the Desire of All Nations, and I will fill this temple with glory," says the LORD of hosts (Hag. 2:6-7).

Through our focused prayers for God's intervention in a particular place, God draws people to Him for His glory. He shakes us to serve Him better. He challenges us to go to new heights and to be courageous Christians and leaders (see Heb. 12:26-28).

Positioned to Receive Divine Direction

As the helmsman or helmswoman of the church, the strategic leader positions the church to receive divine direction and specific spiritual breakthroughs. This positioning is accomplished through prayer (see Ezra 8:31). What wasn't reality suddenly is. What hadn't worked suddenly does. The unwanted situation or object that was there suddenly is not there. The relationship that was unloving becomes loving. The job that hadn't materialized suddenly materializes. No weapon formed against you will have final or ultimate success over you. A weapon might be permitted for a time to come against you, but that weapon will never have final and complete success (see Isa. 54:17).

When I took high school biology, I learned about human genetics, which was a still-developing field. One thing that always fascinated me was DNA, a simple but complex string of units that determine your hair color, your eye color, how quickly your body heals from a cut, and so on. A person starts as a ball of cells that have this DNA inside them and develops into a full-grown person as DNA replicates to form new cells. Without DNA, the body cannot grow.

Cells have a process for replicating DNA, obviously called DNA replication. What happens is that the cell produces all these nucleotides (units that comprise DNA) that need to be organized into a strand. For that organization to happen, a catalyst has to be introduced in the right position at the right time. Once that piece is in place, then the rest of the units start coming into place and growth takes off. For the church, prayer is that catalyst. It's that one necessary element needed to position the pieces in the right place to initiate and accelerate growth. Without the catalyst, there are just random pieces of valuable genetic material scattered throughout the cell. But get that unit in the right position and, suddenly, the pieces make sense.

Prayer releases breakthroughs in understanding dilemmas and in solving problems—new ideas, insights and thoughts suddenly take shape. Because God's thoughts are not our thoughts, we need His comprehension and understanding to overtake ours (see Isa. 55:8-9). The way we invite Holy Spirit inspiration into our places is through prayer. We get the veil lifted from our eyes by spending time in God's presence, praying the Scriptures and waiting for Him to impart His thoughts.

THE POWERFUL PRAYER OF AGREEMENT

The prayer of agreement releases something that is special and specific in the invisible realm, touching the visible realm. Agreement prayer is the act of partnering with God. It employs the prayer of faith as we open new doors, shut old ones and release supernatural strength through powerful, unified praying.

At City Bible, we regularly practice agreement prayer. I typically write a prayer for each series that puts the whole church in agreement as to what we want the Holy Spirit to do in our hearts. We recently finished a series called "Courageous Generosity," which was the theme of a season called "Faith Harvest," which we do yearly. The prayer went like this:

> *Holy Spirit of the living God, come breathe upon me. Fill me with a courageous heart and a generous spirit. I confront adversity with an open hand, knowing that every good thing comes from You, and You will provide all my needs. I willingly open my hands and give You what comes from Your hand.*

That prayer put the church in the mindset that we were going to resist the apparent lack around us and to trust that God will provide all our needs as we extend our gifts to Him. Whenever we make these proclamations together, I feel a sense of unity and accountability arise. I am not alone on this journey, and there are people around me who are making the same determination to resist lack and to give courageously. The prayer was biblical and when we spoke it together, we agreed with the Word of God and with each other. That is a powerful combination.

All church prayer with a unified focus intensifies our faith and pushes prayer to new levels. Jesus taught about agreement prayer in this famous passage: "Again I tell you, if two of you on earth agree (harmonize together, make a symphony together) about whatever [anything and everything] they may ask, it will come to pass and be done for them by My Father in heaven" (Matt. 18:19, *AMP*). The word "agree" is translated from the Greek word *sumphoneo*, which means to be in unison with, having one accord, to champion the same vision agreed upon, and to regard something as settled; to speak the same thing–as in a verbal agreement–and to be harmonious and make united declarations. Notice the language of sound in this definition? We say that a choir is in harmony when they sing different notes that balance each other to make a pleasant sound. Agreement prayer harmonizes with the Word of God. That harmony is established when

God's people declare the will of God to be done on earth as it is in heaven. The SC practices this kind of unified prayer.

Be Ready to Change the World

When the SC stands together in unity, powerful things happen. Cohesive prayer declares the Word of God that something specific will be done. Once the request is made, the pray-er trusts God to grant the request. In 1791, a group of refugees gathered in Herrnhut, Germany, and established two praying bands. One band was all male and the other band was all female. Each group had 24 members, and every member was designated one hour when they were supposed to pray. It was designed so that the men in their place and the women in theirs were praying continuously for 24 hours. This double prayer, unbroken every day, was maintained for 100 years. After 6 decades of uninterrupted prayer, the Moravians had sent over 300 missionaries into the world. Thus emerged the Moravian Mission Movement, during which the missionary church grew three times as large as the home church. Their reach extended to John and Charles Wesley, who, inspired by the Bible truths demonstrated by the Moravians, preached God's Word and a revival that swept England reached America. Millions of people were eternally changed—all because a band of refugees agreed to pray.

Our churches today need the power of agreement prayer to transform lives and communities. Prayer is not just for the retired grandmothers, the super-spiritual or the lead pastor. Agreement prayer requires that everyone get involved in, agree on and focus on the God vision. For the church to be in agreement, there are a few areas that need to be aligned.

Agree with Your Heart

To agree with your heart is to be in unity with yourself, or to stand with your own heart. This is the discipline of not letting your heart be divided or double minded. You secure a unified heart that aligns thoughts, will and emotions with the mind. Scripture teaches that we use our hearts to seek God and that He desires to grant our hearts' desire. This is what the psalmist says: "When You said, 'Seek My face,' my heart said to You, 'Your face, Lord, I will seek' " (Ps. 27:8). Notice that the heart speaks to God, affirming that the person intends to seek Him.

Your heart is where your treasure lies and where your future is shaped. The psalms tell us that as we delight in the Lord, He gives us the desires of our hearts (see Pss. 20:4; 37:4). Therefore, it is vitally important to "keep your heart with all diligence," because God looks into your heart to find out what you truly want (Prov. 4:23; see also Gen. 17:17; 24:45; Deut. 7:17; 2 Chron. 16:9; Prov. 16:23). As the deepest desires in your heart align with kingdom of God desires—sharing the salvation message with lost people, bringing food and shelter to the homeless, ministering in such a way as to include all generations and ethnicities, and so on—then you will see breakthrough in your church and answers to those desires. Out of your heart, prayers will be prayed and destinies will be won (see Matt. 12:3,5). Keep your heart clean and strong in spiritual flow and meditate on and ponder what God has set in your heart (see Luke 2:19; Rom. 8:27).

Agree with God's Greatness

Agreement prayer is agreeing with God's greatness and clearly seeing His unlimited power. This is why we should study and preach the attributes of God. It builds our faith for praying. People's lives are short and the universe is perishable, but God is eternal, the everlasting God, the creator of the heavens and the earth. When we pray agreeing with God's greatness, we see things from the eternal perspective. We see how much bigger God is than our seemingly impossible situations. That renewed perspective raises our faith to trust Him to remove the obstacles, to turn the hard heart, to release resources into our lives and churches, and to do what we thought was impossible!

God is all powerful and thus He has unlimited authority and influence. He has the ability to do whatever His will dictates. Bottom line, He is God (see Pss. 68:14; 91:1; 115:3)! God has both the resources and the ability to make His will happen in the whole universe. In America today, more than 77,000 tons of food goes wasted. Piles of nutritious, carefully grown crops sit unharvested in fields and heaps throughout the nation. But at the same time, 78 percent of children living in countries with food surpluses are malnourished.[5] All around these children, food is rotting because the children do not have access to the sustenance. The problem is not that food is lacking but that there is limited ability to distribute the food. Our God has all the materials, the buildings, the people, the talent, the finances and the resources we need to do His will of building His church. Not only does He have the resources, but He also has the ability to get them into our hands. Part of God's greatness is that He can distribute His unlimited wealth. It does not sit wasted in heaven.

Recognize that God Is Able

God is able! He is able to do everything He needs to do or wants to do. The Scriptures are full of testimony to His grandeur: "Ah, Lord God! Behold, You have made the heavens and the earth by Your great power and outstretched arm. There is nothing too hard for You" (Jer. 32:17). The angel who appears to Mary to give her the news that she will birth the Messiah confidently states that "with God nothing will be impossible" (Luke 1:37). After Job came through a time of unthinkable emotional, physical and spiritual attack, he proclaimed, "I know that You [God] can do everything, and that no purpose of Yours can be withheld from You" (Job 42:2). For a man to lose his family, livelihood and good health and then proclaim that God is able to do anything, he must be either insane or have a strong conviction that God is fully capable. I think it is the latter.

God is the true and living God. He is not inactive, idle or, as Nietzsche said, dead. He is able to do what we ask because He hears our prayers. He is able to do what we imagine because He reads our thoughts. Sometimes we imagine things for which we do not dare to ask. But He can do those things anyway! He knows it all and He can perform it all.

Dream Bigger

Renowned theologian and Bible translator J.B. Philips once wrote a book titled *Your God Is Too Small.* The trouble facing us today is that we have not found a God big enough for our modern needs. We need a vision for the greatness of God as depicted in Scripture. We need to see a God who is big enough to command highest admiration and respect, who can inspire our faith and enlarge our prayers. The SC is full of people who say to God, "How awesome are Your works! Through the greatness of Your power Your enemies shall submit themselves to You" (Ps. 66:3). When we agree with God's greatness, we have assurance that nothing is beyond the power and control of almighty God.

One name for God that has been an anchor point for me is the name El Shaddai. This name means "Almighty God" and was first used in Genesis when God made a covenant with Abram (see Gen. 17:1). There are times when I feel discouraged or tired or I get upset when God doesn't do things on my timetable. When that happens, I lock myself in my library, grab a couple of theology books and start reading about who God is. I read that He is bigger, He is higher, He is unlimited. Then if reading those attributes does not lift my spirits, I pick up a book on the universe and read about the stars, the planets and the unfathomable breadth of our universe. On a clear night, you can see maybe 3,000 stars. There are over one hundred billion stars in our Milky Way galaxy alone, and there are over one hundred billion galaxies in the observable universe. The quantity of stars outnumbers the number of grains of sand on the seashore. Even though the number of existing stars is astronomical, science proves that each star is unique. With that in mind, think about this verse: "[God] counts the number of the stars; He calls them all by name" (Ps. 147:4).

If that's not enough to make your head spin, think about this: Our sun, which is a star, is so big that it can fit one million Earths inside of it. Yet at over a million miles in diameter, the sun is tiny in comparison to other stars. The largest star ever discovered to date, VY Canis Majoris, is a billion times bigger than our sun. Do you feel a little small right now? My small brain cannot begin to comprehend the vastness of the universe, let alone the incomprehensible power of God. When I start to think about how big the universe is and how small I am, suddenly my frustrations seem infinitesimal. My worries dissipate. It is impossible to see my "problems" as totally devastating in light of the perspective of God's greatness.

There is nothing too hard for God. Our prayers need to be saturated with attributes of God so that we agree with the God revealed in Scripture. He is revealed as eternal, incomprehensible, infinite, self-sufficient, sovereign, wise and loving (see 2 Kings 6:17; Isa. 46:10; Eph. 3:20). This is our God! What would happen if you prayed large prayers? Philip Brooks, clergyman and author, was known to encourage people to pray for "wings instead of crutches." He said that when God answers the largest prayers we imagine, we will wish that we had made a bigger request!

God knows what He can accomplish through us, so He expects us to dream big! Whatever you dream for your church, dream bigger! Whatever reach you think you can extend to, think farther! Agreeing with God's greatness means expecting something far greater than what you can do in your limited imagination and capacity. When we pray, we take our eyes off our finite limitations and lift our eyes to the greatness of God—to His ability, not ours (see Gen. 18:14; Isa. 40:29).

Agree with Prayer Partners

Agreement prayer with prayer partners activates one of the greatest principles of power in the kingdom of God. As Scripture says, "How could one chase a thousand, and two put ten thousand to flight, unless their Rock had sold them, and the LORD had surrendered them?" (Deut. 32:30). One person can wield incredible power in prayer, but two people can double their level of effectiveness. This kind of praying can pull down strongholds, touch lives, change churches and engage in spiritual warfare (see Acts 12:5; Col. 4:3-4; 1 Thess. 5:25).

Pearl Goode was a legend to the staff members of the Billy Graham Evangelistic Association (BGEA). A widowed nurse about 65 years old with grown children, in 1949 she joined a group of volunteers to pray for the success of the Christ for Greater Los Angeles meetings that Billy Graham was leading. But Goode felt called to pray, not only for those meetings, but also for all other Billy Graham meetings. From that start in 1949 until her death in 1972, she went to every city in the United States where a Billy Graham campaign was being held. There she met with other volunteers to pray before, during and after the meetings. When that campaign finished, she packed up and went to the next city where Graham planned to hold meetings. She traveled an estimated 48,000 miles on Greyhound busses before starting to travel by plane.

Goode started praying and traveling on her own initiative and at her own expense. There was no public recognition or financial assistance for what she was doing. She did it because she believed in the power of joining with people in prayer for a specific request. Eventually, BGEA members noticed that she was at every meeting, and they helped her with travel and hotel expenses. Billy Graham also attributed his success to her faithful praying.

Pearl Goode demonstrated that praying with others is effective, necessary and even simple. Prayer partners can be friends or people who are drawn together to pray regularly for a pastor, missionary, Christian leader or any other specific need they feel. Prayer partners can also be a prayer shield around leaders who are advancing the kingdom of God. Every leader needs these people to surround him or her. The apostle Paul asked for prayer partners emphatically: "Now I beg you, brethren, through the Lord Jesus Christ, and through the love of the Spirit, that you strive together with me in prayers to God for me" (Rom. 15:30). He asked for partners because he knew that through agreement prayer, doors are opened, chains are broken, and things change (see 2 Cor. 1:11; Phil. 1:19). It was when the Early Church was in agreement prayer that an angel broke Peter's prison chains, released him from the jail and led him past the barred doors. Why did this happen? While Peter was in prison, "constant prayer was offered to God for him by the church" (Acts 12:5). The whole church was in agreement, and God answered their prayers.

All forms of prayer should be employed when praying with partners. Partners can intercede for others, focus on others' needs, effect change and engage in warfare when needed (see Eph. 6:11,18). Their prayers release miracles, especially as they believe for answers when they pray (see Matt. 21:22; Heb. 11:6).

Seven Hedges of Agreement Prayer

Prayer in the strategic church must be implemented systematically and specifically to develop for the local church a prayer shield, which consists of what I call prayer hedges. Isaiah 62:6-7 says, "O Jerusalem, I have posted watchmen on your walls; they will pray day and night, continually. Take no rest, all you who pray to the LORD. Give the LORD no rest until he completes his work, until he makes Jerusalem the pride of the earth" (*NLT*). Our mandate as leaders and believers is to pray often and pray hard!

Over the last several years, we at CBC have set into place seven specific prayer hedges, which can be activated at anytime to release needed prayer. I have leadership in place to signal other intercessors to be praying about everything from my personal life to major issues facing the church to specific individuals in the church. It is comforting to know that a systematic prayer arsenal is in place.

The seven hedges have been identified and developed over the years as the Holy Spirit has led CBC's journey. Picture the hedges like the concentric circles that result when you toss a stone into a still pond. The ripples get wider and wider as they move out from the center. Picture the prayer hedges as being dynamic, not static.

Hedge #1: The Lead Pastor's Personal Prayer Team

I have five couples that meet every Sunday morning and pray for me, my family and the services that morning. They have met every week for years, and I can give them specific things to pray for both personally and corporately. I trust them—they have kept all personal issues confidential—and they are faithful to meet every week. There isn't anything I wouldn't entrust this group with. They are focused on my life and all that pertains to me: my family, ministry, health, etc. I'm not present at these meetings, but

I always know I can call on them to pray, and at times I'll call them in to lay hands on me and pray for specific and pressing needs. The best part is that they are always there. A personal prayer team provides the needed air space to allow for expansion.

Hedge #2: The Prayer Ministry Leadership Team (PML)

The Prayer Ministry Leadership Team is the group of prayer leaders within the church that encourages, develops and helps sustain the prayer momentum in the SC. There are between 30 and 40 people on this team. These are leaders I have asked to help and support me in raising up an interceding church. Remember, no church can be strategic without prayer, and no church can be strategic in prayer without leaders who pray. I lead the prayer in our church, but I also need a team to help me. After realizing that everyone is an intercessor and that I needed a leader to help put into operation all that was in my heart, I implemented a prayer pastor and have an elder functioning in that role. I emphasize help, because I take the full responsibility for prayer in our church. The PML Team does not do all the prayer but provides strategic support to the leadership team and the church to assist in the assignment to grow more prayer in the SC. They meet regularly and are a vital part to the prayer arsenal and the team. Those in the PML lead various prayer meetings and work to cover all church events with prayer before, during and after the event. They have a specialized assignment in the SC and carry out their assignment under the leadership of our Eldership Team. The PML Team has been set up to pray at a moment's notice for any need that arises in my life or the life of the church. I utilize this team often both in forward thinking and planning as well as when a crisis or need arises. They are always in ready mode.

Hedge #3: Watchman Prayer and E-Prayer

The Watchmen and E-Prayer teams are two large companies of pray-ers that can be alerted to the needs of the church. The Watchmen, a team of about 150 people, are trusted leaders from our All Church Leadership Team and among the church. They pray for a variety of needs related to the church and also cover my travel. I use this unit to pray for the finances and all major events of the church. Whenever I travel, they are activated to pray. Watchman prayer is a strategic ripple to all the prayer needs that surface in our church. Only a few leaders are responsible for activating this prayer hedge.

The E-Prayer Team is an even larger company of pray-ers that is administrated by a couple who are part of the PML. There are about 500 people on an email list who receive the general prayer requests that arise out of the church. These requests are communicated directly from the leader via email. Those with prayer requests call or email the leader who edits the request as needed and forwards it on to the e-prayer administrators. Any church member can sign up to be on this prayer team, and anyone can ask for prayer. All kinds of needs are sent out, from requests for healing to salvation for loved ones to success on an impending job interview. This prayer team can also receive prayer requests for upcoming events and any other general or specific need facing the church. When those on the E-Prayer Team get a request, they take a moment and lift up the need immediately after reading it. They join with hundreds of others doing the same when they check their email. Powerful ripple!

Hedge #4: Campus-Specific Prayer Meetings

Campus-specific prayer meetings are prayer meetings with a specialized focus that happen on our various church campuses. As needs arise, prayer meetings are held to meet the particular need or burden. For example, one of the leaders of our PML Team has a prayer meeting for our nation and the leaders of our land. This has been maintained for years on one of our campuses. Another prayer group meets weekly on Friday night and prays for our church and the weekend services. That's an amazing prayer time! We have lots of specialized and specific prayer meetings going on at all different times during the week. The PML Team that leads these prayer meetings can receive specific direction from me if an emergency need arises. I can do this by alerting our prayer pastor.

These campus-specific groups make up a growing number of prayer meetings in our church. All prayer meetings first start by going through a specific process before being approved and promoted. These prayer meetings are all part of raising up an interceding church, and they comprise one of the most strategic hedges.

Hedge #5: Leadership Prayer

Leadership prayer encompasses all the leaders of our church. I personally lead a team of teams and I ask each one of my leaders to develop his or her own personal prayer team so that that leader is covered in prayer. All my leaders are also responsible for encouraging, developing and maintaining prayer in their areas of responsibility and influence. The prayer done by the leaders at their various meetings sustains a level of prayer that serves to cover the leaders and our congregation. This prayer trickles down to all levels of leadership and helps promote and build the prayer shield. I am constantly leading these teams in prayer and releasing them to pray. I encourage them to take prayer into everything they do. Every one of our leaders sees the responsibility and opportunity to build this hedge of prayer. The leadership prayer hedge is a key component to raising up an interceding church. Each leader influences and directs his or her facet of the church. Prayer through these leaders is vital, as is their consistency to build it into others. Strategic praying leaders reproduce strategic praying leaders. Programs don't fuel prayer; prayer fuels programs!

HEDGE #6: CHURCHWIDE PRAYER EVENTS

Churchwide prayer events are powerful meetings of agreement prayer where believers meet in one place to pray for each other and for church needs. An example in our church is Worship, Prayer and Presence, a churchwide prayer event that meets several times a year and is open and promoted to the whole church. The PML Team oversees this particular event that brings together from all campuses people who not only receive prayer but who also pray for others in turn. Churchwide prayer events have times of refreshing in the Lord's presence and times of aggressive warfare-type intercession. They also include prayer for the lead pastor. People are released to flow in the gifts of the Spirit. Each prayer event can have a variety of expressions, depending on the desired purpose for the meeting.

HEDGE #7: ALL-CHURCH PRAYER

All-church prayer is a hedge that is activated when the entire congregation prays as a corporate body. The direction comes from the lead pastor and the leadership team. A simple example of this is a prayer card that CBC distributes three or four times per year. This card contains 7 to 10 targets of prayer. The church as a whole focuses together and believes God to accomplish the set targets. This is large-scale unified prayer. In Acts 12 the church prayed for Peter who was in prison, and God sent an angel to deliver him. There is amplified power when the whole church has focused prayer–like how the light that forms a laser can cut steel. Focused prayer by the whole can move the hand of God to bring forth His purpose in miraculous ways. The prayer card is a simple and effective way to do that!

Mega Prayer Night at CBC is another example of this hedge. It is an annual the-first-of-each-year all-church prayer service led by me that follows a season of all-church fasting and prayer. We do a fast at the beginning of every year. Some people do a Daniel fast, some fast from things such as media, and others do a full abstain-from-food fast. This, again, focuses the entire local church family on prayer and seeking the Lord. There is power in this kind of agreement. Starting the year with corporate agreement in prayer and fasting sets the tone for the rest of the year to be one of power and victory.

There are many other corporate emphases on prayer throughout the year at CBC. The key to releasing the power of prayer in any SC, though, is planning these prayer events on an annual basis. Because prayer is usually resisted, you must be intentional to make it happen on the congregational level. More prayer is better than less prayer!

It is so vital that the SC is a praying church. Strategic leaders will inspire others toward agreement prayer, resisting prayerlessness in the church and treating it as a spiritual disease. There is no room for procrastinating, for excuses or for waiting for a good feeling. Whether it is intercession, thanksgiving, warfare or agreement prayer, make prayer a habit and an integral piece of your church atmosphere. As Nike says, just do it. Start now. Start today. Become a praying church.

Strategic Pursuit of the Supernatural

I cannot remember seeing a single miracle of any kind or any supernatural activities in the church during the first 17 years of my life. I was raised Baptist, my dad being a Baptist pastor and my mom's side of the family also Baptist. My upbringing did put me under the Word of God every Sunday for corporate service and Sunday school as a kid and as a teen. I just had never seen a miracle or anything that could be described as supernatural.

It wasn't until the Jesus movement in the late 1960s that I encountered the miraculous. It was 1967 and I was swept into this undefined controversial youth revival that had many non-traditional practices, non-traditional music, and a nonreligious way of praying. It was during this time I saw my first miracle, and it changed my worldview on the spot. The invisible realm became a reality. God was made real to me in a way I had never experienced before. I had been touched by the supernatural, and it proved to be a vital force in my life and, ultimately, in the ministry God had called me into.

Through the years following that encounter, I began to study what the Scriptures said about miracles, signs, wonders, healings and the invisible realm. I have seen many supernatural miracles happen throughout my life, and I believe that seeing the supernatural is one of the great cries of the human heart. It is the profound need of the church today to press the door of the supernatural.

The Power of the Cross

There is substantial evidence showing that the healing ministry and miraculous spiritual gifts are the chief demonstrations of the redeeming power of the cross that accompanied the preaching of the gospel in the

New Testament church. The cross is the heart of the gospel, the gravity of the New Testament faith. It is first and foremost. We must preach the cross and all the power in and through the cross. That includes the atonement and forgiveness of sins and the manifestation of miraculous deeds.

The cross is the basis for all God's works in our world today. It is the basis to forgive, restore lives, heal brokenness in people and touch our physical needs. Signs and wonders reveal the nature of God. A primary purpose for the release of the supernatural to move us into the invisible and powerful miracle realm is for people to see and believe God. The potential for releasing the supernatural is in and through the cross—the fountainhead from which all blessings flow, including miracles, healings and the power of the kingdom of God.

As leaders of the SC, we must press against the door to the supernatural, the door that opens all of God's resources and power. The word "supernatural" refers to that which exists outside of the natural realm and above and beyond the human realm. The supernatural is God's divine nature and power bringing heaven to invade earth. We have a supernatural Christianity, a supernatural God, a supernatural Jesus, a supernatural Holy Spirit, a supernatural Bible, supernatural prayers, a supernatural mindset and supernatural power. The SC is built upon the premise of the supernatural existing in our natural today. The Scripture speaks clearly about the supernatural's prevalence in our world. Look at these versions of 1 Corinthians 4:20:

> For the kingdom of God is not in word but in power (*NKJV*).
>
> For the kingdom of God consists of and is based on not talk but power (moral power and excellence of soul) (*AMP*).
>
> God's Way is not a matter of mere talk; it's an empowered life (*THE MESSAGE*).

Let us believe in the full range of Holy Spirit activity throughout the church age as a vital part of preaching the gospel, including miracles, healings, signs and wonders. Let us believe, teach, equip and release people to unlock the supernatural power of a living God: supernatural praying, supernatural strength, supernatural dreams and visions, supernatural breakthroughs, supernatural provision and supernatural business turnarounds.

Proclaiming the Full Gospel

We are people of the supernatural. Together in prayer we stand at the door to the realm where all things are possible, and by faith we press forward into this realm. We as leaders must believe and press into the full manifestation of the kingdom of God. Mark 16:20 says that the disciples "went out and preached everywhere, the Lord working with them and confirming the word through the accompanying signs." The phrase for "the Lord working" is translated from the Greek word *sunergo,* a word of partnership, uniting parts to achieve something great. The Lord desires to work with us and confirm His Word, to establish and make sure it inspires confidence in the invisible God we serve. Here are just a few examples from Scripture of the supernatural happenings in the Early Church:

> Then Philip went down to the city of Samaria and preached Christ to them. And the multitudes with one accord heeded the things spoken by Philip, hearing and seeing the miracles which he did. For unclean spirits, crying with a loud voice, came out of many who were possessed; and many who were paralyzed and lame were healed. And there was great joy in that city (Acts 8:5-8).

> Now it came to pass, as Peter went through all parts of the country, that he also came down to the saints who dwelt in Lydda. There he found a certain man named Aeneas, who had been bedridden eight years and was paralyzed. And Peter said to him, "Aeneas, Jesus the Christ heals you. Arise and make your bed." Then he arose immediately. So all who dwelt at Lydda and Sharon saw him and turned to the Lord (Acts 9:32-35).

> And in Lystra a certain man without strength in his feet was sitting, a cripple from his mother's womb, who had never walked. This man heard Paul speaking. Paul, observing him intently and seeing that he had faith to be healed, said with a loud voice, "Stand up straight on your feet!" And he leaped and walked (Acts 14:8-10).

The proclamation of the Word is powerful when we add the supernatural element to it. The New Testament pattern of preaching the gospel consists of more than verbally communicating the rational content of the gospel. It also includes proclaiming the full gospel, which includes demonstrations of the cross and the power of God. It is preaching with full authority and power with faith for the supernatural to break out among us. We must use teaching, preaching and power just like Jesus did, going "about all Galilee, teaching in their synagogues, preaching the gospel of the kingdom, and healing all kinds of sickness and all kinds of disease among the people" (Matt. 4:23; see also Matt. 9:35; 11:4-5; Luke 9:6; Acts 10:36-38; 1 John 3:8). The miracles of Jesus were part of the invading rule of God, which Jesus brought with preaching and acting. Together they were and are the rule of God overcoming and pushing back the demonic. The whole satanic realm of influence is crushed by divine intervention (see Matt. 10:27; Mark 3:14; Acts 4:29; 5:12; 14:3; Rom. 15:18).

The church today needs the demonstration of the power of God in a world that does not know God or understand the God of the Scriptures. Paul wrote that "[his] speech and [his] preaching were not with persuasive words of human wisdom, but in demonstration of the Spirit and of power, that [our] faith should not be in the wisdom of men but in the power of God" (1 Cor. 2:4-5). Demonstration is the proof of what we are preaching, the evidence. We are Christ's witnesses and we are to be witnesses for God. To give witness is to represent God. This actually is the church re-presenting God. We cannot re-present God without demonstrating His power. It would not be an adequate or accurate witness. We need more of the power of God today, now. We can't do it without the power. The gospel is not "in word only, but also in power, and in the Holy Spirit and in much assurance" (1 Thess. 1:5; see also 1 Cor. 1:17-18; Gal. 3:5; Eph. 1:18-20).

One of the foundational Scriptures I quote and pray and declare to the church I lead is Hebrews 13:8: "Jesus Christ is the same yesterday, today, and forever." I believe in this word "today"—not just in the past ("yesterday") and not just in the future ("forever"), but today, in this moment, right now, right here. I want to see the supernatural happen now.

A Supernatural Perspective

A supernatural perspective is a way of thinking, reasoning and considering that is based on the Word of God. It comes through having your mind renewed by the Word so that you view all things based on what God says, fully seeing and believing Him. Several forces shape perspective:

- *Worldview*—Our worldview consists of the culturally structured assumptions, values and commitments underlying our perception of reality.

- *Our experiences*—All of us are hampered to a greater or lesser extent in our attempts to understand the experiences of others that we ourselves have not had.

- *Personality or temperament*—Our predispositions, motivations, degrees of openness to new ideas, conservative or liberal views of life, and optimistic or pessimistic outlooks on life shape how we think and accept possibilities.

- *Our will*—The will factor simply means that we will choose to view a given thing as we have been taught to view it or we will choose to view a given thing differently from how we have been taught to view it. In other words, when confronted with new information or a new experience that may challenge our present views, we will either reconsider our positions or remain unchanged in our opinions.

- *Church background*—Our experiences with and in church—both good and bad—influence how we feel about church, about how church operates and about how we see the church. We may have some faulty teachings or no teachings on certain subjects such as prayer, worship, healing and gifts. Thus we choose a certain perspective because of our Christian or church experiences. We may ask, "Why is my experience of Christianity so different from what I read in the New Testament? What is wrong with my 'brand' of Christianity? Is there more?"

- *Bible knowledge*—We are shaped by what we know and what we think we know about the Bible. An individual's knowledge and understanding of Scripture will greatly change the way he or she thinks about and views everything: God, the devil, sin, hell, heaven, the church, the Holy Spirit, authority, etc. My perspective is connected to my understanding of the Word of God. Teaching that says healing, miracles, and gifts of the Spirit are not for today can greatly negatively influence a person's perspective.

- *Spiritual health*—Our spiritual health has a lot to do with our spiritual eyes. The way we see things will be deeply colored by our level of spiritual maturity—at peace with God, in love with God, a great prayer life, positive outlook, living in victory, encouraged by the Holy Spirit, enjoying the things of God, a happy and healthy church member, functioning faithfully, and so on.

All these factors shape perspective and affect our level of openness to the supernatural.

Supernatural Healings

There is no doubt in my mind that the church has suffered from a faulty theology concerning miracles, healings and the supernatural. Generally speaking, a large number of theologians, teachers and preachers have taught that the age of miracles ceased with the apostolic period of the church and that God no longer heals people as He did in the first century. I lament the fact that we—the whole church—have descended to the level of only teaching the primary power of the natural realm and talents, and we use only natural communication styles to preach, win souls and do church in general, especially in the area of healing and miracles. The gifts of the Spirit have been supplanted by the arts of logic and rhetoric.

Richard Foster has emphasized a balance in ministry and has pointed out that a healing and gift-based ministry is simply a normal and biblical part of the life of faith in Christ:

> Healing prayer is part of the normal Christian life. It should not be elevated above any other ministry in the community of faith, nor should it be undervalued; rather, it should be kept in proper balance. It is simply a normal aspect of what it means to live under the reign of God.[1]

Lift Expectations for Healing

There has been, and remains today, a strong academic community that resists the healing ministry as an unbiblical, erroneous ministry. Extremists, frauds and charlatans have caused a reproach upon the healing ministry that has resulted in questions about its validity and even denials of healings. People have not heard from the pulpit in most churches a strong, biblical and theological preaching of healing. Thus a spirit of faith or an expectation for healing to operate within the church today has never been created. There seems to be a suppressed attitude toward expectation, and the church is afraid to expect much from God because they have been disappointed so many times in the past. This is the stronghold of no expectation and it should be eradicated.

Dr. Paul Chappell has studied the healing movement in America. He makes these remarks about expectation and healing:

> Bushnell observed that Christian souls were falling into "a stupor of intellectual fatality. . . . Prayer becomes a kind of dumb-bell exercise, good as exercise, but never to be answered." The word is good to be exegetically handled, but there is no light of interpretation in souls, more immediate; all truth is to be second-hand truth, never a vital beam of God's own light. . . . Expectation is gone—God is too far off, too much imprisoned by laws, to allow expectation from Him. The Christian world has been gravitating, visibly, more and more, toward this vanishing point of faith, for whole centuries, and especially since the modern era began to shape the thoughts of men by only scientific methods. Religion has fallen into the domain of the mere understanding, and so it has become a kind of wisdom to not believe much, therefore to expect as little. . . .
>
> Let Him [God] now break forth in miracle and holy gifts, let it be seen that He is still the living God, in the midst of His dead people, and they will be quickened to a resurrection by the sight. Now they see that God can do something still, and has His liberty. He can hear prayers, He can help them triumph in dark hours, their bosom-sins He can help them master, all His promises in the Scripture He can fulfill, and they go to Him with great expectations. They see, in these gifts, that the Scripture stands, that the graces and works, and holy fruits of the apostolic ages, are also for them. It is as if they had now a proof experimental of the resources embodied in the Christian plan. The living God, immediately revealed, and not historically only, begets a feeling of present life and power, and religion is no more a tradition, a second-hand light, but a grace of God unto salvation, operative now.[2]

Expectation must lift if healings are going to be seen! Throughout Scripture and history, the supernatural is used as the gateway to the harvest of souls. There has been and remains a spiritual war fought within the context of natural man, a war that fights against God's will, God's best and God's plan for humankind—everyone's soul, spirit and body. That is why spiritual resistance to healing, signs and wonders has confronted the church and believers for centuries.

Regain the Theology of Healing

We must gain back ground in the theology of healing and equip our churches to think right about this nonnegotiable doctrine. Fortunately, we do have some scholars who have stayed the course and believe in the supernatural.

F. F. Bruce, well-known evangelical British New Testament scholar, concluded that Jesus' healing ministry was an integral part of the message He preached: "While the miracles served as signs, they were not performed in order to be signs. They were as much a part and parcel of Jesus' ministry as was his preaching—not . . . seals affixed to the document to certify its genuineness but an integral element in the very text of the document."[3]

Alan Richardson, British New Testament scholar, argued that healing ministry was a necessary and integral adjuvant of Jesus' preaching:

> The working of miracles is a part of the proclamation of the Kingdom of God, not an end in itself. Similarly, the sin of Chorazin and Bethsaida [Luke 10:13; Matt. 11:21] is spiritual blindness; they do not accept the preaching of the Kingdom of God or understand the miracles which were its inevitable concomitants. . . . Can we interpret the remarkable connection which this Q saying establishes between the miracles and repentance in any other way than by understanding the miracles as the necessary concomitants of the preaching of the Kingdom of God?[4]

Hendrik van der Loos, Dutch New Testament scholar, held that:

> The miracles were therefore not works or signs which happened for the sake of the apostles, but originated in the point at issue, viz. the proclamation of salvation by Jesus Christ and the coming of His Kingdom. They did not accompany the preaching of the gospel as incidentals, but formed an integral part of it; in the healing, as a visible function of the Kingdom of God, something that could be experienced, God's will to heal the whole of man was manifested.[5]

Saint Augustine, one of the most influential founding fathers of Christianity, wrote:

> Once I realized how many miracles were occurring in our own day and which were so like the miracles of old and also how wrong it would be to allow the memory of these marvels of divine power to perish from among our people. It is only two years ago that the keeping of records was begun here in Hippo, and already, at this writing, we have nearly seventy attested miracles.[6]

Justin Martyr, the courageous apologist, wrote:

> For numberless demoniacs throughout the whole world, and in your city, many of our Christian men exorcizing them in the Name of Jesus Christ . . . have healed and do heal, rendering helpless and driving the possessing devils out of the men, though they could not be cured by all the other exorcists, and those who used incantations and drugs.[7]

SUPERNATURAL MIRACLES TODAY

The God of miracles is the God revealed in the Scriptures. The reality of God is the fundamental fact. God is! This is the basis for everything else. "In the beginning God" (Gen. 1:1). The Scripture is a record of God's being and mighty acts: creation, redemption, miracles—God at work.

THE GOD OF MIRACLES IS A REALITY

God is living. God is not like any idol, philosophy or great man that leads people into deception. Our God is the true God. Our God is the only living deity (see Jer. 10:10). He is the everlasting King. We do not worship a dead object or an empty philosophy. We worship the living God. He gives life and breath to all things, even bringing life back to that which was dead, thus restoring life. As Peter confessed, Jesus is "Christ, son of the living God" (Matt. 16:16).

God is personal. God is not a god of impersonal energy or blind fate. He is the God who knows us and can be known by us. He is a personal God involved with every aspect of our lives. He searches and knows us (see Ps. 139:1), and He calls us friend (see Jas. 2:23).

God is infinite. God is unlimited, unbounded. We are finite, confined to space and time. God has no confinement and no limitation. He is high and lifted up, exalted above everything earthly or human. From His seat in heaven, God declares, "Can a man hide himself in hiding places so I do not see him? . . . Do I not fill the heavens and the earth?" (Jer. 23:24, *NASB*). We can go to the heavens and He is there; we can go to the depths of the earth and He will be there (see Ps. 139:7-8). He knows no boundaries.

God is love. God loves us with an everlasting love. He desires to work for us because He loves us. This love is not based on our merit and not based on our worthiness. He loves us in spite of ourselves. We don't deserve His love and we can't earn His love (see Rom. 5:6-8).

The God of Miracles Is a God of Power

God is omnipotent, meaning all powerful. He is mighty in His providential activity wherein He sustains the universe "by His powerful word" (Heb. 1:3, *NIV*). Nothing is too hard for Him and His mighty power (see Gen. 18:14; Job 42:2; Jer. 32:17; Luke 1:37; Rom. 1:16; Eph. 1:19). God is fully able to go beyond His ordinary works to perform extraordinary, supernatural works. God is God Almighty for whom nothing is impossible that He wills to do. He can cause the sea to open up so that people walk through on dry ground (see Exod. 14:22). He can lengthen a day beyond the normal 24 hours (see Josh. 10:12-14). He can restore a physically dead person to life again (see 1 Kings 18:38). He can heal incurable diseases and infirmities (see Luke 5:22-26).

The God of miracles is our God. We have assurance that nothing is beyond the power and control of almighty God. We can expect God to be powerfully at work, not only in the ordinary events of daily life, but also in the performing of mighty works. God is able to lead people to salvation, perform miracles of healing and deliverance, and destroy every force that comes against His work!

Anticipating Miracles In and Around Your Life

Miracles are around you even now. They are headed your way from the throne of God. Let's discuss what miracles are.

A miracle is an extraordinary event manifesting divine intervention in human affairs. Peter Marshall, a popular preacher in the 1940s and 1950s, pastored in the historic Fifth Avenue Presbyterian Church in Washington, DC. During his boyhood in Scotland, Peter visited a friend who lived some distance away. As boys often do, he lost track of time and stayed too late. Dusk came and Peter started for home. To save time, he took a shortcut across the moors. Darkness fell. Lost and terrified, Peter began to run. Suddenly, he thought he heard a voice call his name, "Peter!" He ran on. Again the voice called, "Peter!" Turning to see who was calling as he ran, he stumbled and fell in the darkness. Reaching out to raise himself, Peter touched nothing but air. Groping fingers examined the ground. Suddenly he knew where he was: at the edge of an old stone quarry. A few more steps and he would have fallen to his death. Peter Marshall always felt that God had saved his life by calling out to him! It was a miracle that he did not fall from the cliff.

A miracle is also an extremely outstanding or unusual event, thing or accomplishment. A 75-year-old man who is perhaps the most remarkable survivor of a devastating tsunami that rolled through the Indian Ocean is alive today thanks to a crocodile who towed him to safety. A tsunami washed into his home and swept him away. He desperately grabbed at a nearby log, only to discover it was a crocodile! The crocodile took off through the water, dragging him with it. It eventually deposited him on a riverbank where he was saved. The man looks back at that wild trip down the river and the whole situation as "divine providence" that saved his life. It was an unusual event.

Miracles are acts of God that are obviously supernatural. Providential acts in our lives—divine intervention—happen when God uses natural things in a supernatural way, choosing to work within the framework of natural laws. George Müller, legendary father of the faith, had many stories about God's supernatural intervention in his orphanages. One of my favorite stories is about the miracle breakfast. One morning, all the children in the orphanage were sitting at the breakfast table with an empty plate and glass in front of them. Little did they know that the orphanage was out of food and there was nothing to eat. Regardless, Müller sat down and prayed for the food they were about to receive. Immediately, there was a knock on the door. Müller opened it to see the local baker standing there. "Mr. Müller," he said, "I couldn't sleep last night. Somehow I felt you had no bread for breakfast, so I got up at 2 o'clock and baked fresh bread. Here it is." Soon a second knock was heard. It was the milkman. His cart had broken down in front of the orphanage. He said he would like to give the children the milk, so he could empty the cart and repair it.

The bread and milk showing up at the precise moment can be explained as being the result of divine intervention. Miracles are powerful, mighty actions of God done on behalf of people. This is another characteristic of God that sets Him apart from all other false gods: He cares about people. Jesus fed the 5,000 men who came out to hear Him preach, because He loved them and had compassion for them. God cares enough about the wellbeing of His people that He will perform mighty miracles to provide for their needs and desires according to His will. He also performs miracles to challenge and stretch our faith. The disciples did not believe that the multitude of people in front of them could be fed, but Jesus challenged them to stretch their faith to believe that it was possible–and their faith grew. God can do mighty, miraculous things with what you give Him, and He can provide more than enough.

A miracle is an unusual event that triggers awareness of God's presence and power. On February 5, 2008, a massive tornado ripped through Union University in Jackson, Tennessee, a small Bible college known for its Christ-centered teaching. It leveled most of the campus in a matter of mere minutes, damaging 33 of the 42 buildings. Yet of the 1,200 people there during the tornado, only 51 were injured and there was not a single fatality. One student remarked, "You can't help but say that is a miracle and God was here protecting us."

At CBC, we have had our own share of miracles. I taught a series and wrote a book called *Miracles* that lays a biblical foundation for the presence and prevalence of miracles today. I could give countless stories of miracles that happened in our church during this season where we really pressed into the supernatural realm. One year, we had a young man who was dealing with scoliosis, a disease that causes the spine to curve, resulting in a variety of complications from respiratory problems to spinal cord or nerve damage. The disease had stopped his growth for three years and left an annoying pain in the lower back area, which required surgery to straighten. He came to the youth conference at our church and proclaimed healing over his spine. After the conference, he went back to the doctor for an examination. The doctor expected to find the young man's spine to be worse than the last time it was checked, but to his surprise, it was straight! A miracle! Something unusual that sparks an awareness of God and what He is doing.

Cultivating an "It's Possible" Mindset

How do we get the miraculous, supernatural power of God into our church today? To start seeing the supernatural, there are a few facts we need to realize.

You have the capacity to imagine. First, empty out the old assumptions and presuppositions in your heart and mind. Put away vain imaginations that evolve from past hurts and conditions that put a lid on your imagination. Ask yourself about the assumptions you have made unconsciously that are defining your future—your vain imaginings instead of God-inspired imaginings. How will God stretch your mind to believe?

You have been given the ability to dream. You have the Holy Spirit, the Word of God, the same spirit of faith as the people before you, and you have opportunity! What new dream does God desire to birth in you? What creative resources will God bring into your life?

You are a dreamer in the making. Don't allow yourself to think and live in the rut of sameness with no change or challenges and then allow that "sameness" feeling to become your security blanket. Be willing to do those things that feel illogical to your normal practices and understanding.

What do you imagine will happen in your church? Do you have vision for hundreds and thousands of lost souls to come, be discipled, and turn around and win more souls? Is your vision to see broken lives healed and marriages restored? Whatever you dream, it is possible! There are six "It's possible" attitudes and actions that each leader should own so that he or she can see the supernatural happen in the church.

1. See the Future Without Limitations or Restrictions

Our senses are great tools for hearing, smelling, tasting, touching and feeling; but they cannot get us to the level of the supernatural. What would you do if you knew you could not fail? An "It's possible" mindset sees a future that no one else has ever laid hold of, a future that necessitates miracles and will impact generations to come. This future is between highly unlikely and nearly impossible! A future with no proof as of now that it will ever be a reality but one that you believe can happen is one declared by faith, and it is the future God has planned for you (see Gen. 12:1-3; Jer. 29:11).

2. Let the Holy Spirit Open Your Heart to Reveal His Secrets

Scripture tells us that no one has heard or seen what God has in store for His people, but He "has revealed them to us through His Spirit" (1 Cor. 2:10). God has a purpose, a design, for each individual and for every church; and He wants you to know it so that you will be encouraged, inspired to greatness, and hit the mark He set for you. To do that, you must first open your heart to the Holy Spirit, the written Word and the quickened Word.

You can start with confessing that God has cleansed you from all sins and that you are pure and holy, whole and beautiful. God has bought you with His blood and you are important, significant and special. He has destined you to be blessed, favored and fruitful; and He is committed to changing you so that you can live your dream. God has indeed given you a dream and a hope for the future.

3. Believe that What Was Impossible in the Past Is Now Possible

Think about the father who brought his demon-possessed son to Jesus, described in Mark 9:14-29. He had heard that Jesus had the ability to heal people who unexpectedly throw themselves on the ground or into a fire or become totally rigid. He started to hope that maybe Jesus would be the answer to his son's problem. He started to believe that what was impossible in the past is now possible. Then, the father ran into a group of Jesus' disciples! "Maybe they can help my son," he probably thought. So he probably walked up to a group of them and asked, "Can you help my son?" The disciples tried, unsuccessfully, to cast out the demon, and the father left them, disappointed.

A little while later, the father was in a crowd of people as Jesus came by. He complained to Jesus that the disciples were unable to cast out the demon. So Jesus told him to bring Him the son. The father, stirred with hope, begged, "If You can do anything, have compassion on us and help us" (Mark 9:22). Jesus' response was that if you can believe, anything is possible. Then the father took a brave step and cried, "Lord, I believe; help my unbelief!" (Mark 9:24). Jesus cast out the demon and the boy was healed. Why? Because the father believed that what was impossible in the past is possible now. The supernatural power of God was present in his world, and he grabbed the opportunity to get freedom from lifelong oppression for his son. Believe that, in spite of past failures or human incapability, all things are possible with God (see Matt. 17:20; Mark 10:27).

4. Lift the Lid Off Your Mind and Resist Old Assumptions

In the book of Isaiah, God speaks a very interesting command to Israel: "Do not remember the former things, nor consider the things of old. Behold, I will do a new thing, now it shall spring forth; shall you not know it? I will even make a road in the wilderness and rivers in the desert" (Isa. 43:18-19). To remember, here, means to ponder—to reflect and meditate on—what has happened. Continually pondering the past puts an unhealthy frame on the future, because you assume that whatever happens in the future will be no different from the past. If you prayed for someone to be healed and they did not instantaneously recover, then the same will happen the next time you pray for someone, so why bother? Your church gave money to another struggling church and when you needed funds, no one sent any money to you, so why give?

As we do the ridiculous, God does the miraculous. In our present economy that is in so much turmoil and uncertainty, it makes no sense to human minds that we should sow money into the church with tithes and offerings. Yet in the supernatural realm that says "It's possible," we step up in faith and sow our seed, knowing that God will do something miraculous with it and return our seed to us in ways that we did not imagine.

I have a friend who was so scared to pray with other people for healing because every time she prayed for someone, that person would die. She would lay hands on a person and pray in faith; and then, a month later, the person would pass. After quite a number of times that she prayed for someone and they didn't recover, she decided that she would never pray for healing again. So when a friend brought a sick person to her for prayer, she flat out refused. "Don't let me pray for you, because if I do, you'll die." But her friend insisted that she pray, so she did, and the man died right in front of them.

However, this time she had faith to believe God could raise someone from the dead. Laying her hands on the corpse, she prayed for life to reenter that body, and the man was resurrected. That event caused a complete turnaround in her life, and today, astonishing miracles of healings and deliverance follow her and her husband's ministry.

What happened that she was able to pray for a healing and resurrection miracle, even though she had not yet seen one happen through her prayers? She took the lid off what was impossible naturally speaking, resisted the assumption that God could not do something miraculous through her, and prayed with courageous faith.

Through the Holy Spirit, we have the power to do more than what we have experienced so far. Don't let your lack of good experiences rule out what God seeks to do in your life and in your church. Most of the time, the worst conditions provide the best atmosphere to act in faith. Take yourself out of the equation and invite the Holy Spirit to come and cover the ministry time, revealing His power, His wisdom and His insight, taking charge.

5. Let Go of Lesser Ambitions and Reach Beyond

Ask anyone who has been around church for a while and he or she will probably agree that the apostle Paul was a man who had great ambition and achieved a great deal in his life, which he certainly did. However, one reason why he accomplished so much is because he always pressed beyond what his human reasoning told him was adequate. From the Philippian jail he wrote, "I do not count myself to have apprehended; but one thing I do, forgetting those things which are behind and reaching forward to those things which are ahead" (Phil. 3:13). Paul had plans and ideas for what he could do for God's kingdom with his intellect, his charisma and his writing ability. But when he was sailing in a ship on his way to visit a church, thinking about his future and life goals, he probably did not think that his writings, under Holy Spirit inspiration, would make up much of the New Testament that we read and preach from today! Yet he did not stop reaching, until he died.

What is the "lesser ambition" that you are holding on to? You can't stretch out and reach the God thing that is above your current capacity while you have your own smaller objective in your hand. It's time to move your tent stakes out a little farther, to stretch a little farther, and to do so in faith, knowing that God will expand your reach (see Josh. 8:18; Isa. 54:2-3).

6. Make a Faith Declaration of What You See

There is incredible, life-changing power in words. You might be familiar with the passage in James that talks about the tongue's ability to speak life and death (see Jas. 3:3-12). What you speak about your life and your situation shapes your attitude and outlook on life. If you wake up and confess that today is a good day and you will rejoice throughout the day that God is faithful, that He has given you health and that you woke up that morning, then your attitude will reflect that confession. If you wake up, stub your toe as you climb out of bed, and sarcastically say, "What a great start to the day. Today is going to be awful," then you will pout and complain the whole day long.

A faith declaration produces a breakthrough when no physical evidence that something is happening exists. It does this by pushing out a space and making room for the possibility of a new reality. It produces a spiritual ripple in the invisible world by saying it, declaring it and putting it into motion. Making a faith declaration mimics what God does when He "gives life to the dead and calls those things which do not exist as though they did" (Rom. 4:17). You see the vision through the Spirit's eyes and trust that God can make it happen, because you know He has proved His faithfulness in the past. Therefore, you make a faith declaration that what God has revealed to you, He will do, and then you start making steps toward that vision (see Job 22:28; Ps. 40:10).

What do you want to happen in your church and in your life? It's possible! Divine intervention is headed your way. Position yourself to press open the door to the supernatural and receive what is coming your way. Lift your vision and open your spirit to see miracles happen in your life and church today.

Strategic Blending of Spirit and Word

My hunger and interest in knowing and understanding the Word of God have led me down the path of education, including Bible colleges and seminaries. As I mentioned earlier, I earned my Master of Divinity and Doctor of Ministry from Oral Roberts University. I also took classes at other schools, both Evangelical and those with charismatic, or Pentecostal, orientations. The two camps were well defined and each had a perspective and a way to define the other group. The Evangelicals would say that Charismatics have little or no scriptural foundation and that they are shallow and driven by personalities and unscriptural spiritual manifestations. The Charismatics would criticize the Evangelicals as having no spiritual power, being spiritually shallow—as dry as Ezekiel's bone yard—and driven by knowledge not power.

While taking courses at these various institutions, I found myself caught in an interesting position, because I was a blend of both—raised Baptist, swept into the Jesus movement and then captured and filled with the Holy Spirit. My Baptist roots instilled a deep conviction of sound doctrine and the supremacy of the Scriptures. The Jesus movement and my encounter with the Holy Spirit ignited a passion for evangelism, preaching the Word and seeing miracles, healings and powerful works of the Holy Spirit. My journey has kept me loving both the Spirit and the Word.

As I study the church in Scripture, I am convinced that an effective, God-pleasing church is not exclusively Spirit driven or exclusively Bible exposition driven but a precise blend of both. It is a church built on solid biblical knowledge, proper interpretation and respect for hermeneutics and doctrine, and energized and anointed by the Spirit so that the gifts of the Spirit flow through every person. A determined balance of the Spirit and the Word should characterize our preaching, teaching, corporate services and leadership training. The Spirit-Word balance is a defining characteristic of a Strategic Church.

From the beginning, the Spirit and the Word have worked together, as seen in Genesis 1:2-3: "The earth was without form, and void; and darkness was on the face of the deep. And the Spirit of God was hovering over the face of the waters. Then God said, 'Let there be light'; and there was light." The Spirit of God hovered over the deep, preparing the way for the coming of the Word. What followed was a universe created with a word (God's word) and given life through the Holy Spirit. Likewise, the SC is a place where a group of believers who have accepted Christ (the Word) are bonded together by new birth through the Holy Spirit and are endued with His power to effectively carry out the work of God. Our lives and churches must have both. It's right, it's biblical, and it's strategic.

The Spirit-Word balance is one that is important to me and to CBC. I begin my speaking time by having the congregation stand, hold their Bibles and pray together, asking the Spirit to illuminate the Word and make it practical to us. This puts us in mind that we can read the Word and study it, but it is the Spirit who gives us inspiration and helps us practice what it says.

We also have a tradition of reading a Scripture before we give our tithes and offerings and then praying the Scripture. For instance, we will read a verse like Psalm 112:3-4: "Their houses brim with wealth and a generosity that never runs dry. Sunrise breaks through the darkness for good people–God's grace and mercy and justice!" (*THE MESSAGE*). Then the service emcee will teach for a few minutes from that verse. Next the congregation prays over their gifts with a prayer inspired by the Scripture just read. It could be something like: "Lord, my life, my work and my dwelling place are Yours to fill with Your abundance. When I face the dark days, I believe that Your light will break through. Pour Your graciousness into me so that my giving overflows with a willing and generous spirit."

The practice of praying God's Word back to Him is part of our culture. It says that we value the Word and we believe it has practical, life-changing applications for our unique situation. This is just one way to demonstrate the interaction of the Spirit and Word in a corporate service.

THE SPIRIT-WORD CHURCH IN ACTS

The Spirit-Word balance is a God idea and it is seen throughout Scripture, particularly in the book of Acts, as the norm for church life. Here are a few Scriptures that demonstrate that blend and balance of the Spirit and Word (emphasis added).

THE SPIRIT CHURCH

- Acts 1:8: "But you shall receive power when the *Holy Spirit* has come upon you; and you shall be witnesses to Me in Jerusalem, and in all Judea and Samaria, and to the end of the earth."
- Acts 2:4: "And they were all filled with the *Holy Spirit* and began to speak with other tongues, as the Spirit gave them utterance."
- Acts 2:33: "Therefore being exalted to the right hand of God, and having received from the Father the promise of the *Holy Spirit,* He poured out this which you now see and hear."
- Acts 4:8: "Then Peter, filled with the *Holy Spirit,* said to them."
- Acts 4:31: "And when they had prayed, the place where they were assembled together was shaken; and they were all filled with the *Holy Spirit,* and they spoke the word of God with boldness."
- Acts 6:3: "Therefore, brethren, seek out from among you seven men of good reputation, full of the *Holy Spirit* and wisdom, whom we may appoint over this business."
- Acts 8:17: "Then they laid hands on them, and they received the *Holy Spirit.*"
- Acts 9:31: "Then the churches throughout all Judea, Galilee, and Samaria had peace and were edified. And walking in the fear of the Lord and in the comfort of the *Holy Spirit,* they were multiplied."
- Acts 10:44: "While Peter was still speaking these words, the *Holy Spirit* fell upon all those who heard the word."
- Acts 11:15: "And as I [Peter] began to speak, the *Holy Spirit* fell upon them, as upon us at the beginning."
- Acts 13:2: "As they ministered to the Lord and fasted, the *Holy Spirit* said, 'Now separate to Me Barnabas and Saul for the work to which I have called them.'"

(See also Acts 1:2,4-5; 2:17-18,38; 5:32; 6:10; 7:55; 9:17; 10:19,38; 11:12,24; 13:4,9,52; 15:8,28; 19:2; 20:23,28; 21:4,11.)

THE WORD CHURCH

- Acts 2:41: "Then those who gladly received his *word* were baptized; and that day about three thousand souls were added to them."
- Acts 4:4: "However, many of those who heard the *word* believed; and the number of the men came to be about five thousand."
- Acts 4:29: "Now, Lord, look on their threats, and grant to Your servants that with all boldness they may speak Your *word*."
- Acts 4:31: "And when they had prayed, the place where they were assembled together was shaken; and they were all filled with the Holy Spirit, and they spoke the *word* of God with boldness."
- Acts 6:7: "Then the *word* of God spread, and the number of the disciples multiplied greatly in Jerusalem, and a great many of the priests were obedient to the faith."
- Acts 8:4: "Therefore those who were scattered went everywhere preaching the *word*."
- Acts 13:5: "And when they arrived in Salamis, they preached the *word* of God in the synagogues of the Jews."
- Acts 15:35-36: "Paul and Barnabas also remained in Antioch, teaching and preaching the *word* of the Lord, with many others also. Then after some days Paul said to Barnabas, "Let us now go back and visit our brethren in every city where we have preached the *word* of the Lord, and see how they are doing."
- Acts 19:20: "So the *word* of the Lord grew mightily and prevailed."

(See also Acts 8:14,25; 11:19,26; 16:17; 17:11,13; 18:11; 19:10; 20:20; 28:31.)

The strategic leader and the leadership team must highly esteem both the Spirit and the Word as equal strengths for building every aspect of the church (see Matt. 16:16-18; Acts 2:1-4). These leaders will model both aspects in their lives and ministry. They will show spirit leadership by living in the Holy Spirit and being full of the Spirit (see Judg. 6:34; 2 Kings 2:9; 1 Thess. 1:5). Leaders demonstrate Word leadership by living in and being full of the Word of God (see Acts 6:2,4; 1 Tim. 4:2).

Distinctives of the Spirit-Word Church

A church cannot be expected to rise above the level of Spirit-Word capacity that the church leaders have not achieved. Spanish essayist and thinker Miguel de Unamuno wrote, "The would-be leader of men who affirms and proclaims that he pays no heed to the things of the Spirit, is not worthy to lead them."[1] As leaders, we must continually evaluate and make course adjustments to keep the healthy balance and blending of the Spirit and the Word (see 1 Thess. 5:19-21; Titus 1:9).

The birth of the church described in the beginning of Acts 2 bursts with the outpouring of the Spirit. From this founding experience, we can draw several distinguishing characteristics, or distinctives, of a church that is born by the Holy Spirit and is formed and empowered by Him. In the event described in Acts 2, the Spirit used wind and fire to manifest His presence and establish the church. When we believe God is truly present in our churches by His amazing presence and power, the SC is ready to build. That means we continue to live out the book of Acts, a book God is still writing, because it is the Acts of His apostolic people.

In the book of Acts, we see the need for distinctives that form a church built on the Spirit and the Word.

- *Spirit-forming distinctives*: prayer, worship, gifts of the Spirit, waiting upon the Lord, a prophetic spirit, corporate fasting and prayer, asking and believing for a fresh touch of the Holy Spirit (see Joel 2:28; Acts 1:8; 2:1-4,42; 1 Cor. 12:4,7,13; Phil. 3:3).

- *Word-forming distinctives*: teaching, preaching, devotions, discipleship, disciplines of study, Bible-honoring praying, decisions made with and by the Word of God, and teaching and modeling principles taken from the Word of God (see Matt. 7:24-27; John 1:1,14; Acts 6:2,4,7; 12:24; 18:11; 19:20).

The Equal Blending of the Spirit and the Word

The Spirit and the Word share in a marriage made in heaven. To hold to both equally is, as church history proves, an intensely difficult and elusive challenge that we cannot afford to fail to meet. A strategic leader builds a church that is committed to interfusing and intermixing the Spirit and the Word in equal parts. This is a commitment to blend:

- Holy Spirit *activity* and Word of God *basics,*
- Holy Spirit *ministry* and Word of God *principles,*
- Holy Spirit *speaking* and Word of God *guidelines,*
- Holy Spirit *worship* and Word of God *substance,*
- Holy Spirit *power* and Word of God *parameters,*
- Holy Spirit *presence* and Word of God *approach,*
- Holy Spirit *guidance* and Word of God *disciplines,*
- Holy Spirit *creativity* and Word of God *authority,*
- Holy Spirit-*inspired vision* and Word of God *definition of the vision,* and
- Holy Spirit *revelation* and Word of God *interpretation.*

The Spirit-Word foundation provides any church builder with a solid base and a clear path to follow. Consistently following biblical, proven principles over an extended period of time leads to authentic breakthroughs and long-lasting spiritual fruit. There are no shortcuts. Break the cycle of multiple levels of decline in the church by returning to the proven basics of the Word of God that will, in due season, produce right results. Don't seek the one defining action, the grand program, the one killer cutting-edge idea, the miracle moment that would allow the church to skip the hard work of building by the Word. Know and stick with the basics. Tremendous power exists in commitment to continual improvement and delivering steady results step by step, little by little. There are no shortcuts to true breakthroughs. Trust in and build with the Spirit and the Word. Breakthroughs come by making a series of good decisions, disciplined actions grounded in the Word, patience, and movement in the right direction with faith. When we become impatient and begin to follow trends, shortcuts or the one-big-breakthrough idea that takes us away from the disciplined work of building with the proven principles of the Word and Spirit, we may be tempted to break the rules.

A Word Formula for Health and Growth

You probably remember the first day of kindergarten or grade school. You bounced into the classroom for the first day of school with your new backpack, carefully sharpened pencils and a paper lunch sack with your name written on it. Class began and the first thing the teacher said was his or her name. Then the teacher unveiled a giant poster with a long list of rules on it: "No chewing gum," "No fighting," "Look both ways before crossing," "Don't raise your voice," "No talking when the teacher is talking"—and you can probably remember several more. There were probably several students who took the rules very seriously and strictly adhered to them. (We called those kids teacher's pets.) Then there were those mischievous ones who wanted to press the rules as far as they could just out of spite and because they were strong willed.

What we were probably too young to comprehend at that age was that rules were there to help us. If we didn't fight, we wouldn't get hurt. If we listened to the teacher, we would learn something and also get into a healthy habit of respecting people while they are talking. If you look both ways before crossing the street, you are less likely to get hit by a car! Follow the rules, succeed. Break the rules, damage yourself and possibly many others who depend on you.

Breaking the rules of biblical church building that we are talking about produces a wrong formula for spiritual health and growth in the church and causes only harm:

Figure 11.1

The Wrong Formula

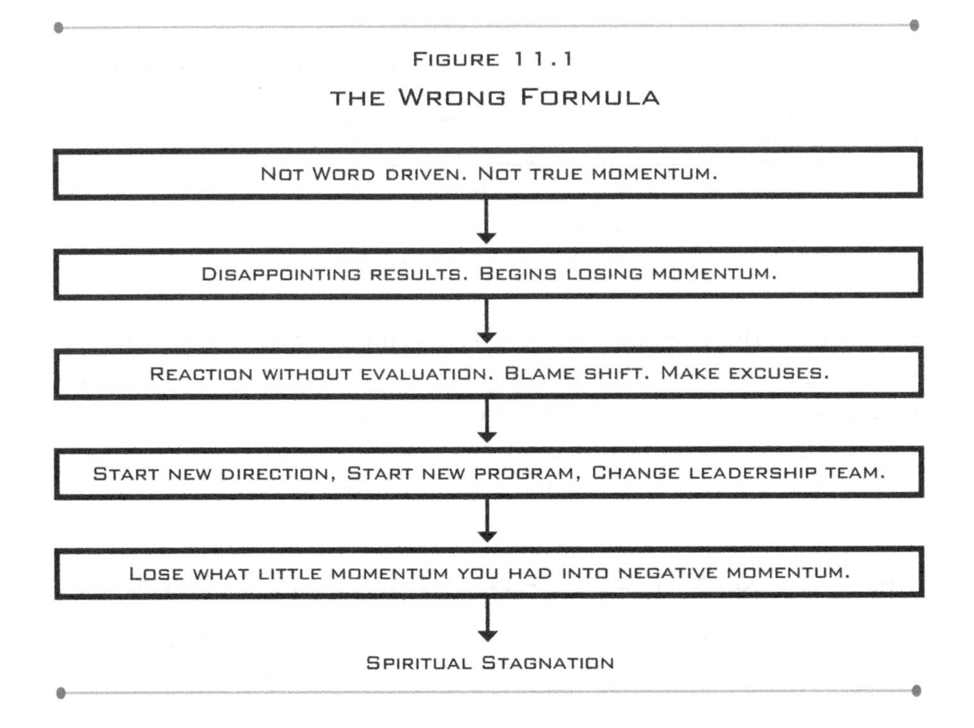

When you start something without a good foundation, you have to keep making little adjustments in order to keep everything balanced, because your base is always teetering. You have to keep trying new programs, moving leaders around and shifting the pieces. Thus, what little momentum you had when you started ends up backfiring, and you end up stagnating. This is not health.

When we as leaders honor the Spirit-Word principle, we produce a right formula for building strategic churches:

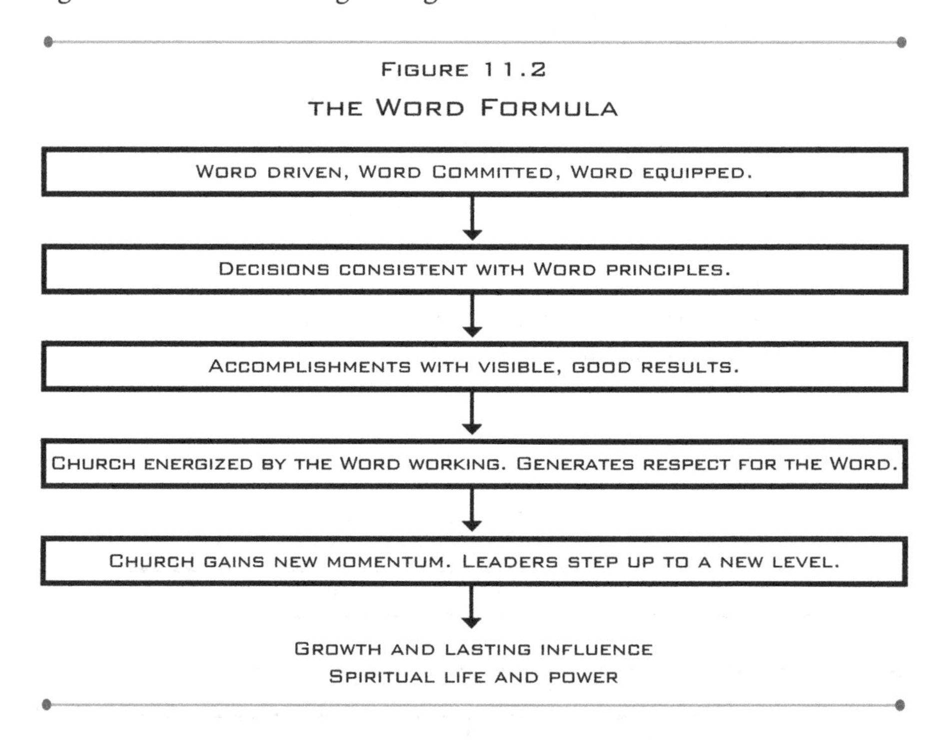

Every level of this flowchart is a solid beam laid on a concrete foundation. Every step relates back to the foundation, which is the Word. You don't have to keep shifting from program to program. You stick to Word principles, gain momentum and see lasting growth and lasting influence. Let's now get into the precise elements of the Spirit-Word balance in the SC.

ELEMENTS OF A SPIRIT-WORD CHURCH

Forming the SC with the power of a Spirit-Word foundation requires that the leadership team be on the same page with how their church should look. They are the ones who must form and empower every aspect of the church into a cohesive whole, guided by the lead pastor. The lead pastor sets the vision, identifies values, structures the church with proper organization, trains leaders, mentors next-level leaders and uses the pulpit to feed, lead, inspire and equip. These are the Spirit-Word elements the lead pastor and leadership team should communicate:

1. *Spirit-Word-Centered Vision*—A vision that originates with the clear teaching of Scripture and is structured around strong, biblical values will outlive and outlast personality-driven visions or trend visions. Vision that is Spirit-Word-centered should be birthed in prayer and Holy Spirit activity in the leader and the team. The very essence of leadership is that you have a vision that is inspiring, motivates others, is clearly articulated and is based on God's Word and Holy Spirit confirmation (see Hab. 2:4; Acts 26:19). (For a more detailed discussion of vision, see chapter 2.)

2. *Spirit-Word-Centered Decision Making*—Decision making that is Spirit-Word centered begins with the clear principles of integrity and of consistency with overall Scripture. Whether in values or principles, Spirit-led decisions do not violate the Word of God. The Word is the measuring rod against which all decisions are made. It forms our principles and sets our priorities.

3. *Spirit-Word-Centered Worship*—Worship that is Spirit-Word centered is worship that flows from a clear understanding of biblical principles. Expressions and styles coincide with the core value of what Scripture says worship is to be. True worship is having an encounter with God that transforms a person's soul and spirit (see John 4:24; Eph. 5:19). The believer is not a spectator but a participator. All worship flows from this conviction.

4. *Spirit-Word-Centered Church Growth*—Church growth that is Spirit-Word centered begins with a clear understanding of what true growth consists of as seen in the Scriptures and a Word-governed discipleship program. One of the main themes in the book of Acts is the growth of the church. True growth flows from true spiritual health (see Acts 2:41,46; 4:4; 5:14; 6:7; 9:31; 11:21).

5. *Spirit-Word-Centered Children's Ministry*—Children's ministry that is Spirit-Word centered begins with the core value that children are people with souls to be grown. They can and should have an encounter with Christ, a true salvation presentation and a steady diet of the Word of God. Careful consideration should go into choosing curriculum and structuring weekly services for them. Children should leave their service with a feeling of fun and excitement, but they should also come away knowing who Jesus is, what the importance of the Bible is and how to practice principles such as obedience and grace. Children's ministry is not babysitting or childcare; it is discipleship. Children should be led into encounters with the Holy Spirit.

6. *Spirit-Word-Centered Youth Ministry*—Youth ministry that is Spirit-Word centered begins with the same core values that mold the adult congregation: prayer, worship, purity, doctrine, the Word, character and integrity. These are kept as the core values of youth ministry so as to build a strong relationship between youth and the local church. Various methods and services can be planned to serve this group. CBC holds weekly Wednesday night services for youth. We also host small-group meetings that happen throughout the week. This gives the students time for closer interaction with a trained leader. With this strategy of large corporate gatherings and smaller Bible study groups, we fulfill our goal of training the next generation to live spiritually healthy lives and to be servant-leaders in the local church. Youth ministry must be a pipeline, not a pond.

7. *Spirit-Word-Centered Pastoring*—Pastoring that is Spirit-Word centered begins with seeing the church from a right perspective. A church is not just a gathering; it is a family. Pastoring is the sheep and shepherd relationship, and it necessitates certain kinds of qualified leaders who take a biblical approach to counseling, discipleship and mentoring. Pastoring is believing in the gifts of the Spirit to pastor and help people (see Isa. 11:1-3; 1 Cor. 12:7; Eph. 4:11-12).

8. *Spirit-Word-Centered Evangelism*—Evangelism that is Spirit-Word centered begins with an understanding of the lost souls that believe in a heaven and a hell. This is a belief system that sees eternal destinies as a reality, thus moving the entire congregation into a place of taking responsibility to win the lost in an atmosphere of compassion and confidence to share Christ. The gospel of the kingdom starts with repentance. Believe in Spirit-led, Spirit-empowered evangelism (see John 14:6; Acts 8:29).

9. *Spirit-Word-Centered World Missions*—World missions that are Spirit-Word centered begin with the conviction that every church in every nation is responsible to establish churches in their culture and in their nation and then to train national leaders to send to all the nations of the world. These churches should become nationally independent, self-supporting local churches.

10. *Spirit-Word-Centered Preaching*—Preaching that is Spirit-Word centered begins with the feeder (or feeders) of the flock starting with the Word, working into the Word with proper research and working out from the Word with proper interpretation, and preaching from the Word with appropriate preaching skills.

Blending Spirit and Word for Powerful Preaching

On every level, the strategic leader is one who communicates the Word. Weekend services, leadership training and special events are all driven by the Word being preached and by the power of the Holy Spirit. The SC must have a Spirit-Word preacher.

There's an old Puritan saying about preaching: "Thou art a preacher of the Word; mind thy business." Heavy biblical or theological materials gleaned from books and commentaries but not digested or assimilated into the preacher's spirit will fail to produce Spirit-anointed, biblical preaching. We all face busy schedules, busy minds, fast study styles, tired emotions and the temptation to throw a message together. Hoping the

Holy Spirit will anoint our lack is not going to help hit the target of Spirit-Word preaching. Word leaders should not give interpretations of Scripture that are far-fetched and violate good hermeneutics in the name of "The Spirit showed me." Powerful preaching comes from continual study of the Word and inspiration from the Holy Spirit as He illuminates your heart. Through Holy Spirit prayer, we receive insight and are burdened to connect the human condition with the Word of God and then meet needs by His Word with power and passion. You have to get a conviction based on the Word first. You can threaten and cajole to tithe, and church members will tithe that week; but they revert to normal behavior unless the Holy Spirit has the preached word to use in order to bring conviction.

Several words are used in the Bible to describe preaching. There is "announce," meaning to bring the message down; "charge," to leave the message beside them; and "publish," to put the message through, to penetrate. Then there is "inform," meaning to lift the people up; and "report," which is something coming from the presence of God to the people. The first church emphasized continual teaching and preaching (see Acts 5:42; 6:7; 20:20; 1 Cor. 12:28). We bring people a message of hope, a word of encouragement, victory, freedom and yoke-breaking anointing (see Isa. 40:9; 52:7). As Paul says, "Preach the word! Be ready in season and out of season. Convince, rebuke, exhort, with all longsuffering and teaching" (2 Tim. 4:2). Preach, announce, inform, impart and bring the Word with power. I think Charles Spurgeon summed it up nicely:

> It is idle merely to let the eye glance over the words, or to recollect the poetical expressions, or the historic facts; but it is blessed to eat into the very soul of the Bible until, at last, you come to talk in Scriptural language, and your very style is fashioned upon Scripture models, and, what is better still, your spirit is flavored with the words of the Lord.[2]

Stay away from novel or sensational interpretations of Scripture, and stick with preaching the Word.

Three Keys to Maintain a Biblical Balance

Martin Luther once wrote, "The devil does not mind the written word, but he is put to flight whenever it is preached aloud." I have learned three keys that will help you maintain a biblical balance of preaching the Word with the Spirit's power and role in mind.

KEY #1: PREACH WITH REVELATION

Preachers are like excavators. They find something that has been in hiding and buried in the earth and they uncover it and put it in public view. This takes work, but it is Spirit-Word preaching: spending time researching the Word and allowing the Holy Spirit to illuminate truth in your spirit. Truth must be marinated into the speaker and then transmitted to the people. It is easier to make a sermon of the letter, out of skill and study, than to grow a sermon in the depths of your spirit. A sermon that arises out of the inner life will touch the inner life of others. When I read E. M. Bounds or R. A. Torrey, I am compelled to slide off my chair and onto my knees, because they wrote from the Spirit and they touch my spirit.

A woman said to me one day after church, "We've attended here for seven years and look forward to coming every Sunday because every Sunday, something is adjusted in our lives." Preaching is not just a science or an art. It is impartation into life. Some people today want to be entertained and download quick and easy answers. But they need to hear Spirit-empowered, solid preaching. Inhale the breath of the Spirit in research, hermeneutics, homiletics and scholarship. Exhale the fresh life of the Word in practical life application and life-related truths.

KEY #2: PREACH WITH INSPIRATION AND ANOINTING

The specifically placed breath of God is the spring of life. Scripture houses divine vitality—the source of life, as contrasted to human writings, which neither have nor give life. The authority behind preaching resides not in the preacher but in the biblical text, not in emotion but in the Holy Spirit that inspired the text. When you do not feel the anointing, preach on by faith in the Word of God. During a dry season, I preach on the Word and preach my way out of the season. Don't feel your way out of it or prophesy your way out; preach your way out. When you preach the Word, things will happen in people's lives that you could not envision otherwise because the Spirit makes the Word real to the individual.

The Spirit-Word preacher must have a surplus of the Holy Spirit and a unique and powerful anointing. The anointing is a spiritual empowering or outpouring of the Holy Spirit upon us as leaders. It permeates and saturates us, transferring a divine enablement that goes beyond our own capacity and strength. Our ministry must be filled to overflowing with the Holy Spirit at all times so that there is always surplus and more than enough to impart to others (see Luke 4:14,18; Eph. 5:18-19). Our greatest concern is not the devil, the darkness around us or the culture we face. Our greatest concern should be the quality of our anointing, how full of the Spirit we are and how much virtue we have. Our lack of anointing results in an empty spirit and lack of overflow, and it will cause our ministry to falter (see Ps. 23:5; John 7:38).

KEY #3: PREACH WITH TEACHING

Preaching calls for clear, systematic instruction, imparting carefully thought-through material that is gradually developed to meet a definite need (see Mark 1:22). Good preaching has good teaching to it. The usual Greek word for "teach" in the New Testament signifies holding a discourse with others in order to instruct. Good preaching means someone has learned something. This might be learning the principles of warfare or historical facts of the Bible's validity or other spiritual truths. One effective way to teach is by using illustrations and stories. Illustrations can be a very helpful complement to the truth you are sharing. But remember, you are not primarily a storyteller but a truth teacher. Truth should not be tacked onto illustrations as a pretext for telling the story. Stories are important, but truth is primary! The relationship of seasonings and sauces to gourmet cooking parallels the role of introductions, illustrations and conclusions. A simple rule to follow is that illustrations should demonstrate the truth, not elevate the preacher.

The preacher's delivery of the message must have the elements of freedom, flow and spontaneity. He or she must be open to the influence and power of the Holy Spirit to direct his or her thoughts and, at times, not be tied to the message, even though it has been carefully prepared. I do not know how many times I have preached only half my notes or just a small fraction of what I had prepared. When that happens, I can't get upset or frustrated. I'm grateful for the demonstration of the Spirit and open to the inspiration of the moment. Some of the best things a preacher says may not be premeditated or written in the sermon material. We can't hope to speak effectively out of our own understanding, because "our sufficiency is from God" (2 Cor. 3:5). Yes, study and prepare. But let the Holy Spirit confirm what He authored. Anyone can write with ink. Christ alone can write with the Spirit of God. Teach and impart, not clinically or academically, but spiritually.

The Question of Relevance

The relevant church is one that connects to and communicates in a significant, contemporary way to the culture around it. Being relevant is absolutely a right issue for leaders to be concerned about and seek to fulfill—but not at the cost of losing what is biblically right for a church to be and what the message is supposed to bring. When church leaders turn to the experts for marketing, style and standards of what is acceptable by the unchurched in a church, there is a problem. Experts tell us that the best way to reach people who think church is irrelevant is to appeal to something that is undeniably relevant to mass culture: being entertained. So sermons get shorter and wittier, less Scripture is preached, more stories are shared, music gets more contemporary—sometimes even secular songs are used to make a connection—and theology takes a backseat in everything. We see these churches drawing people, but questions have to be asked: "What happened to people? Where are those who love the Word and understand the Spirit? Where are prayer, intercession and worship inspired by the Holy Spirit and glorifying to Him?"

Yes, we can be relevant and incorporate all the elements that the New Testament church models for us: preaching the Word, praying for healing, actively seeing miracles and Holy Spirit encounters, and reaching cities as a fully functioning church. But the leader who seeks to build by the Spirit and Word must do so with a mindset to connect with people in ways that help them understand the Word and the power of the Holy Spirit.

The Spirit-Word quality of the SC is the wineskin that keeps the church fresh and flexible because of the Holy Spirit's presence. A church without this power and presence will become rigid, inflexible, old and brittle. The old wine and old wineskin metaphor is Jesus' own, found in Luke 5:33-39. "Old" here does not refer to age but to a cramping, or tightening, narrowness of the church that has lost freshness and vitality amid the traditions that are practiced. Rather than swinging to the other extreme and losing theological ground in the name of relevance, the Spirit-Word leader bases the church's principles of ministry on a core of biblical truths, listens to what the Holy Spirit is currently saying and then moves out in obedience. We should take our directives from the Word of God and gain the empowerment to fulfill these directives from the Holy Spirit.

The strategic leader combines all the biblical values modeled in the New Testament church into the always fresh Spirit-Word empowered church in a balanced mixture. Blending prayer, worship, praise, Word preaching and a contemporary atmosphere is truly a challenge for leaders desiring to build

Spirit-filled, Word-filled, relevant churches. The SC should be biblical and spiritually powerful and expand the kingdom of God, reach people for Christ and disciple believers. Build a Spirit-Word culture that has strong roots in the Word and has Spirit-empowered leaders.

Strategic Culture of Generosity

The strategic leader understands a culture in the church is much deeper and broader than any event or any sermon given on a topic. Culture is rooted in the deep convictions of the congregation, resulting in a corporate attitude, behavior and lifestyle. The SC develops a culture of generosity that becomes a "heart style" and a spiritual lifestyle that reflects the generous God we see in Scripture, a God who sets the example by being outrageously liberal with His unlimited resources. A generosity heartbeat in the church makes the church look and feel as if Jesus lives in that place.

Building a culture of generosity into the congregation is a choice the strategic leader makes. When we were planting our church in Eugene, Oregon, we had to build this culture and attitude of generosity from the foundation up. People who came to Christ in our church—prodigals, new converts and transplant Christians from other churches—all had to be nurtured into this new way of doing life. Generosity is an attitude, a lifestyle, and it is mixed with faith and a conviction that generosity is God's idea. Generosity is about more than giving money, but it does involve money. Anything that deals with money takes a spirit of faith. People must be discipled into becoming generous. It is not a natural inclination of the soul to be generous. The natural part of us is the Adamic nature, the old nature, and it is a taker, not a giver. It is stingy, self-serving and tight-fisted.

To take people from this stronghold nature of keeping all they have to becoming givers—and to be liberal, generous givers at that—is a strategic process. If you as a leader seek to build a culture of generosity, then you must be committed to a longer process than the preaching of one sermon on giving. The leader-preacher or primary feeder must sow the Word as seed, water the Word with prayer and be patient to reap the harvest of the seed sown. For me, this was and has been a disciplined journey of pastoral instruction and a well-planned preaching series that builds a mindset and conviction that result in biblical generosity.

The preaching series on generosity is intended to encourage every person to develop a biblical perspective on managing their resources (see Prov. 24:3-4; Matt. 6:19-34) and to expose money problems as indicators that things are out of order (see Prov. 12:1,15,25; 14:12; 15:19). The giving of our resources starts with understanding how to manage what we already have in a biblical way so that God can bless and increase what we have. Teaching generosity without first teaching the discipline of money management only creates a false sense of generosity. A true culture of generosity is started by building into the congregation the biblical management of their resources and then adding biblical generosity to this foundation. The leader must understand that this takes strategic preaching with a vision to build a culture into the church. The culture of generosity happens when the leader chooses generosity, models it, values it, believes in it and imparts it into the congregation.

Seven Components of Generosity Culture

The place I have always started with in leading the congregation into a culture of generosity is what I call the seven components of generosity culture. These make up the preaching approach I take in building a strong foundation for a congregation lifestyle of generosity.

Let's look at a few of these components in more detail.

Generosity Culture Starts with Stewardship

Russell Herman was beyond generous. When his will surfaced, this simple carpenter had left a staggering $2.4 billion to the tiny town of Cave-In-Rock, Illinois. He also left the same amount to the impoverished community of East St. Louis as well as vast amounts for dredging rivers to prevent flooding, for preservation of the national forests and for other projects in southeastern Illinois. Russell's generosity is matched only by his inability to fulfill his promises. Despite leaving a will that gave away billions of dollars to those who really needed it, Russell only owned a dilapidated 1983 Oldsmobile when he died.

Figure 12.1

The Seven Components of Generosity Culture

1. STEWARDSHIP

The careful and responsible management of that which God has entrusted to our care: our time, strengths, talents and money. (Matt. 25:21; Luke 16:10)

2. WORKING

Working with diligence and integrity is biblical, and God promises to reward hard work. (Prov. 22:29; 13:11; Eph. 6:5-8; Col. 3:23-24; 2 Thess. 3:6-15; 1 Tim. 6:1-3)

3. GIVING

Giving activates divine law that releases the blessings of God in our personal world. (Prov. 3:9-10; 11:24; Luke 6:38; Acts 20:27,35; 1 Cor. 16;1-2; 2 Cor. 9:7)

4. RECEIVING

God responds to our giving by opening opportunities to receive divine provisions both directly and indirectly from His hands.(Deut. 28:8; Prov. 10:22; Isa. 40:8; Mal. 3:9-10; Matt. 7:8; Mark 10:30; Rom. 4:21)

5. MANAGING

God expects and requires believers to biblically manage their lives, including their money. (Josh. 1:8; Ps. 1:1-3; Prov. 16:32; Matt. 25:14-30; Luke 16:1-13; 2 Tim. 1:7)

6. PROSPERING

God desires that we receive abundantly and have more than enough so as to become liberal givers. (Gen 39:2,23; Deut. 28:13; Prov. 3:6; 1 Chron. 4:10; 2 Chron. 26:5; 31:21; Neh. 1:11; 2:20)

7. BEQUEATHING

God desires that we live wisely and leave an inheritance to continue His work into and through the next generation. (Job 42:15; Ps. 16:6; Prov. 13:22; 19:14; Ezek. 46:16-17)

A church can desire to be generous, but they can't give away what they don't have. At the base level of generosity culture is stewardship, which is the bedrock of generosity. Stewardship has to be in place and functioning before the culture of generosity can take root. We are stewards of the earth, that is, all things God entrusts to us that we inherit or earn. That includes our wealth and possessions. Generosity culture starts with the leader encouraging every person to have a biblical perspective on managing their lives, including their money, in a biblical way (see Ps. 49:16-17; Prov. 24:3; Matt. 6:19-34).

When a person comes to Christ as savior, he or she is also coming to Him as lord (see Acts 2:36; 16:31; Rom. 10:19). Accepting Jesus as savior and not yielding to Him as lord is an incomplete conversion. A call to salvation is a call to accept Jesus as savior, submit to Him as lord and become a disciple, a disciplined follower of the Lord Jesus Christ. Money problems are indicators that something is out of order, and spiritual and biblical principles that may be violated should be exposed (see Prov. 12:1,15,25; 14:12; 15:19; 22:5).

We cannot expect a miracle on our finances if we are not managing our finances in a biblical way. The path to generosity is an honest evaluation of life habits that bring about a change of mind and heart in the way we think about money and use money (see Prov. 13:6; 28:6; 2 Cor. 8:7). God has given us life, health and talents and has allowed us to work and receive money and possessions. It all comes from His goodness. God can bring prosperity into our lives, give us more than enough and allow us to receive abundance as we learn to wisely manage our money and understand that the purpose of prosperity is to be generous (see Deut. 8:13-17).

Generosity Needs Defining

To build a generosity culture, you first have to understand what generosity is. Generosity is liberality beyond normal giving, characterized by a magnanimous spirit that lives with an open hand. It extends beyond just giving money; it reaches everything a person has. Generosity taps the Christ virtue and flows from that virtue into abundant and over-the-top giving. Like any action, giving one's resources is the outworking of an inner spiritual conviction that just as God is actively generous, so too will the individual freely extend everything he or she has with a willing heart and a joyful spirit. Willingness is fundamental to generosity. The willing heart is a generous heart made ready to give (see Ps. 112:5; Prov. 11:24-25; 21:25-

26; 2 Cor. 8:7). It expects good things from the Lord and proclaims this expectation with strong prayers and praise, saying, "God shall supply all [my] need according to His riches in glory by Christ Jesus" (Phil. 4:19). God's Word says that He "crown[s] the year with [His] goodness, and [His] paths drip with abundance" (Ps. 65:11). You can willingly and joyfully give because you know God's character is one of eager generosity (see Pss. 34:8; 107:37; Gal. 6:9).

Generosity Culture Loves the House of God

The generosity culture builds upon the stewardship foundation by encouraging a dynamic generous heart that is passionate about the house of God. Love for the house is a deep root in the heart of every generous giver. This heart is "a willing heart" (see Exod. 35:5; see also Exod. 25:2; Ezek. 1:4), a "stirred" heart (Exod. 35:21), a sacrificial heart (see Exod. 35:22-29), a rejoicing heart, and a heart that desires to give the best (see Gen. 4:5; 22:2-8,13; Rom. 12:1-2).

When the people's hearts are stirred to love the house they are building together, generosity flows and grows. Speaking about his generosity for God's house that was motivated by his love for it, King David said it well: "Moreover, because I have set my affection on the house of my God, I have given to the house of my God, over and above all that I have prepared for the holy house, my own special treasure of gold and silver" (1 Chron. 29:3). When God's people are joined together, they become the habitation for the Holy Spirit, a place of life and power, a house where God works, a special place indeed (see Pss. 26:8; 27:4; Eph. 2:21; 1 Pet. 2:5). God's house is a special house. We should give generously without reservation. His house is called to be a place where essential things happen:

- People love people.
- There is room for everyone.
- Every person finds hope and a future.
- Life can be lived together.
- Dreams are encouraged.
- Brokenness is healed.
- Lifelong friendships flourish.
- Generations serve God together.
- God's Word is honored.
- God's presence is powerful.

- Prayer is believed.
- Vision is always expanding.
- Worship is expressive and genuine.
- Shepherds love their sheep.
- Faith can be experienced.

God's house is the house we love, and our love overflows with generosity. Leaders who build a generosity culture are convinced that God's house is their place to give their lives without hesitation. We can give our all without fear. This is our place to make beautiful, as the psalmist writes:

> But I am like a green olive tree in the house of God; I trust in the mercy of God forever and ever. I will praise You forever, because You have done it; and in the presence of Your saints I will wait on Your name, for it is good (Ps. 52:8-9).

God's house is your place to serve with abandonment, love others, carry the vision, be a participator, and build with your heart and your hands (see Ps. 122:1). God's house is made to be a house where people can love, feel passion for and joyfully be part of a culture of generosity. Remember that generosity has to start somewhere. Let it be in you and then flow through you to your church.

David, a man after God's heart, modeled willing generosity: "I know, dear God, that you care nothing for the surface—you want us, our true selves—and so I have given from the heart, honestly and happily. And now see all these people doing the same, giving freely, willingly—what a joy!" (1 Chron. 29:17, *THE MESSAGE*). Note that David recognized first that God's character is genuinely concerned about the heart, the inner person. Therefore, David willingly gave from his heart, and his actions prompted others to do the same. Willingness is contagious, and it starts in the heart of the leader.

Strategic Leaders Model the Generosity Lifestyle

King David built a culture of generosity because he had a generous soul and he loved God's presence. Listen to his heart: "Furthermore, because my heart is in this, in addition to and beyond what I have gathered, I'm turning over my personal fortune of gold and silver for making this place of worship for my God" (1 Chron. 29:3, *THE MESSAGE*). David set his affections on God's house, prepared his generous gifts and gave an amazing 110 tons of gold and 260 tons of silver. That was from his personal valued possessions!

The culture of generosity has leaders who give like King David—leaders who love God's house and instill a culture of generosity into the congregation by leading the way. The Matthew 6:21 principle is true: Where your treasure is, there your heart will be also. Our giving doesn't simply indicate where our hearts are; it determines where our hearts go. Money leads, and the heart follows. Loving God's house with your generosity is crucial to cultivating a generosity culture. As a leader, keep your eyes and heart fixed on God and point the church to fix their hearts on God:

> Both riches and honor come from You, and You reign over all. In Your hand is power and might; in Your hand it is to make great and to give strength to all. I know also, my God, that You test the heart and have pleasure in uprightness. As for me, in the uprightness of my heart I have willingly offered all these *things*; and now with joy I have seen Your people, who are present here to offer willingly to You. O Lord God of Abraham, Isaac, and Israel, our fathers, keep this forever in the intent of the thoughts of the heart of Your people, and fix their heart toward You (1 Chron. 29:12,17-18).

Generosity Culture of the Macedonian Churches

In 2 Corinthians 8:1, Paul refers to the Macedonian churches: "Moreover, brethren, we make known to you the grace of God bestowed on the churches of Macedonia." The Macedonian churches are Philippi (see Acts 16:12), Thessalonica (see Acts 17:1), and Berea (see Acts 17:10). These churches were planted by the apostle Paul with his grace and God's grace stamped upon them. They had a history of giving and helping Paul. In AD 50, Philippi entered into a financial partnership with Paul after his first visit. Late in AD 50, Silas and Timothy brought financial help from the Macedonians to Paul in Corinth (see Acts 18:5; 2 Cor. 11:9). In AD 56, the Macedonians contributed to Paul's collection for the Jerusalem church's needs (see Rom. 15:26), and in AD 60, the Philippians sent Epaphroditus to Rome to bring Paul relief supplies (see Phil. 4:18). The Macedonians were always flowing with the grace of giving sacrificially, liberally and beyond themselves. Let us pray for this same grace to be upon our churches!

God's Grace Empowered the Macedonian Grace

The Macedonian churches had experienced severe trials, national crises, breakdowns in economy, lack and huge challenges. Yet they pleaded for the privilege to give, and they gave with a level that amazed everyone. They believed God's grace was sufficient to take weaknesses and, through them, display His power. The Macedonian churches had Paul's heart—his own special apostolic spiritual DNA—deposited in them. His grace for giving and for amazing generosity is seen in these churches. Their grace was one of liberality that was not of themselves but from God (see Phil. 4:10,14-19; 1 Thess. 3:7).

Paul describes the courageous generosity of these churches in his letter to the Corinthians: "Fierce troubles came down on the people of those churches, pushing them to the very limit. The trial exposed their true colors: They were incredibly happy, though desperately poor. The pressure triggered something totally unexpected: an outpouring of pure and generous gifts" (2 Cor. 8:2, *THE MESSAGE*). The great trials that tested them only exposed their heart of generosity and proof of their genuineness. They were pushed to the limits yet responded with grace. They had lack of means by the natural eye that looked at the circumstances, but they turned their lack into an abundant grace of generosity.

The Macedonian Grace Can Be Our Grace

We can have the same grace that rested on the Macedonians. Second Corinthians 8:3 says, "For I [Paul] bear witness that according to their ability, yes, and beyond their ability, they were freely willing." They abounded in riches of liberality, their generosity exceeded and overflowed, and they had more than enough to excel in the grace of generosity. Their lack and needs had a positive effect of abounding liberality, not a negative effect of stingy gifts. Rock-bottom destitution did not rock their world. No computer can analyze this amazing formula:

GREAT AFFLICTION + DEEP POVERTY + GRACE =
ABUNDANT JOY + ABOUNDING LIBERALITY

Paul describes this kind of giving, not with business words or banking language or accounting terms, but in terms of a dynamic, spiritual experience. Paul calls this act in various ways:

- Grace (see 2 Cor. 8:1,6,7,9)
- Partnership (see 2 Cor. 8:4)
- Service (see 2 Cor. 8:9; 9:1,12-13)
- Earnestness (see 2 Cor. 8:8)
- Love (see 2 Cor. 8:7-8,24)
- Willingness (see 2 Cor. 8:11-12,19; 9:2)
- Generosity (see 2 Cor. 8:2; 9:11,13)
- Abundance (see 2 Cor. 8:14)
- Lavishness (see 2 Cor. 8:20)
- An undertaking (see 2 Cor. 9:4)
- Blessing (see 2 Cor. 9:5)
- Good work (see 2 Cor. 9:8)
- The yield of righteousness (see 2 Cor. 9:10)

The Macedonian generosity grace motivates us to build churches that give generously at all times in any and all circumstances. Giving is the alternative to spending or hoarding, and it breaks the back of materialism. The act of giving is a reminder that it is all about God and not about us. We should be motivated to give generously by the generous giving culture of the New Testament churches (see Acts 2:42-47). The purpose of our giving is to build vibrant, life-changing churches that will impact our cities and nations. Let us believe that God is good and does good things for His people. Let us believe that as people learn a lifestyle of generosity, they will be fulfilled and God will do great things for them also (see Ps. 27:13). "For the LORD God is a sun and shield; the LORD will give grace and glory; no good thing will He withhold from those who walk uprightly," says the psalmist (Ps. 84:11). Let us see our generosity as a pathway to releasing God's abundance so that we can propagate the gospel worldwide, plant churches, send missionaries, feed the poor and rebuild our cities.

Generosity Culture Powered by Sowing Our Seeds

In 2 Corinthians, Paul teaches the Macedonian church that generosity faith believes that God supplies our seed, waters our seed and multiplies our seed:

> But this I say: He who sows sparingly will also reap sparingly, and he who sows bountifully will also reap bountifully. Now may He

> who supplies seed to the sower, and bread for food, supply and multiply the seed you have sown and increase the fruits of your righteousness (2 Cor. 9:6,10).

Seeds are one of nature's mighty miracles, for they contain a fierce force of life. They are living guarantees of continuity between generations. More than 250,000 plants and 800 trees produce seeds. Henry David Thoreau once wrote, "I have great faith in a seed. Convince me that you have a seed and I am prepared to expect wonders."

The seed is used throughout Scripture as a multifaceted symbol. It represents the people of God (see Jer. 2:21), the Word of God (see Luke 8:11), the kingdom of God (see Mark 4:26-28), the salvation experience (see 1 Pet. 1:23), prosperity and favor (see Ezek. 17:5; Zech. 8:12), faith (see Matt. 17:20), and finances (see 2 Cor. 9:10). God is the supplier of our financial seed, as seen in Isaiah 55:10: "The rain comes down, and the snow from heaven, and do not return there, but water the earth, and make it bring forth and bud, that it may give seed to the sower and bread to the eater." We may choose to keep our seed in our barn and not sow it, or we may choose to eat our seed and enjoy it just once. We may choose to sow it in the wrong place, or we may choose to plant our seed in a fertile place, believing that God will water it, grow it and multiply it.

A missionary living in Africa encountered a farmer who knew how to properly use his seed:

> The Sahel . . . [is] a vast stretch of savannah . . . just under the Sahara Desert. In the Sahel, all the moisture comes in a four month period: May, June, July, and August. After that, not a drop of rain falls for eight months. The ground cracks from dryness, and so do your hands and feet. The winds of the Sahara pick up the dust and throw it thousands of feet into the air. It then comes slowly drifting across West Africa as a fine grit. It gets inside your mouth. It gets inside your watch and stops it. The year's food, of course, must all be grown in those four months. . . .
>
> October and November . . . the granaries are full—the harvest has come. People sing and dance. They eat two meals a day. . . .
>
> December comes, and the granaries start to recede. Many families omit the morning meal. Certainly by January not one family in fifty is still eating two meals a day. By February, the evening

meal diminishes. The meal shrinks even more during March and children succumb to sickness. You don't stay well on half a meal a day. April is the month that haunts my memory. In it you hear the babies crying in the twilight. Most of the days are passed with only an evening cup of gruel.

Then, inevitably, it happens. A six- or seven-year-old boy comes running to his father one day with sudden excitement. "Daddy! Daddy! We've got grain!" he shouts.

"Son, you know we haven't had grain for weeks."

"Yes, we have!" the boy insists. "Out in the hut where we keep the goats—there's a leather sack hanging up on the wall—I reached up and put my hand down in there—Daddy, there's grain in there! Give it to Mommy so she can make flour, and tonight our tummies can sleep!"

The father stands motionless. "Son, we can't do that," he softly explains. "That's next year's seed grain. It's the only thing between us and starvation. We're waiting for the rains, and then we must use it."

The rains finally arrive in May, and when they do the young boy watches as his father takes the sack from the wall and does the most unreasonable thing imaginable. Instead of feeding his desperately weakened family, he goes to the field and with tears streaming down his face, he takes the precious seed and throws it away. He scatters it in the dirt! Why? Because he believes in the harvest.

The seed is his; he owns it. He can do anything with it he wants. The act of sowing it hurts so much that he cries. But as the African pastors say when they preach on Psalm 126, "Brothers and sisters, this is God's law of the harvest. Don't expect to rejoice later on unless you have been willing to sow in tears."

I want to ask you: How much would it cost you to sow in tears? I don't mean just giving God something from your abundance, but finding a way to say, "I believe in the harvest, and therefore I will give what makes no sense. The world would call me unreasonable to do this—but I must sow regardless, in order that I may someday celebrate with songs of joy."[1]

The farmer understood that properly used seeds produce greater fulfillment than improperly consumed seed. He exercised great self-discipline by planting the seed instead of eating it. He was able to wait because he knew that on the other side of his patience and obedience was harvest growth. Seed in our hands is natural; seed in God's hands is supernatural. This farmer had faith for scattering the seed.

Generosity Culture Scatters the Seed

Paul describes how scattering the seed (see 2 Cor. 9:6) sets in motion something miraculous. The generosity culture understands the power of scattering the seed, believing it is a faith-filled experience. Ezekiel 17:5 says, "Then he took some of the seed of the land and planted it in a fertile field; he placed it by abundant waters and set it like a willow tree." When we sow our finance seed, we sow into the future. If no seed is sowed, no future is reaped.

The kingdom of God is an invisible realm, but it touches the visible world. Faith plants a seed and believes for a harvest before it can be seen, waiting with confidence for the invisible possibilities to become reality through the miraculous and supernatural provision of God. We put the seed in the ground and hope that it grows. Faith for the seed gives substance to our hope. It is a way of seeing things. To have faith is to be sure of what we hope for (see Heb. 11:1).

There are realities for which we have no material evidence of their existence, but faith enables us to know with certainty that they exist. J. Oswald Sanders said, "Faith enables the believing soul to treat the future as present and the invisible as seen." Faith apprehends as a real fact what is not revealed to the senses and prompts action in the face of all that seems to contradict it. In the end, faith is real seeing. By faith, Moses "forsook Egypt, not fearing the wrath of the king; for he endured as seeing Him who is invisible" (Heb. 11:27). A SC has faith that sees the invisible God as visibly acting in their world, meeting their needs in real ways. Contrary to popular belief, faith is not blind; it perceives the great power that lies at the source of the visible universe, which is the Word of God (see John 6:11-13; Heb. 11:3).

Generosity Culture Sees a Seedtime and Harvest

Seedtime and harvest is God's principle that is stamped into nature and into His kingdom:

> There is one who scatters, yet increases more; and there is one who withholds more than is right, but it leads to poverty. The generous

soul will be made rich, and he who waters will also be watered himself. The people will curse him who withholds grain, but blessing will be on the head of him who sells it (Prov. 11:24-26).

There are four seed-sowing actions that make up the principle of seed-time and harvest, as explained in God's Word:

1. *God supplies seed to the sower.* Faith for the seed is recognizing Jesus as Lord of your seed, Lord of your harvest, Lord of your field and Lord of the future.

2. *God expects you to sow your seed.* Giving is sowing your seed by faith, knowing that you have to sow before you can reap and that you will reap even more than you sow. You must scatter your seed with handfuls. Giving is the planting of your seed, believing God will move your mountains.

3. *God waters and grows the seed sown.* Under God's mighty hand, the seed is watered and caused to grow. Only God, the giver of all life, can quicken the life within the seed and make it live (see 1 Cor. 3:6). Only God can make the seed grow, increase and multiply.

4. *God promises a miracle harvest.* Giving is the act of seeding for your miracle from which God the source will multiply, and you must be ready to receive.

George Müller testified to the principle of seed multiplication: "I took one shilling out of my box in the house. This was all our money . . . so I gave it. I needed to feed over 100 people. I sowed by last seed and then prayed by faith, believing the seed would produce. We fed all the people with the blessing pouring in."

Remember this: A farmer who plants only a few seeds will get a small crop, but the one who plants generously will get a generous crop. Seed sowing is a supernatural act that can turn the tide, turn losses into victories and change the future. David Trueblood once said, "It takes a noble man to plant a seed for a tree that will someday give shade to people he may never meet." Be courageous and plant the seed.

ACTIONS FOR STRATEGIC LEADERSHIP TO TAKE

We are leaders who can and will lead God's people through storms of turbulent economies and uncertain times. Trying times necessitate strong and faith-filled leaders. We know God is in control, but we also know we must respond with a right leadership attitude and God's wisdom. Strategic leaders make hard decisions in hard times and lead the church through those times. This is our time to stand in the gap with a spirit of faith and an exceedingly hopeful perspective of confidence and trust.

1. LEAD IN AND THROUGH THE STORM

Chaotic times call for leaders to lead with faith, wisdom and courageous optimism. Leadership is judged in times of crisis, and leaders are expected to have the capacity to lead a congregation through a crisis. Leaders take people to the other side, through the storm, and by faith experience a God kind of miracle in the storm (see Job 26:12; Ps. 107:29; Isa. 4:6; 25:4; Nah. 1:3).

2. LIFT UP THE GREATNESS OF GOD

The attributes of God need to be clearly set before the people at every available occasion and in every possible way: in public services, songs, Web communication, letters, cards and sermons. We must declare the greatness of God as people feel their hope has been destroyed and their dreams are gone. They must be reminded that God is unlimited, unbound and unconfined. He is high and lifted up, unchanging, dependable, constant and all-powerful. All things are possible with a sovereign God (see Jer. 32:17; Matt. 19:26; Heb. 1:3; Jas. 1:17).

3. BELIEVE GOD FOR THE UNUSUAL IN TIME OF LACK AND FAMINE

God has everything we need and is ready to work in our situation in a miraculous way. We must believe that miracles are on their way. God's miracles are manifestations of His unlimited resources to do the unusual when the unusual looks impossible (see Gen. 26:2,12-13; Deut. 2:7; Mark 8:25; 1 Cor. 2:9-10; 2 Cor. 8:15).

4. POSITION THE CHURCH WITH AN ATTITUDE OF FAITH

Pastor-leaders must lead from a faith perspective, sharing a faith outlook on the future and consistently articulating this faith spirit to the congregation. Leaders must communicate the message that God is with us and that we will indeed thrive in this season. And leaders must stay filled with faith in spite of the obvious challenges. Leaders must have the Luke 7:16 attitude: "They all realized they were in a place of holy mystery, that God was at work among them. They were quietly worshipful—and then noisily grateful, calling out among themselves, 'God is back, looking to the needs of his people!'" (*THE MESSAGE*).

5. War Against Fear, Anxiety and Vain Imaginations

Financial fear sends nations' stress levels soaring as people try to digest news of the economy every day. Most financial analysts say that fear is also the driving force behind the continuing financial crises. Anxiety levels rise and cause panic; and attacks of fear, worry and vain imaginations cause physical predicaments. The pastor-leader must put on the armor of God and go after these faith killers. Overcome these enemies every day and every week and in every church service. Worry is a chokehold that harasses and torments people (see Ruth 3:11; Prov. 1:33; 4:12; Isa. 41:10; Matt. 8:26; Heb. 13:6; 1 John 4:18).

6. Make Church a Place of Hope and Encouragement

When people decide to visit the church during a time of personal crisis, life pressures and life challenges, the church must be ready to speak words of hope and encouragement. The church atmosphere and attitude must be one of lifting people up and filling people with a God hope and a God help. The purpose of the church in the world is evident in the nature of the church: to reconcile people to Him and to restore people's lives to working order, in harmony with His design (see Job 14:7; Pss. 31:24; 42:5; Mark 2:1-2; Rom. 4:18).

7. Keep the Church Looking Beyond Itself

We are the people of God and we have a clear purpose and mission to fulfill. We are called by God to reach out, not to shrink back. We are not a narrow "bless me" club trying to survive and "just keep the lights on." We are here to win people to Christ, to reach into our communities and cities. This is a time to expand our ministry to people, not to pull back. With today's challenges come greater opportunities for our people to demonstrate love, kindness and support to one another and to those outside the church (see Prov. 29:11; Acts 6:1,7; 4:16,33).

8. Inspire Generosity in Giving

Pastor-leaders must embrace the roles of leader and teacher within the church in the area of finances and generous biblical giving. No one else can pastor this area better than the pastors who are to feed and lead the flock. Generous giving must be seen as a biblical attitude and pastors are to lead people into the opportunity of experiencing this biblical principle (see Exod. 25:2; Prov. 11:24-26; 1 Tim. 6:18-19).

9. Establish Intentional Prayer Ministry over Finances

The usefulness of prayer is obviously known. We all probably believe in prayer. The intentional, focused prayer team must take on praying over the church's giving. This team should meet to target definite financial goals concerning the tithe goal, missions and special projects. The team should systematically pray for the release of finances and for open heavens over the church, over area businesses and over all area jobs. Prayer lays hold of God and influences Him to work. It puts God's work in His hands and keeps it there (see Isa. 56:7; 60:11; Acts 4:23,31; 1 Tim. 2:1; Rev. 5:8).

10. Focus on the Biblical Worldview of Life

A biblical worldview must be kept in clear focus as we move through a time of financial lack that threatens the things we treasure in life. Pope Benedict XVI said, "The one who builds on sand builds only on visible and tangible things, on success, on career, on money. . . . The one who builds his life on these realities, on matter, on success, on appearances, builds upon sand."[2] We are now seeing in the collapse of major banks that money vanishes. It is nothing. All these things that appear to be real are in fact unsubstantial. A worldview is a way of thinking about truth and reality. It is the sum total of what we believe about the most important issues of life. Focus on a biblical worldview (see Matt. 7:24-27; 25:44-45; 2 Cor. 4:18; 5:7; 1 John 2:15-17).

11. In Every Service, Pray for People in Need of Jobs and Career Changes

People are faced with the reality of losing jobs and maybe never gaining back the dream jobs they had. People have lost heart and hope for their futures. We must pray for God to open doors that will provide work—not just any work, but work with purpose and ample provision. Pray for the wisdom of God to be released into their situations and for them to have clarity in decision making. We the leaders must speak words of life and encourage expectation in the heart of every person. Every service should be focused and have powerful prayer for breakthrough in these areas (see Isa. 59:16; Matt. 21:11; Rom. 1:9; 12:12; Eph. 6:18).

12. During Every Corporate Service, Pray for all Businesspeople

Marketplace people are in financial crises that are changing the world around them into a totally different market playing field. These people need all the prayers and encouragement we can give them—and they are needed all the time. These people are surrounded all day with negative news, financial complexity and the gloom and doom of American financial structures. Where can they go for a cold drink of the water of Holy Spirit encouragement? Our churches! Strategic agreement prayer for businesspeople can be life changing for them (see Lev. 26:8; Deut. 32:30; Isa. 56:7).

13. Make the Offering Time a Faith-Filled and God-Focused Homerun

Celebrate the goodness of God and build an atmosphere that giving is an opportunity rather than an obligation. It is a time to celebrate God's faithfulness, sovereign power and creative provision. Celebrate victories in giving and financial breakthrough. Purposefully build up the believers' faith boldly and biblically. Generosity is a spirit and a biblical approach to life that should be continually pastored into the church. Lead pastors should be the people who make this part of the service powerful, Holy Spirit driven, fresh, creative and fruitful. This is the perfect time to speak faith, trust, courage and right perspective into the world of every person. This could be one of the most important pastoral encounters you have with the congregation every week (see Gen. 4:4; Exod. 35:21; Luke 21:1-2; 2 Cor. 8:1-4).

Bill Bright, the great leader and founder of Campus Crusade for Christ, once said, "If God can get it through you, He can get it to you!" When Bright was given the Templeton Prize for the advancement of religion in the world, he was also given a $1 million check. When asked what he would do with this million dollars, he answered, "What I've always done. All my means have been dedicated to Christ." Let us endeavor to build such a culture of generosity that church members live for others and give to a cause beyond themselves. What we do with our resources in this life is our autobiography: The book we write with the pen of faith and the ink of works will go into eternity unedited, to be seen and read by the angels, the redeemed and God Himself. Let us be ready to hear the words of Matthew 25:21: "Well done, good and faithful servant."

The SC leader can build a culture of generosity. Take heart and begin to teach, preach and exhort people toward a generosity lifestyle and a "heart style." God is good, and He desires to do good things to and for the people of God (see Pss. 31:19; 34:8; Matt. 7:11). "All sunshine and sovereign is God, generous in gifts and glory" (Ps. 84:11, *THE MESSAGE*). Let us believe this and build with great faith.

Strategic Reaching of Cities, Regions and the World

It was several years ago on a cold winter day when I hopped in a van with six other pastors and drove around our city of Portland, Oregon, praying. I had been making a shift in my own thinking and prayer life for our city and the metro area. The heart at our church had changed toward our city. We were feeling an alteration in our approach to reaching the Portland metro area and this prayer meeting in a van was part of the journey. We had never really done anything like this before, but we were on a pursuit to break out of our church ruts and see our city in a new way. The van had pastors from different churches and various denominations. We were all very different, yet we came together to pray and reclaim our city.

The method we chose to make a visual and real declaration was to put wooden stakes in the ground at pivotal border points. We pinpointed our locations, made some stakes that were two feet long and wrote a city proclamation prayer and Scripture on each stake. Then we pounded them into the ground, poured oil on top of them and joined hands to declare blessing, favor, revival and spiritually open heavens over our city. It was one of the most memorable days I can think of in my ministry as a city pastor. We prayed on the basis of Scripture and the power of the Cross, asking that God would secure the boundaries of our city.

Repent, Request and Resist

As we traveled around Portland that day and drove our stakes into the ground, we prayed three things: repent, request and resist.

Repent (See Daniel 9:4-9)

We asked the Lord Jesus to forgive us for sins that have taken place in our state, in our city and specifically in our northeast and southeast regions. We asked for forgiveness for the sins of political corruption, racial prejudice, moral perversions, witchcraft, the occult and idolatry. We prayed the blood of Jesus to cleanse our hands from shedding innocent blood in the acts of abortion, euthanasia and any other ways the innocent have been destroyed. We asked for forgiveness for divisions in the church, for spiritual pride, for sins of the tongue and for anything that has hurt the church of Jesus Christ. We repented, humbled ourselves and asked for mercy to be poured out upon our land, our community and our churches.

Request (See Jeremiah 29:7)

We asked for God's kingdom to come and His will to be done in our city and region. We asked in the name of the Lord Jesus Christ for a spiritual outpouring of God's grace, mercy and fire upon our city. We asked for true spiritual revival to come and cover our community, causing a turning to God, a cleansing, a brokenness, a humility, a hunger for the one and only true God. We asked God for mercy here. We asked for our destiny to not be aborted. We asked that God visit our city, our churches and our homes. We asked that God not pass our city by. We asked for restoration of the foundations of righteousness to our city.

Resist (See Ephesians 6:10-17; James 5:7)

On the basis of our submission to God, we in faith resisted the devil and his work. We resisted all forces and powers of evil that had taken hold of our city. We resisted the spirit of wickedness that had established strongholds in our city region—the dark places, the hidden works of darkness, the mystery places where the enemy has set up encampments. We called on the name of the Lord to destroy all spiritual strongholds. We proclaimed that day that the city of Portland, especially the southeast and northeast regions, was now under the power and ownership of the Holy Spirit. All other spirits were given notice and evicted from the property by the power of the name of Jesus. We stood in the gap and rebuilt a hedge of protection around our city:

> *We claimed Isaiah 58:11-12:* The Lord will guide you continually, and satisfy your soul in drought, and strengthen your bones; you shall

> be like a watered garden, and like a spring of water, whose waters do not fail. Those from among you shall build the old waste places; you shall raise up the foundations of many generations; and you shall be called the Repairer of the Breach, the Restorer of Streets to Dwell in.
>
> *We claimed Isaiah 1:26:* I [God] will restore your judges as at the first, and your counselors as at the beginning. Afterward you shall be called the city of righteousness, the faithful city.
>
> *We claimed Matthew 16:18-19:* And I [Jesus] also say to you that you are Peter, and on this rock I will build My church, and the gates of Hades shall not prevail against it. And I will give you the keys of the kingdom of heaven, and whatever you bind on earth will be bound in heaven, and whatever you loose on earth will be loosed in heaven.

Then we prayed that our city would be reclaimed, restored, revived and set on a path of righteousness. We prayed that our borders would be secured on that day and that God would give us grace, protect us and allow His angels to encamp round about us. This we did in humility and faith.

What we did for the metro Portland area may seem a little strange, but it was done with a heart for the city. Jesus loves our cities, our metro areas, all people and all races. Jesus has one true church in the city. All congregations make up one church that reaches the city together. As pastors, we often live by trying to balance the needs of our local congregation. This requires feeding, discipling, counseling, community, building up, and encouragement for looking outside to the city with a "go to, find and meet the need" attitude.

We are called to serve our city. The Early Church father Jerome advised his monks to avoid city life and cities altogether. Tertullian, the Early Church theologian, taught that Christ was against the city and that Christians should escape the pollution and idolatrous decay of city life. I believe that we are salt and light—called to the city, not away from the city (see Matt. 5:13-16). Our desire should be to bring peace to the city, as we are commanded in Jeremiah 29:7: "And seek the peace of the city where I have caused you to be carried away captive, and pray to the Lord for it; for in its peace you will have peace." Cities are strategic places of mission, and the SC is a missional church, which means that we need to get into our cities.

Because of sin, cities today are human centered and often violent and filled with friction, greed and carnality. Sin runs freely through the streets and markets. It sits enthroned in high places of civic life. Cities are characterized by many broken covenants—most of all, the broken covenant with God. In this humanistic context, the church is called to bring hope, healing and restoration of God in the city.

A Vision to Reach Our Cities and Regions

A biblical strategy is to reach cities, towns and villages with the gospel of Christ. This strategy involves developing a place where God's presence dwells and His ways are known. Revolution happens when God becomes the dominant force in our cities, resulting in people who are changed by the power of the Holy Spirit. We make God famous by ministering hope to our region, proclaiming God's destiny for it, and bringing solutions and answers to the area's problems. Timothy Keller, pastor of a multiethnic congregation in New York, has a unique and (I think) biblical perspective of the city:

> The city is God's invention and design, not just a sociological phenomenon or invention of humankind. . . . City building is an ordinance of God just like work and marriage. And indeed, cities draw together human talent and resources and tap the human potential for cultural development as nothing else does. . . . It is quite wrong to see the city as intrinsically evil! It was designed by God to "draw out" and to "mine" what God made.[1]

Cities were designed to build civilizations where people come together and share in the marketplace of ideas in such a way that those people meet with God and help others in the community.

God loves our cities! Jesus' last words to the crowd before He ascended was a command to "be witnesses to [Him] in Jerusalem, and in all Judea and Samaria, and to the end of the earth" (Acts 1:8). As a SC, our strategic mandate is to reach our Jerusalem, which is the responsibility we have to our primary city. We aim to reach our Judea, which is our burden for our primary region. We must reach Samaria, which is our privilege and commitment to ethnic diversity. Finally, "the end of the earth" signifies our duty to impact the world.

The starting place of this strategy is your city (town or village). You must believe that grace will abound in your city. Scripture affirms that "where sin abounded grace abounded much more" (Rom. 5:20). There is hope for your city. To believe that grace will abound, you have to start seeing your city the way God sees it. God's plan began in the Garden, but it ends in a city. He has a vision for your city, a vision to make it a place where the church becomes a voice and a place of hope. In His vision, the city receives this hope by believing in the God of hope.

If we will pray and ask God to open our eyes, we will see that our cities already have the mark of God's sovereign purpose upon them. A city, like a person, has a soul. Arnold Toynbee, in his book *Cities of Destiny*, says that "in order to become a city, it would have to evolve at least the rudiments of a soul. This is perhaps the essence of cityhood." What is the soul of your city? What is the mindset? Emotional status? Having a vision for the city requires being in tune with the city's soul so that you can see its needs and aim at meeting them. We have to develop vision that sees the biggest need of all: salvation. Scriptures warns that "Where there is no vision [no redemptive revelation of God], the people perish" (Prov. 29:18, *AMP;* see also Isa. 40:1-2). We need a vision, and that vision should be one where God is in our city.

God's Perspective of the Church in the City

In Matthew 16:18, Jesus says, "I will build My church." As leaders, we must acknowledge that "the church in the city" refers to the whole church. All congregations that are biblically consistent with the New Testament revelation of Christ, the cross, redemption and salvation for all humankind are part of the same unit called "the church in the city" (see Acts 20:28; 2 Cor. 8:1; Gal. 1:2; Eph. 5:32; Rev. 1–3). The church is not national, international, denominational, nondenominational, sectarian or nonsectarian. It is one new person, a new thing. Every city has local churches that make up the one church Jesus is building. Each local church has its own divine calling, set leadership and determined destiny. Moreover, each local church is unique and is called specifically to fulfill its exclusive God-ordained destiny.

We see the uniqueness of local churches displayed throughout the book of Acts: in the Jerusalem church, Antioch church, Corinthian church and Ephesian church. Each had its own unique personality and calling of God. That uniqueness was perfect for its city. The Antioch church would not have been as effective in Corinth as it was at Antioch, and vice versa. God builds churches to match the city. He chooses, equips, anoints and gives special grace to the churches He raises up that will impact the city. It's the Lord who knows our cities and what the keys are to reach it. At Jericho, it was a miracle trumpet blast and mighty shout that knocked down the walls of the city (see Josh. 6:5,20). In Samaria, it was the conversion of one woman with a deep broken life that moved the whole city to accept Jesus (see John 4:28-30,39). In Corinth, it was God giving a vision to one man that opened the city to the gospel (see Acts 18:9-10).

We should not compare or judge another church because it is different from ours. Each local church will have its own dominant, distinctive features, which is the practical outworking of its leadership gifts, specific vision, pastoral philosophy, theological roots, history and heritage. God chooses local churches and uses these churches with their specific strengths to reach a city.

God's Relationship to Your City and Region

God hears the cry of our cities. He heard the cry of Sodom: "And the LORD said, 'Because the *outcry* against Sodom and Gomorrah is great, and because their sin is very grave, I will go down now and see whether they have done altogether according to the *outcry* against it that has come to Me; and if not, I will know' " (Gen. 18:20-21, emphasis added). In Job, we read that "the dying *groan in the city*, and the souls of the wounded *cry out*" (Job 24:12, emphasis added). If we would tune in our hearts through prayer, we would hear the sounds of our cities coming to us through the cries of people. God weeps over our cities:

> Now as [Jesus] drew near, He saw the city and wept over it, saying, "If you had known, even you, especially in this your day, the things that make for your peace! But now they are hidden from your eyes. For days will come upon you when your enemies will build an embankment around you, surround you and close you in on every side, and level you, and your children within you, to the ground; and they will not leave in you one stone upon another, because you did not know the time of your visitation" (Luke 19:41-44).

We must feel the burden of the cities and our hearts must be broken for the cities. When your heart is moved, you will find a place of intercessory prayer. God looks at the earth and searches for intercessors: "[God] saw that there was no man, and wondered that there was no intercessor; therefore His own arm brought salvation for Him; and His own righteousness, it sustained Him" (Isa. 59:16). He searches for "a man among them who would make a wall, and stand in the gap before [Him] on behalf of the land, that [He] should not destroy it" (Ezek. 22:30). God will raise up intercessory prayer churches that penetrate the darkness of cities. Those churches will be full of people who hear cities calling out and have a burden to answer the cries. The divine principle of intercession is demonstrated through Abraham's prayer for the city: It takes only a minority to change the destiny of a city (see Gen. 18:22-23; Exod. 17:9-11; Isa. 59:16).

God has spoken and will speak to us about our cities and He will use us to speak to our cities. The Lord's voice is heard through His people, both individually and as a corporate body of believers (see Prov. 1:20-21; 8:1-3; Mic. 6:9). God loves our cities and sends the right missionaries there. You were sent to your city, not just to your church (see Jon. 1:3; Luke 9:51-56).

City Reaching Churches Have No Roof and No Walls

A church with no roof and no walls has no obstructions standing in the way of a free flow of God's love, forgiveness, power and blessings. It is a church with open heavens and intercessory prayer. It is not isolated from the unsaved and the unchurched. There is an unobstructed flow of the gospel to the multitudes. This is the church that goes into the highways and the hedges and compels people to come in so that God's house will be filled (see Luke 14:23).

We are called to reach the multitudes—whole cities and regions. It's mind-boggling to try grasping that task, but that is what the first churches succeeded in doing. This is what Jesus' ministry did: reach the multitudes. "But when He saw the multitudes, He was moved with compassion for them, because they were weary and scattered, like sheep having no shepherd" (Matt. 9:36).

The first church as seen in the book of Acts reached and ministered to the multitudes. Countless times, we read how the "multitudes" gathered together and their needs were served (see Acts 6:2,5; 14:1; 15:12; 17:4). Acts

4:32 records that "the multitude of those who believed were of one heart and one soul; neither did anyone say that any of the things he possessed was his own, but they had all things in common." Out of the thousands of people who were part of this multitude of believers, not one had a need that was not met. What a miracle!

At present, there are cities that are larger than some countries. Some metro areas would make up a thousand towns and villages in Christ's time. The church today must have a vision to see every neighborhood and strata of society in our metro areas penetrated with the love, compassion, truth and joy brought by the gospel of Christ. Only then will each of us start to fulfill the Acts 1:8 mandate to reach our city, region, nation and world. Mother Teresa was once asked, "What's the biggest problem in the world today?" Without hesitating, she answered that the biggest problem in the world today is that we draw the circle of our family too small. We need to draw it larger every day. Stretch out, expand your borders, and make room for more people.

Drawing a Bigger Circle

To expand your circle of influence, you have to have passion for the multitudes, passion to include them and bring them into God's family. To do this, you must see with Jesus' eyes. The eyes of Jesus are the eyes of the Holy Spirit, which must become our eyes. His eyes see the multitudes of people with broken hearts, broken souls, afflictions and spirits of harassment attacking them (see Mark 3:7-11). When He saw these people, He responded with compassion and also a strategy.

The miracle of feeding the 5,000 men provides a great example of how supernatural vision results in a faith attitude that produces a strategy for reaching the multitudes. John sets the stage for this lesson in developing supernatural vision: "Jesus lifted up His eyes, and seeing a great multitude coming toward Him, He said to Philip, 'Where shall we buy bread, that these may eat?' But this He said to test him, for He Himself knew what He would do" (John 6:5-6). This situation exposed a few flawed perspectives:

1. *Philip's attitude*—"It's not within our budget, and we can't afford the multitudes. We are comfortable where we are, so let's just stay within our means" (see John 6:7). Philip's perspective was logic driven. He calculated the numbers and saw that at

the present moment, they did not have the capacity to expand to serve more people. So he closed his mind to alternative solutions. It was not convenient for him to sacrifice a little more in order to reach thousands.

A friend of mine tells a story about an encounter he once had with a lady in his church. The church was growing to several hundreds of people coming every weekend as they were aggressively pursuing the poor and people in their city who were being exploited. One day after service, a woman approached the pastor and said, "Pastor, our church is getting too big. We need to stop letting all these people in here."

He was caught off guard a little by this remark, but he quickly recovered and gently asked the woman a question: "Ma'am, do you have any family members who are not saved or who you would like to see in church?" The woman paused and said, "Well, I do have a young nephew who needs to be saved. And I have a few friends that need Jesus." His soft reply was, "Do you think we can make a little more room for them?"

If everyone were able to sacrifice just a little more to make room for a few more people, we would expand our reach and bring the lost into God's family.

2. *Andrew's attitude*—"It's not within our power or our resources. We only have enough for five loaves and two fish" (see John 6:8-9). Andrew decided that because their resources were limited, they couldn't get enough to give people. The Andrew attitude rules out the possibility of God using what is in your hand to do something supernatural. It assumes that growth is incumbent upon the individual alone. Certainly, everyone has a part to play and needs to participate in bringing people to church or bringing church to them. But, ultimately, it is God who draws the people to Him. As Paul said, he "planted, Apollos watered, but God gave the increase" (1 Cor. 3:6).

3. *The Disciples' attitude*—"Send them away." There were thousands of people ready to receive more of Jesus' teaching and the disciples' response was, "Send the multitude away, . . . for we are in a deserted place here" (Luke 9:12). It had been a long day,

> Jesus had just given a heavy sermon, and the disciples were hungry, tired and probably a little dirty. The last thing they wanted to do was find a bakery with enough bread for thousands of people, cart in the food and, on top of all that, foot the bill. It would be much easier to just send everyone home and let them fend for themselves. Does that sound familiar?
>
> For several years, City Bible has been running a ministry called Stitches. Every week, hundreds of volunteers and staff spend their evenings and mornings connecting with families and helping them understand the love of God. Teams drive busses into communities and pick up children and families for church and other weekday activities. Kids get connected to the City Kids ministry, youth get plugged into small groups and services fitted for them, and adults get to attend Sunday services. They also receive support from life recovery programs that coach them on parenting, financial management and work skills.
>
> These volunteers who drive busses every week and sit with underprivileged families to share the message of hope probably get a little tired every once in a while. They might have been tempted to see the inconvenience of driving a bus to someone's neighborhood every week as a little burdensome, but they have a faith attitude that says, "We can enlarge our capacity. We have room for more families, more kids, more youth."

The harvest is ready. Our task now is to go out there and bring them in. We cannot afford to be comfortable with our current state. Spread out your borders and make some more room!

Developing Faith for the Multitudes

The disciples' responses to the multitudes were flawed reactions that came from wrong attitudes. We must not let those same attitudes keep us from wining the multitudes. Let us take a faith attitude that believes we can reach our cities. To develop eyes that see the multitudes and develop a strategy to reach them, the leadership and the church need to have an attitude that says, "We care, we can, we have, and we will!"

WE CARE

The We Care attitude has compassion for the multitudes of people. When Jesus saw groups of people, He was "moved with compassion" for them (Matt. 14:14; Mark 1:41; 6:34). Matthew records that Jesus was moved because the people were "weary and scattered, like sheep having no shepherd" (Matt. 9:36). He didn't see them as a nuisance or a band of freeloaders but as people who were wandering aimlessly and desperately in need of someone to lead and protect them. He cared.

A church with a We Care attitude starts with a leadership team that asks God to enlarge their capacity and make them city-reaching people (see 1 Chron. 4:10). The vision for city reaching is the capacity to see both the needs and the possibilities and then see the church growing and increasing. A city-reaching leader sees the opportunities for growth, whereas a non-growth leader sees only the problems and becomes complacent, accepting a non-growth environment. Growth leaders look at the multitudes and see them as sheep who need a shepherd.

The SC has an attitude that asks God to increase their faith to believe in multiplication growth. One of the greatest killers of growth is unbelief. God has a track record of making His people increase:

> [God] increased His people greatly, and made them stronger than their enemies (Ps. 105:24).
>
> May the LORD give you increase more and more, you and your children (Ps. 115:14).
>
> You have increased the nation, O Lord you have increased the nation; You are glorified; You have expanded all the borders of the land (Isa. 25:16).

There is a link between increased faith and growth. The apostle Paul understood this principle. In his missionary journeys, he made sure to challenge the faith of each church and community he visited, and the result was growth. Luke records that the churches Paul toured "were strengthened in the faith, and increased in number daily" (Acts 16:5). Paul later wrote to the Corinthians, "As your faith is increased, we shall be greatly enlarged by you in our sphere" (2 Cor. 10:15). Faith increased and the church grew. We must ask God to increase our faith to believe for growth in order to realize it in our churches.

Jesus' vision for the multitudes in John 6:5 is a vision for the multitudes that every strategic leader should have if he or she is going to see expansion and development in the church. There are three phases in developing this kind of vision.

First, you must lift up your eyes. You can't see the multitudes if you don't pull your head up from looking exclusively at where you are right now. Lifting your eyes is the look of faith toward the harvest of thousands that are ready to respond to the gospel and build a New Testament, twenty-first-century church. Some may not want to look up because they don't think there is anything out there. You won't be disappointed. "Lift up your eyes and look at the fields, for they are already white for harvest" (John 4:35). Raise your eyes and observe the fields (see Gen. 13:14-15; Ruth 2:9; Isa. 60:4; Jer. 13:20).

After you lift up your eyes, you then must see in the spirit. See into the realm of the supernatural. This is the spirit realm where all things are possible, where you can see the future before it happens.

Finally, when you lift up your eyes and see in the spirit, you must then see a great multitude coming. Do you see the great harvest field of people within your metro area who are already on their way to Christ, who are already on their way into the church? This is strategic imagination. It is having a dream inspired by the Spirit to expand the reach of the gospel.

Two men walked together on an orange grove of over 160 acres. One had a vision of a place where families could have fun together in an amusing yet educational environment. He thought of building attractions like a jungle cruise where participants could get into a makeshift boat and tour the world's exotic jungles, guided by a fearless captain. He envisioned hundreds of families and children coming to play and make memories there. The other man could not see this vision at all. A few years later, the first man saw his vision become reality, as thousands of families poured into Disneyland in California. Years after Disneyland opened, Walt Disney had a dream to open another similar theme park on the East Coast, and 16 years later, Walt Disney World Resort opened near Orlando, Florida.

By the time Disney World was completed, Walt Disney had passed away. When the park opened, someone remarked, "Isn't it too bad that Walt Disney didn't live to see this?" Mike Vance, the creative director at Walt Disney Studios, replied, "He did see it—that's why it's here."

To experience growth in your church, you have to see that growth taking place. Lift up your eyes, see in the spirit, and see the multitudes coming to hear the gospel and become disciples. Increase your faith.

We Can

The We Can attitude believes that we have everything we need to minister to the people's needs. We can handle all this brokenness. When the disciples suggested to Jesus that He send away the multitudes so that they could go eat, He replied, "They do not need to go away. You give them something to eat," implying that the disciples already had what was needed in order to meet the need in front of them (Matt. 14:16). Still, they had to work together to serve everyone. Jesus multiplied the bread and fish, but the disciples labored together to distribute the food to the multitudes. It is important that we understand the necessity of working as a team. The sum product from the team is much greater than the sum total of all the achievements by the individuals on the team.

Teamwork reinforces the We Can attitude because it draws from every individual in order to carry out the mandate. It is the principle of synergy: joint working and cooperation that result in increased effectiveness and advancement as a result of combined action or collaboration. You don't have to go to the state or the church next to you to find small-group leaders or instrumentalists. God has positioned the right people in your place to meet the specific needs in your community. Moreover, He has the resources you need and is ready to release them. He has unhindered and unlimited possessions (see Mal. 3:10). He is poised, ready to throw open His warehouse and make resources suddenly and dramatically more accessible (see Deut. 28:12). God is in our house, and He can let loose whatever we need in order to spread the gospel and help people grow as disciples.

We Have

A We Have attitude recognizes that we possess all the virtue and power needed to touch all. When Jesus came to this earth, He said, "The Spirit of the Lord is upon Me, because He has anointed Me to preach the gospel to the poor; He has sent Me to heal the brokenhearted, to proclaim liberty to the captives and recovery of sight to the blind, to set at liberty those who are oppressed; to proclaim the acceptable year of the Lord" (Luke 4:18-19). Indeed, Jesus taught good news to those who were discouraged, cast out demons, released people who were oppressed by the enemy, and healed the sick. When Jesus ascended, as described in Acts, the virtue and power to touch all people and needs did not leave. Peter taught that "[Jesus'] divine power has given to us all things that pertain to life and godliness" (2 Pet. 1:3). Indeed, "the Spirit of Him who raised Jesus from the dead dwells in you" (Rom. 8:11). Therefore, through the Holy Spirit, we have the capacity to touch every person God puts in our hearts and visions to reach.

Believing that we have all the strength and grace needed to fulfill our divine call necessitates an attitude that believes God has positioned us for great growth. A church may get locked into the status of non-growth or even decline because it doesn't expect growth. Expecting little growth, they achieve it. Aiming at meager advance, they hit it! Accepting slow increase as the norm, they are content with it. To grow, we should expect growth. We should see our position as ready for growth. We should optimistically believe and then move out to accomplish what we believe. We cannot be content with limited growth when possibilities for more abundant harvest exist.

Declarations of We Have

- We have great locations (or a location) to reach more people.
- We have great atmosphere of God's presence and healing power.
- We have a great leadership team with everyone in the right place.
- We have room to grow and are ready to grow.
- We have a great heart for people throughout the congregation.

Promises in Scripture

A We Have attitude asks for the inheritance promised in Scripture. That inheritance is people. Throughout the New Testament, we see a pattern where multitudes of people followed Jesus and the apostles as they taught and worked miracles:

> Great multitudes followed Him—from Galilee, and from Decapolis, Jerusalem, Judea, and beyond the Jordan (Matt. 4:25).

> Then great multitudes came to Him, having with them the lame, blind, mute, maimed, and many others; and they laid them down at Jesus' feet, and He healed them (Matt. 15:30).

> Now it happened in Iconium that [the disciples] went together to the synagogue of the Jews, and so spoke that a great multitude both of the Jews and of the Greeks believed (Acts 14:1).

There are also many examples in Scripture of people who obtained their inheritance (just a few are listed here):

> Be strong and of good courage, for to this people you shall divide as an inheritance the land which I [God] swore to their fathers to give them (Josh. 1:6).

> "Surely the land where your foot has trodden shall be your inheritance and your children's forever, because you have wholly followed the Lord my God." And Joshua blessed him, and gave Hebron to Caleb the son of Jephunneh as an inheritance. Hebron therefore became the inheritance of Caleb the son of Jephunneh the Kenizzite to this day, because he wholly followed the Lord God of Israel (Josh. 14:9,13-14).

We have a good inheritance and that inheritance is the multitudes (see Ps. 16:6). Ask for your inheritance, trusting that God has equipped your church with all the virtue and resources it needs to meet the needs of those coming to you.

We Will

The SC has a We Will attitude that says that "We will be ready for the opportunity." When the harvest floods upon us, we will be ready. We will be prepared to disciple several thousands of new people.

It was June 2, 1925, at a New York Yankees game when the first baseman, Wally Pibbs, said to his manager, "I have a headache. I can't play." Pibbs took a seat and the manager turned to a young man who was a complete nobody and put him in as first baseman. The player stepped in and immediately showed that he was the man for this position. He was alert and quick, and he knew where to throw the ball at the right time. From that first game on, Lou Gehrig played 2,130 consecutive games, a record that stood for almost 70 years. Gehrig had been preparing for the opportunity and when it came, he was ready to step in and change history.

When the time comes, we will be ready! We will reach our cities to reach our regions and the world. Develop a vision for the multitudes to see their need and see them coming in droves. Trust that God has already put in your house everything you need to meet the need, and then go for it! Be ready in season and out of season for the harvest that is on its way.

Strategic Lessons Learned

Everyone makes mistakes. We have off days; we process some decisions in not quite the best way. We hire the wrong staff, create our own problems, go through hard times with a wrong attitude, preach dry sermons, struggle with vision, and more. There is no doubt that the journey of becoming a strategic leader and leading a strategic church is filled with many experiences, both good and bad. It is what you do with those experiences that shape your leadership and your church. Do you learn from situations, or do you ignore them?

One of the best books I have read on leaders' mistakes is *The Top Ten Mistakes Leaders Make* by Hans Finzel, president of WorldVenture and noted author and leadership expert. His list of mistakes include the following: the top-down attitude, putting paperwork before people-work, the absence of affirmation, no room for mavericks, dictatorship in decision making, dirty delegation, communication chaos, missing the clues of corporate culture, success without successors, and failure to focus on the future.[1] These are normal and identifiable leadership mistakes. We've all made some or all of them. Here, however, I want to share with you local church leadership mistakes that my team and I have made and why we made them. I want you to learn from our mistakes. Finzel's perspective comes from being the director of a church planting and leadership training organization in over 40 countries. My point of view is that of a church planter and pastor of a local church and part of a leadership team. My framework for sharing these mistakes is that I live where you live, building the local church.

I have learned several lessons from experience. Experiential learning is the process of making meaning from direct experiences. It is learning by contrasting what you did with what you know or were taught. In 1853, a chef named George Crum was cooking for some wealthy customers in a Sarasota Springs (New York) restaurant. Crum was an accomplished chef, so he was shocked and a little offended when, as one version of the story goes, one customer sent back his plate saying the potatoes were too thick and soft. Crum was upset; but "the customer is always right," so he sliced the potatoes thinner, cooked them and gave the plate back to the server to take to the customer. Still too thick. They went back and forth a few times until Crum was so exasperated that he decided to cut the potato so thin that the customer would not be able to pick up the fried pieces with a fork. The server took out this man's plate of food for the fourth time.

Intrigued by the paper-thin potato wedges on his plate, the man picked one up, crunched into the deliciously thin crisp and loved it! He told all his friends about this one restaurant where they serve potatoes so thin you have to pick them up with your fingers. Word spread and the restaurant became famous for the paper-thin crisps. Eventually chef Crum opened his own restaurant, and several entrepreneurs marketed the potato chips. Crum's initial failure to serve satisfying fried potatoes to a customer resulted in the invention of the popular potato chip. Crum made a learning experience out of a customer's dissatisfaction.

Experience education is the best and the most expensive! We pay with more than money. We pay with pain, with emotions, with regrets, with time and with other people's lives. Experience can be very costly, but it is the way God helps us to change and to learn. As leaders seeking to build the church Jesus desires us to build, we must be willing to be actively involved in all learning experiences in order to reflect and draw out the lessons that make us better leaders. Wisdom is gained, not only by learning from our own experiences, but also from the experiences of others. The ability to learn rapidly and effectively is the hallmark of great leaders. Let us decide to be learners—to reflect on our experiences and learn, observing others' lives and learning from their examples.

Lesson #1: Find Your Blind Spots

We all have blind spots. For a variety of reasons, those spots happen most when we do not listen and we refuse to learn. Learning can be both painful and time consuming. As a result, we often avoid it.

We may surround ourselves with people who won't confront what is wrong or won't influence us in a direction we do not want to go. Leaders tend to surround themselves with these people because they are usually highly resistant to change. Yet change must happen, and it often comes in the form of blind spots. From a physiological perspective, a blind spot is an area on the retina that lacks the receptors that respond to light. If an image falls into this area, it will not be seen. In psychology the term is "metaphorically." It is based on the notion that there are parts of ourselves that we simply do not wish to see, even though they are apparent to those who know us. What we know about ourselves may be different from what others know about us. For example, others may notice that I do not make eye contact when talking with people, but I am completely unaware of this. It is only through the process of receiving feedback that such blind spots can be addressed and changed.

Blind spots also refer to areas where people remain stubbornly fixed on their views. A person with a blind spot in a particular area will dismiss sound arguments, refute evidence and refuse to change his or her views in any way. This kind of a leadership blind spot will frustrate anyone and everyone with whom you work. The *Oxford Dictionary* defines a blind spot as "an area in which a person lacks understanding or impartiality."[2] The *Chambers 21st Century Dictionary* defines a blind spot as "any subject which a person either cannot understand, or refuses even to try to understand."[3] We all have blind spots, and we need others to help us.

Mistake: Leader Not Seeing Blind Spots

Because I am bent toward being a visionary-type leader with a huge amount of faith and an attitude of "expect great, achieve great," I am set up to push things ahead, climb the mountain, overcome the obstacles—get on with the vision! My blind spots become apparent to the team when I don't see an issue with what I was planning. They will kindly point out to me, as they just recently did when I laid out a plan to start campus number five, there are some other factors we should consider.

City Bible is blessed with having good success with our multisite model, and I was ready to get on with the next campus, stepping closer to our agreed-upon vision of nine campuses in our metro area. The vision is right, the plan was good, the timing was wrong, and I missed a very vital piece. Our staff needed to be upgraded to the next level of compensation, and opening a new campus would delay that process. When the team pointed out my blind spot, I concurred with them. I had felt a God nudge, had a surge of faith and had an inspiring plan;

but I was blind to a vital piece that my retina had no light on. I couldn't even see it.

Recently, Robert Schuller's famous church the Crystal Cathedral was in real trouble. Unpaid creditors were left in suspense, and the church had to lay off a huge number of staff and face a property sale, bankruptcy and failed fund-raising attempts. The final step was to sell the building for $50 million to a college so that the creditors could be paid. There was, unfortunately, one very little—but very wrong—mistake that was made in the midst of all this financial turmoil. Robert Schuller's wife was ill. They didn't want get well cards, but they did need and did ask for something a little more practical—meals. The email the Schullers sent to the church asked people to bring meals to the church so a limo driver could then transport the meals to the house. Can you guess what phrase set everyone off? "Limo driver." Could a church that owes creditors $50 million not see that the fact that their founder was still utilizing a limousine driver would be problematic? Blind spot! The newspapers and hundreds of irate people sent letters of disbelief and outrage over this incident. It was a total blind spot.

MISTAKE: CHURCH NOT SEEING BLIND SPOTS

We as leaders have blind spots and we as a church have blind spots. What would it take for you to find out what your church's blind spots are? Our church had blind spots with honoring and promoting both male and female future leaders. We adjusted our perspective on the gender issue and have since seen our leadership pipeline filled with both men and women coming up and impacting our church. We also had a blind spot in regard to having an almost totally Caucasian church membership. We then saw that being multiethnic was God's plan, and we decided to make a concentrated effort to bring in people from all ethnicities. The journey was difficult, and many more blind spots surfaced. We faced our flaws and made attitude changes, and slowly our darkened retinas realized the light. Today we have hundreds of people of different nationalities coming to City Bible. We have services in Burmese, Spanish, Laotian and Sudanese; and we offer translation in Russian during English-speaking services. Now we see how far off track we were.

SOLUTION: SEE AROUND YOUR BLIND SPOTS

If you take the driver's license qualification test in America today, the evaluator will watch to see how aware you are of your blind spots. I have a friend who took the test and knew that this was part of the evaluation. So when she was told to change lanes or do anything that required a course adjustment, she clicked on the blinker and cranked her head around to look around the blind spot and make it obvious that she was trying to avoid any unforeseen obstacles. She checked the side mirrors and rearview mirrors and then made her move.

When you are steering the course of your church, you need to crank your head around and look intently at your surroundings for unexpected roadblocks. Simply ask the team of leaders you work with, "Would you please point out my blind spots?" This will get the ball rolling, though it may also be a little uncomfortable. Find the blind spots that you may have no idea exist, and find them right now. These may be holding you and the church back from being the church you desire.

LESSON #2: HAVE A DECISION-MAKING PROCESS

In their book *In Search of Excellence: Lessons from America's Best-Run Companies,* Thomas Peters and Robert Wakerman say that the leader's understanding of the environment can sometimes be up to 10 years out of date. The leader has to update his or her mental process with new ways of thinking that fit the environment where he or she currently resides and does church. Our decisions are housed in our mental perception of the environment of our decision making. As a leader, I have to align the discipline of comprehensive understanding of the people process, the strategy and the operating plan. Whenever I miss any of these three important components of making decisions, I usually have trouble.

Good decisions involve getting the right person in the right place who has the right DNA at the right time with a budget and plan in place. There is no shortage of materials on strategy, vision, leadership, development or innovation. Such resources are endless. There is an abundance of tools and techniques for getting things done, approaches to organizational structure and how to grow a church. It is the gap between initiation and execution that gets leaders in trouble and causes some problems. It's the implementation gap—getting it done with wisdom and with grace. Implementing involves consistent good, even great, decisions.

Great decisions concern every area—Church life: volunteers, staff, budgets, programs and weekend services; Church planting: when and where; Missions: who to send when; Buildings: acquiring new ones or moving to a new location; City ministry: how much involvement, where and with whom. All these concerns have a decision-making component that will either build great momentum or miss the mark. Sometimes you have the right timing but the wrong person. Sometimes it's the right person to lead a new ministry, but there is no strategy and no budget. No worthwhile strategy can be planned without taking into account the organization's ability to execute it. The discipline of executing a systematic approach—investigating the hows and the whats, questioning, tenaciously following through and ensuring accountability—is what makes a great idea work. It is leadership ability to make decisions that recognizes and has all these pieces in place. No exceptions.

Mistake Almost Made: Making a Decision Without a Process

In one situation, I was leading our core leadership team in a deep evaluation of our church's complexity and how we need to always simplify. We went through a process of discussing all ministries, all programs, the church calendar, budgets and how much time leaders were spending in leadership meetings. I made an assumption about one main ministry we were doing that would clear the calendar, refocus staff and use volunteers better. To me, it seemed like a great forward-moving decision. My salvation was to follow my decision-making discipline of not pulling the trigger until we heard from the person who led this ministry. That meeting took us three hours, along with a lunch and another few hours discussing why we may or may not change the function of this particular ministry. By the time we finished, the leader had slowly changed our perceptions, our perspectives and our decision. We hardly changed anything. In fact, I think he got more help and more heart from us.

This kind of meeting leaves me feeling like a stockholder who held on to his stock when things looked bleak, and then one day his investment doubled. I felt a nervous relief, a scary feeling that we had almost made a very wrong decision. If we as leaders fail to have a discipline of decision making that always includes a process, then we will likely make many poor or bad decisions.

Solution: Don't Make a Decision Without Looking at All the Angles

We leaders make decisions about everything from something that has to do with a lofty and high vision in the making to a mundane decision like whether to budget for a new laptop computer for the graphics people on the church team. Any and all decisions—whether big or small—should be made by using a well-thought-through procedure that looks at the concern against the framework of the big picture, which is the overall vision of the church. I have always tried to keep the big decisions in the Executive Leadership Team meetings, knowing that certain sizable decisions must also be submitted to the eldership team of our church. A leader must know all the facts and all the people whom the decision affects before a final decision is made.

Decisions made by a leader or leadership team should be made with the understanding that you would never risk all your resources on one decision. You do not have an unlimited supply of energy, time and money; and you cannot risk more of these resources than you possess. Any decision can use one or more of these resources, but no action should deplete all your resources in any given area. Good decisions are those that open up more possibilities for future choices. Be wise. Expect the unexpected. Prepare for the challenges before you face them. Work with a team, surround yourself with wise leaders, be teachable, be humble, and commit to a disciplined process. Then you will be a good decision maker.

Lesson #3: Technology Is Not the Same as Personal Touch

We leaders are in the people business, so to speak. We are pastors and leaders of people, congregations; and within this context, we do other organizational work, which involves technology. We have certainly moved into a new era of technology usage as a way of life: cell phones, Facebook, iPads, Twitter, laptops, YouTube, texting, emailing, blogging, and who knows what's coming next. Google's CEO Eric Schmidt estimates that a blog is created every second! We are now sending more text messages in America than we are making phone calls.

Mobile customers send and receive an average of 357 text messages per month. Americans use cell phones to send 75 billion text messages per year, which amounts to about 2.5 billion messages sent per day. Facebook now has over 800 million active users and more than 50 percent of those users log on to Facebook every day. The average user has 130 friends on this popular social network. Over 250 million photos are uploaded every day, over 70 languages are used, and more than 350 million people access Facebook through their mobile devices. It is mind-boggling and pure insanity to try keeping up with all the ways to do modern social networking!

Mistake: Putting Convenience of Technology over Sensitivity to the Message

The pastors and leaders of the church today should most definitely learn how to use many of the new technological methods of connecting to people. The 25-year-old and under group uses every technologically available means of communication, and we pastors must connect with them every way we can. Having said all that, we must keep the personal, pastoral, good old-fashioned in-person way of meeting with people in our repertoire of ways to communicate. People do feel valued when they get face time. Emails are quick and great, but emails are not the best way to handle certain personal issues and situations. I have sent texts to different staff people when it was easier and faster for me to make a decision and let them know about it only to have the text message cause misunderstanding and, a few times, discouragement.

Solution: Take Time to Make Personal Contact

Even though we live in a world of now-communication where we demand a response in seconds, we should not let that atmosphere rob us of the proper personal touch and the patience to give it. Texts, emails, tweets and the like simply cannot communicate the emotion and the right spirit you often wish to convey. Using cell phones to text while in counseling or in a meeting with your team leaders can also send the wrong message in regard to where your heart focus is. Take the time to give personal attention to people. Hang out after the church service and shake some hands with people. Ask your staff about how they are doing and then listen to what they say. Find out a few interesting facts about each one—maybe hobbies they have—and then when you are in conversation, bring up those little bits of information you unearthed. This shows that you care about the person. I also write letters of encouragement to my staff. I name certain sacrifices they have made and thank them for what they do to lead our church. Those small gestures go a long way in building unity and value.

Lesson #4: Keep the Main Thing the Main Thing

American historian James Harvey Robinson once stated, "Greatness, in the last analysis, is largely due to bravery—courage in escaping from old ideas and old standards and respectable ways of doing things." A good leader knows how to move into the new and better zone while staying connected to the healthy roots of the past. Good leaders are not weak or defective in character or ministry skill. They are adequate in most areas of leadership function and are able to accomplish what they set out to do. God has called every leader to be good and also to become a great leader (see Josh. 1:9; Pss. 34:10; 37:23). None but leaders of strong passion are capable of rising up to greatness.

Great leaders are always growing and reaching to better their leadership and everyone around them. They take responsibility for their own failures as well as successes. There is no situation that does not have a lesson somewhere to be learned and great leaders know that. Great leaders push the boundary lines and move beyond what is normal or usual. By nature, leaders are pioneers, venturing into new, unexplored territory and guiding people to new and often unfamiliar destinations. With all the vision, risk taking and exploration of new territory, they also know the core nonnegotiable factors of who they are and what they are building. Great leaders are able to strip away much of the noise and clutter and just focus on the few core things that would have the greatest impact.

Mistake: Making a Simple Thing Complex

The book that really helped me to focus and clear the clutter was Jim Collins's *Good to Great*. This book inspired the theme of one of our All Church Leadership Team retreats that I led. We had so many activities happening at our church of 60 years. We had a full K-12 school and a full-blown four-year Bible college with dorms, classrooms, a library, a cafeteria and a whole lot of work. One of our campuses was fairly large and hosted a publishing company, an office complex for the fellowship to which our church founder belonged and led, and most of the office space for church operations. We had missions, church planting, city ministries, a multisite campus model, and everything that goes with all those ministries. It was at this time that we needed to do the hard thing: We had to become a hedgehog.

A hedgehog is a small animal similar to a shrew. When it senses an attack, it rolls into a ball and sticks out the quills from its spiny coat. It stays focused on that one thing. Its opposite is a fox. A fox is a quick animal that pursues many things at the same time. That is what we had become. We were running after so many different ministries and pursuits that we had lost focus and become entangled in a web of complexity. The fox mentality is one that is scattered and diffused, moving on many levels and never really integrating all the circulating thoughts into the one overall unifying vision. Guilty! We were found guilty on all charges. We had to move toward becoming a hedgehog church, but how? We were so varied and scattered and doing so many good things.

The hedgehog church simplifies a complex world and focuses on a simple organizing idea, a basic principle or a concept that unifies all the teams and guides all the church into one vision. It took us four days to press down all our thoughts, accompanied by teaching and open discussion. I was amazed—actually, more like shocked. Why could we not just say, "This is our hedgehog and these are our foxes"? Simple. But those leading the fox-type ministries had a very difficult time being called foxes.

Solution: Focus on the Main Thing

We went through three questions with each ministry leader: What are you deeply passionate about? What drives your resource engine? What can you be best at in the world? When these were answered in a small discussion-group setting, we then came together (about 130 leaders) to put all our conclusions on a whiteboard. We finally ended our week with a definite unified hedgehog: We are church builders. Our hedgehog is our church, not the publishing, not the schools, not all the other things that are good things to do but do not make up the core of the church. The core elements are people, discipling, prayer, worship, small groups, things we would do if we had no property and no money. So simple, yet so profound. Yes, we have a hedgehog and that is the church.

Our conclusion set into motion various changes in how we related to and structured the schools, publishing—all ministries. We had learned a most important lesson. Our vision was recast. We would become the best at being the church. Our reason for existing was to build and impact our world with a great church. So now we are doing just that.

Lesson #5: Don't Violate Your Own Principles

Principles and values provide the shared roadways on which leaders exercise their influence and followers respond. Shared values provide the criteria for what ought to be done and what ought not to be done. Every church should have guiding principles for the church leadership team to see, understand and abide by. Principles are based on the core values that create the church culture and build great trustworthy leaders. These principles guide all decision-making and leadership functions.

Mistake: Violating the Principle of Owning the Church Vision

City Bible has a principle of choosing leaders based on a journey where the potential leader owns the vision, values and principles that our church is built upon. The assimilation of these things takes time, training, classes, mentoring and adjustments. Much is shaped during this time.

Whenever we violate our own principle by choosing and placing leaders before they have gone through this process, we have been burned. We have looked back and said to ourselves, "That was our own violation that caused the problem." The person looked good and had gifting, great charisma and seemed so right that we didn't think we needed to wait for the process to finish. Violation of a principle usually always comes back in the end to get you and the team.

Solution: Stick to the Principle

Keep to principles that have proven to build the church safely, slowly and solidly. If you have a membership track, then every leader must go through it. Everyone starts with the basics. If you believe water baptism is a basic requirement for a person to be a growing disciple, then get people baptized. If serving is a principle for proving one's heart and character, then everyone should serve before they lead. If you choose a leader before you know if a foundation is in place, you are violating the principle of proving a person and waiting to see his or her fruit. Everyone wants to lead but not all want to serve. Positions and titles can motivate people to be spiritual and look spiritual, but underneath they may be performance driven, not heart driven. Growing your own leaders is by far the best way to multiply and equip effective leaders.

Underdeveloped leaders are not leading to their full potential, and it takes specific steps to get them to where they need to be. That means time! Work! Energy! Frustration! These are the words that both describe and explain why leaders sometimes violate their own principles and put someone into a ministry to lead and pastor people when the person hasn't been in church long enough to know the leader or to know the vision and principles of the house. Failure! That's another word that comes into play when we violate principles. We fail. The leader fails, the church is hindered and people get hurt. Build on principles that allow you a safe selection process for people you will develop, and create a development track for these people. Leaders are made. It takes time and work.

Lesson #6: Define Your Ministry Focus

City Bible has always been a church with a heart for global missions activity, just as many churches today are. We take seriously the Acts 1:8 mandate to reach into different areas of our world and society. We have planted churches both nationally and internationally and sent missionaries around the world. We have also "adopted" missionaries and church plants that were not sent from our church. This relationship may not be apostolic in its sending, but there is an apostolic relationship, connection and an impartation of resources.

Mistake: Making Unfocused Choices

Our mistake was to allow ourselves to join with many different people and places where we could not give resources and proper input. The leadership team had to admit we were unfocused and the vision we were seeking to fulfill was blurry. We had diluted our focus and spread our resources around to meet all the needs but had not effectively connected to the nations God had called our church to bond with. The mistake was unintentional and, in fact, was a mistake of trying to love and help everyone. We decided to begin choosing where we would plant churches and to what nations we would send missionaries a little more carefully. As we went through the decision-making process, it became clear that not every mission vision in the heart of the individual may be in alignment with the strategy of our church's mission. We had to back up, refocus, redefine and relate differently to those who did not align with our strategy of what our leadership team had laid out.

Solution: Face the Brutal Facts and Make Drastic Changes

It is difficult to make drastic changes involving past decisions, because it involves people's lives. But we rewrote our missions policy to bring definition to our church plants, missionaries, extension ministries and network relationships. These were the four categories we would work with at different levels. We tried several times to redefine but kept complicating ourselves with a blurry definition. We were still trying to make our old mistakes fit in our new policy, but we soon learned we still had a problem. We had to face the brutal facts. We were not leading with clarity and we were causing confusion. After several rewrites, we finally landed on a clear definition and a clear process. Now we have a clear way for church-plant monies and missions monies to be raised, when they can be raised, by whom they can be raised and how those ministries must process the vision and strategy. Missionaries we send need to outline a people focus; define who they intend to reach; identify the geographical focus, location priorities and activities they will engage in or start; and determine what level of ministry they will be doing. Because we learned the consequences of making choices without a clear focus, we have developed a very precise and detailed process that guides the way we carry out the Acts 1:8 mandate.

Lesson #7: Overcome Location Blindness

Location is a vital component of the church building strategy. It affects the type of person you will draw, the number of people who can come to church, and your capacity to reach and have influence. Because of those things, it is imperative that a location be chosen with careful consideration.

Mistake: Letting Location Interrupt the Vision

The church property on which City Bible had built a sizable vision had its challenges and limitations. The parking was built to accommodate only 50 percent of the auditorium capacity. It was meant to be remodeled later but never was. We were in a neighborhood setting with one road in and out, limited parking and several other huge challenges. Decision time. Should we stay, move or change our vision implementation? We were blinded by our location. In fact, the location actually interrupted our vision, our future and our options. Wrong perspective. It was a revelation when we finally broke out with a new idea: Maybe we should change how we do church. So we did.

Solution: Find a Different Location—or Locations

The leadership team researched several different models of how other churches were doing church to see if it would spark any thoughts for our specific kind of church. We eventually came up with some conclusions that opened the door to where we finally wound up. We decided to take church to the people, instead of people to one location. The first piece of our answer came with a vision called the Circle of 15: No one would have to drive more than 15 minutes to find a City Bible Church location with full CBC service ministries. The location blindness turned into location unlimited possibilities. Location became a motivating, even inspiring, word. Our multisite strategy began to take form with the great commission word "Go" as the driving force. A very hard, almost discouraging location blindness had turned into a new door with amazing opportunities.

The multisite model is now growing across our nation and beyond. When we started, there were not many other churches that resembled our church's size and specific spiritual DNA. We researched the video model, video-cast model, teaching team model and partnership model, but in the end, we created our own model. We now use a simulcast regional campus model that reproduces all vital ministries in each location. The lead pastor is the primary feeder, with a live simulcast into that location. We now do this with four locations and many services per week.

Our location blindness problem opened us up to doing church a new way that has doubled the size of our church with growth possibilities that only the lack of trained leaders could hinder. Parking lots or entry roads do not hinder us. We have overcome geographic barriers, and we have enabled untapped talent to emerge each time a campus is opened. We have mobilized volunteers, improved our church's resources and created different sizes of services; and we do all this with people driving 15 minutes or less to a location. We have one church, one name, one budget, one ministry philosophy, one vision and one DNA, yet it is all spread around to multiple locations. It was one of the greatest learning experiences of my lifetime and one of the scariest. I didn't know if this would work!

After leading a church for over 30 years and planting a church, I have made my fair share of mistakes and learned many lessons. My hope is that you will learn from my journey and become a strategic leader. The world today does not need another model or another cookie-cutter church. The world needs a strategic church where people are transformed and mobilized to live like Jesus and share His love. Commit to building this kind of church!

Conclusion

I trust in the Holy Spirit that He will guide you the leader and the leadership team into a strategic vision to build a strategic church. Strategic churches plan how to build and what to build with all the important elements in place, resisting the pressures of our culture or the fruitless ministries of others. Strategy is the means by which objectives are consciously and systematically pursued and obtained over time. It is a way of thinking that sets a course of action and achieves it.

We as pivotal leaders are church strategists with the mighty help of the great builder, the Holy Spirit. We can do this. We will be like Paul, who "fought the good fight, . . . finished the race, . . . kept the faith" (2 Tim. 4:7). He was so determined to finish that he wrote, "But none of these things move me; nor do I count my life dear to myself, so that I may finish my race with joy, and the ministry which I received from the Lord Jesus, to testify to the gospel of the grace of God" (Acts 20:24). We will be like John the Baptist, of whom it is written, "And as John was finishing his course, he said, 'Who do you think I am? I am not He. But behold, there comes One after me, the sandals of whose feet I am not worthy to loose' " (Acts 13:25).

Be encouraged, and stay the course. Maintain your course strategy, and pursue your vision regardless of any obstacles and all criticisms. Stay the course, finish the race, follow the plan. If the strategy is failing, change it. Don't stay on a failing course. Adjust failing structures so that they fit a biblical pattern. God is not a human that He should lie. He is God and His Word is right, true and unbroken. Trust the blueprint and strategize to build a great, world-changing church. Handle the disappointments, see the distractions, stand strong, and be a world-class strategist!

Endnotes

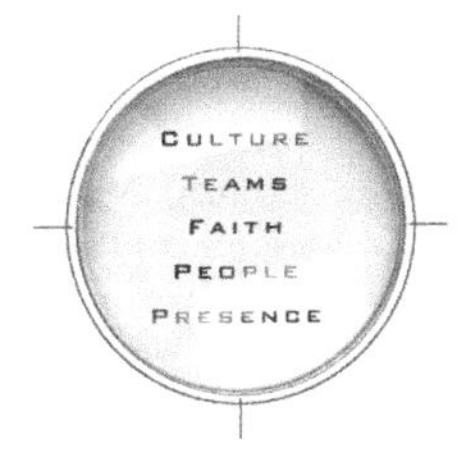

Chapter 1: Strategic Leaders Build Strategic Churches

1. Ed Stetzer and Thom S. Rainer, *Transformational Church: Creating a New Scorecard for Congregations* (Nashville, TN: B&H Publishing Group, 2010), p. 12.

Chapter 2: Strategic Vision

1. John D. Rockefeller, 3rd, *The Second American Revolution: Some Personal Observations* (New York: Harper & Row, 1973), p. 72.
2. George Barna, *Turning Vision into Action: Defining and Putting into Practice the Unique Vision God Has for Your Ministry* (Ventura, CA: Regal Books, 1996), pp. 19-20.
3. "The Only Way Out of This Corrupt World," *Heaven's Gate,* November 28, 1993. http://www.heavensgate.com/book/6-3.htm (accessed December 2011).
4. "Our Position Against Suicide," *Heaven's Gate.* http://www.heavensgate.com/misc/letter.htm (accessed December 2011).
5. Hudson Taylor, quoted in Paul Borthwick, *Leading the Way: Leadership Is Not Just for Super Christians* (Colorado Springs, CO: Navpress, 1989), p. 153.
6. Andrew Murray, quoted by Phillip Brooks, "Prayer," *Speak the Word Church,* January 11, 2003. http://www.speaktheword.com.
7. Harold Chadwick, ed., *E. M. Bounds on Prayer* (Orlando, FL: Bridge-Logos Publishers, 2001), p. 207.
8. Nike Consumer Affairs Packet, 1996.
9. Jim Collins and Morten T. Hansen, *Great by Choice: Uncertainty, Chaos, and Luck—Why Some Thrive Despite Them All* (New York: HarperCollins, 2011), p. 36.

Chapter 3: Strategic Church Growth

1. Charles L. Chaney and Ron S. Lewis, *Design for Church Growth* (Nashville, TN: Broadman Press, 1977), p. 17.
2. Richard J. Krejcir, "Statistics and Reasons for Church Decline," *Francis A. Shaeffer Institute of Church Leadership Development,* 2007. http://www.intothyword.org/articles_view.asp?articleid=36557 (accessed April 2012).
3. Tim Keller, "A Biblical Theology of 'the City,'" *Gospel Community Culture,* 2002. http://nickrynerson.com/2011/11/18/tim-keller-a-biblical-theology-of-the-city (accessed April 2012).
4. Josh Green, "Cops: Empty Gas Tank Foils Burglar's Escape," *Gwinnett Daily Post,* October 7, 2011. http://www.gwinnettdailypost.com/news/2011/oct/07/cops-empty-gas-tank-foils-burglars-escape (accessed April 2012).
5. Ray C. Stedman, "Defense Against Defeat, Part 4," *RayStedman.org,* December 19, 1965. http://www.raystedman.org/new-testament/ephesians/defense-against-defeat-part-4 (accessed April 2012).

Chapter 4: Strategic Dynamic Atmosphere

1. Brad J. Waggoner, *The Shape of Faith to Come: Spiritual Formation and the Future of Discipleship* (Nashville, TN: B&H Publishing Group, 2008), p. 62.
2. Ibid., p. 69.
3. Ibid., p. 201.
4. Ibid., p. 153.
5. Ibid., p. 157.
6. *Hudson Taylor's Choice Sayings: A Compilation from His Writings and Addresses* (London: China Inland Mission, n.d.), p. 13, quoted at OMF International. http://www.omf.org/omf/us/resources__1/omf_archives/famous_china_inland_mission_quotations/hudson_taylor (accessed April 2012).

7. Department for Communities and Local Government, *No One Left Out: Communities Ending Rough Sleeping* (London: Communities and Local Government Publications, 2008), p. 10.
8. Sangeet Duchane, *The Little Book of Mother Teresa* (New York: Barnes & Noble Books, 2004), p. 25.
9. Winston Churchill, "We Shall Fight on the Beaches," *WinstonChurichill.org./The Churchill Centre and Museum at the Churchill War Rooms, London.* http://www.winstonchurchill.org/learn/speeches/speeches-of-winston-churchill/128-we-shall-fight-on-the-beaches (accessed April 2012).
10. Martin Gilbert, *Winston Churchill's War Leadership* (New York: Vintage Books, 2004), p. 27.

Chapter 5: Strategic Unique Culture

1. Frank Newport and Joseph Carroll, "Another Look at Evangelicals in America Today," *Gallup,* December 2, 2005. http://www.gallup.com/poll/20242/Another-Look-Evangelicals-America-Today.aspx (accessed December 2011).
2. C. S. Lewis, *Weight of Glory* (New York: HarperCollins, 2001), p. 26.
3. Karen Pazol and others, "Abortion Surveillance–United States, 2007," *Centers for Disease Control and Prevention,* February 25, 2011. http://www.cdc.gov/mmwr/preview/mmwrhtml/ss6001a1.htm (accessed April 2012).

Chapter 6: Strategic Team of Teams Culture

1. John C. Maxwell and Jim Dornan, *Becoming a Person of Influence: How to Positively Impact the Lives of Others* (Nashville, TN: Thomas Nelson, 1997), pp. 108-109.
2. Michael Useem, *The Go Point: When It's Time to Decide—Knowing What to Do and When to Do It* (New York: Three Rivers Press, 2006), p. 19.
3. Mike Krzyzewski with Jamie K. Spatola, *The Gold Standard: Building a World-Class Team* (New York: Business Plus, 2009), p. xvii.
4. James M. Citrin, *The Dynamic Path: Access the Secrets of Champions to Achieve Greatness Through Mental Toughness, Inspired Leadership and Personal Transformation* (Emmaus, PA: Rodale, 2007), p. 54.
5. Krzyzewski, *The Gold Standard: Building a World-Class Team,* p. 43.
6. Peter F. Drucker, *The Daily Drucker: 366 Days of Insight and Motivation for Getting the Right Things Done* (New York: HarperCollins, 2004), June 9.

Chapter 7: Strategic Emerging-Leadership Culture

1. Martin Luther King, Jr., and James Melvin Washington, *A Testament of Hope: The Essential Writings and Speeches of Martin Luther King, Jr.* (New York: HarperCollins, 1991), pp. 265-266.
2. James M. Kouzes and Barry Z. Posner, *A Leader's Legacy* (San Francisco: Jossey-Bass, 2006), p. 10.
3. Peter Drucker, *The Daily Drucker: 366 Days of Insight and Motivation for Getting the Right Things Done* (New York: Harper Collins, 2004), June 9.

Chapter 8: Strategic Life-Changing Worship

1. Darlene Zschech, *Extravagant Worship: Holy, Holy, Holy Is the Lord God Almighty Who Was and Is, and Is to Come . . .* (Bloomington, MN: Bethany House Publishers, 2004), p. 10.
2. A. W. Tozer, "Whatever Happened to Worship," *Upstream Ministries,* January 7, 2012. http://www.upstreamca.org/whathappened.html (accessed May 2012).
3. Louie Giglio, *The Air I Breathe: Worship as a Way of Life* (Sisters, OR: Multnomah Publishers, Inc., 2003), p. 55.
4. Matt Redman, *resurrected legs* (Ventura, CA: Regal, 2004), p. 13.
5. Joni Eareckson Tada, *Diamonds in the Dust: 366 Sparkling Devotions* (Grand Rapids, MI: Zondervan Publishing House, 1993), August 24.
6. Redman, *resurrected legs,* p. 23.
7. "The Closer Walk: Reflections on Practicing God's Presence" *Light Heart,* www.PracticeGodsPresence.com.
8. Brother Lawrence, "The Practice of the Presence of God," *Catholic Treasury.* http://www.catholic-treasury.info/books/presence_of_God/pr8.php (accessed May 2012).
9. Darrell A. Harris, "John Wesley's Directions for Singing in Worship with Commentary," *Worshipedia,* 2010. http://www.worshipedia.org/node/1494 (accessed May 2012).

10. Tony Campolo, interview by Samuel D. Perriccioli, *Worship Leader* (November/December 2000), p. 25, quoted in *To Know You More: Cultivating the Heart of the Worship Leader* (Downers Grove, IL: InterVarsity Press, 2002), pp. 153-154.

Chapter 9: Strategic Powerful Praying

1. Andrew Murray, *God's Best Secrets* (New Kensington, PA: Whitaker House, 1998), p. 46.
2. E. M. Bounds, *The Weapon of Prayer* (Grand Rapids, MI: Baker Books, 1980), p. 3.
3. E. M. Bounds, *The Necessity of Prayer* (Grand Rapids, MI: Baker Books, 1976), p. 25.
4. *The Art of War by Sun Tzu—Classic Collector's Edition,* trans. Lionel Giles (El Paso Norte Press, 2009), p. 17.
5. Real Time Statistics, "Food," *StoptheHunger.com,* 2000-2011. http://www.stopthehunger.com (accessed November 2011).

Chapter 10: Strategic Pursuit of the Supernatural

1. Richard J. Foster, *Prayer: Finding the Heart's True Home* (New York: HarperCollins, 1992), p. 203.
2. Paul Chappell, *Great Things He Hath Done: Origins of the Divine Healing Movement in America* (unpublished), pp. 10-11.
3. Walter C. Kaiser Jr., Peter H. Davids, F. F. Bruce, Manfred Brauch, *Hard Sayings of the Bible* (Downers Grove, IL: InterVarsity Press, 1996), p. 469.
4. Alan Richardson, *The Miracle Stories of the Gospels* (Norfolk, VA: SCM Press, 1941), pp. 61-62.
5. Hendrik van der Loos, *The Miracles of Jesus,* trans. T. S. Preston (Leiden, Netherlands: E. J. Brill, 1965), p. 220.
6. Saint Augustine, *The City of God,* bk. 22, chap. 8.
7. Justin Martyr, "The Second Apology of Justin for the Christians Addressed to the Roman Senate," ed. Alexander Roberts and James Donaldson, *Believe Religious Information Source,* 2012. http://mb-soft.com/believe/txv/martyr2.htm (accessed May 2012).

Chapter 11: Strategic Blending of Spirit and Word

1. Miguel de Unamuno, *Tragic Sense of Life,* trans. J. E. Crawford Flitch (New York: Dover, 1954), p. 16.
2. Charles H. Spurgeon, *Sermons on the Death and Resurrection of Jesus* (Peabody, MA: Hendrickson Publishers, 2005), p. 385.

Chapter 12: Strategic Culture of Generosity

1. *Leadership: A Magazine for Christian Leaders in Africa,* 1983, quoted at "Missions, Evangelism, Witnessing," *Sermon Illustrations.* http://www.sermonillustrations.com/a-z/m/missions_evangelism_ wit nessing.htm (accessed November 2001).
2. "Address of His Holiness Benedict XVI at the Opening of the 12th Ordinary General Assembly of the Synod of Bishops," *Libreria Editrice Vaticana,* October 6, 2008. http://www.vatican.va/holy_father/benedict_xvi/speeches/2008/october/documents/hf_ben-xvi_spe_20081006_sinodo_en.html (accessed May 2012).

Chapter 13: Strategic Reaching of Cities, Regions and the World

1. Tim Keller, "A Biblical Theology of the City," *Evangelism Now* (July 2002).

Chapter 14: Strategic Lessons Learned

1. Hans Finzel, *The Top Ten Mistakes Leaders Make* (Colorado Springs, CO: David C. Cook, 2007), contents.
2. *Oxford Dictionaries,* s.v. "blind spot." http://oxforddictionaries.com/definition/blind%2Bspot (accessed May 2012).
3. *Chambers 21st Century Dictionary,* s.v. "blind spot." http://www.chambersharrap.co.uk/chambers/features/chref/chref.py/main?query=blind+spot&title=21st (accessed May 2012).

ACKNOWLEDGMENTS

First and foremost, I want to acknowledge the tremendous grace on my life because of what Jesus has done in me and through me. It's all about His working and patience with me. Thank You, Jesus!

I want to thank my executive personal assistant, Sanny Rider, for all her amazing and unfailing energy to get this project finished. A book is never the work of one person. There's editing, researching, re-editing, and always looking for ways to better the book. Thank you, Sanny. You are absolutely the best!

I also want to thank Regal for their vision for this book, and Kim Bangs for her encouragement and for keeping this project on track. Many thanks to all the staff at Regal—you are a home run team.

Finally, thank you to the leaders and the people of City Bible Church. You have enthusiastically responded to the call to build a life-changing church. Together, we are building the Strategic Church.

MORE PRAISE FOR

STRATEGIC CHURCH

In *Strategic Church*, Frank has skillfully presented a complete vision of what the Church is, her purpose, leadership principles, the major truths we must preach and teach, and the vision of reaching our cities, regions and the whole world. Any given chapter could be the basis for in-depth study and teaching of subjects relevant to the Church and, thus, the whole society today. There is hope for America and the West, and we can and must turn back to God and fulfill our destiny. I highly recommend this excellent book.

DENNIS BALCOMBE
Senior Pastor, Revival Christian Church, Hong Kong
Director, Revival Chinese Ministries International, Hong Kong

Pastor Frank Damazio has invested more than 30 years in training and equipping leaders from all walks of life and all ministries. In this book, ministry leaders and church builders will find time-tested wisdom and innovative strategies for building a biblical and life-transforming church. Pastor Frank Damazio is not only a gifted writer but has also become known to the world as a great church builder.

TOMMY BARNETT
Senior Pastor, Phoenix First Assembly of God, Phoenix, Arizona
Co-founder, The Dream Center, Los Angeles, California

Pastor Frank is a world-changing leader who has a heart to see the lost saved and the saved changed. His wisdom and intentional strategy has led City Bible Church to become a *dangerous church* that has pushed back the gates of hell and changed a city. Read this book with your whole leadership team, and when that moment comes—that pivotal, life-altering moment—step out and see God step in.

JOHN BISHOP
Senior Pastor, Living Hope Church
Author, *Dangerous Church*

Frank Damazio is on top of his game in *Strategic Church*. You will grow deeper in your understanding of issues and have real-life biblically based solutions that transcend contexts and cultures. I encourage you and every leader to read *Strategic Church* so you can know, grow and show.

DR. SAMUEL R. CHAND
Author, *Cracking Your Church's Culture Code*

I am told that people go by the *cover* of a book before they buy it. For me, however, I go by the *content* before I buy. A look at the table of contents of *Strategic Church* will do that for many leaders, preachers and teachers of the Church in this present generation. *Strategic Church* is challenging, enlightening and refreshing—indeed, something to really think about!

KEVIN J. CONNER
Former Senior Minister, CityLife Church, Australia

Frank Damazio has a vast amount of wisdom that he has gleaned from decades of life experience, from reflection on the Scriptures, and from ministering in the trenches of local church life. *Strategic Church* is a welcome addition to the leadership conversation and will be sure to provide a wealth of insights for church leaders—both beginners and veterans alike. I highly recommend it!

MARK CONNER
Senior Minister, CityLife Church, Australia

We cannot choose the times or seasons our Lord has granted us to fulfill His divine destiny in our lives, yet we can learn how to read our times, rearrange our plans, and ramp up for greater growth in our ministries. In *Strategic Church*, Dr. Frank Damazio provides us with the strategic blueprint to both create a sequence for success and the steps required to leverage our leadership for maximum impact in our generation.

DR. JAMES O. DAVIS
Co-founder, Billion Soul, Orlando, Florida

This is one of the most comprehensive, palatable, absorbing and informative books that I've come across in recent years. Charles Spurgeon, the notable pastor and preacher of the historical Metropolitan Tabernacle in England during the 1800s, told his students that "in order to *do* better, you must *be* better." No matter where you are in your walk with God, reading *Strategic Church* will motivate you to be better! It's a must-read for every child of God.

MICHAEL DURSO
Senior Pastor, Christ Tabernacle

People are searching for significance, and many are looking to become a part of something big and dynamic that will outlive them. In *Strategic Church*, Pastor Frank imparts this great sense of purpose to the heart and mind. He reveals the strategic church God is building with such expansive energy that all of society will be affected and the powers of hell will not prevail against it.

JUDE FOUQUIER
Lead Pastor, City Church Ventura, California

Frank Damazio is a visionary leader and a trusted voice in church leadership. In *Strategic Church,* he has generously offered the wisdom of his experiences to all of us who are passionate about building Christ-centered churches. This book will lift your faith to see God's vision for your church as you develop a biblical strategy.

STEVEN FURTICK
Lead Pastor, Elevation Church and Author, *Sun Stand Still*

All church leaders aspire to build better churches, but what is it that makes a church truly dynamic? *Strategic Church* synthesizes biblically authoritative and culturally responsive answers to that question. It is the best book on how to lead a life-changing church that I have ever read—a wonderful distillation of the inspirational, practical and biblical!

MICHAEL GIROUX
Pastor and Lawyer, The City Church, Washington, DC

Pastor Frank Damazio's teaching on the Church has consistently and continually helped shape my leadership as a pastor. *Strategic Church* is a must-read.

DANNY GUGLIELMUCCI
Senior Minister, Edge Church International

Strategic Church is a book long overdue. Pastor Damazio's blend of leadership insight, biblical understanding and more than 30 years of experience will provide answers that those who desire to build God's Church are struggling to find. I loved it!

PAUL DE JONG
Senior Pastor, LIFE, New Zealand

After reading *Strategic Church,* I regret only one thing: that this book was not available 15 years ago when I became a new pastor of a church. In this book you will discover clear, profound and practical wisdom from an author who shares his experience and knowledge with those who want to strategically build churches around the world. I highly recommend it to every church leader.

ZHENYA KASEVICH
Pastor, Hillsong Church, Kiev-Moscow

If you read one book this year on church strategy, make it *Strategic Church.* After having the privilege of walking with Pastor Frank Damazio for nearly 20 years, I can testify that the principles in this book are tried, tested and proven. A must-read for church leaders at every level.

DOUG LASIT
Pastor, The Pearl Church, Denver, Colorado

In *Strategic Church*, Frank Damazio makes a fresh contribution to the theory and practice of "doing church" in the twenty-first century. The blueprint for the Church he builds in terms of the principles and guidelines he recommends is biblically sound, theologically balanced and practically applicable. Aspiring church builders will do well to heed his call for orthodoxy, authenticity and strategy.

THOMSON K. MATHEW, D.MIN., ED.D.
Dean, College of Theology and Ministry, Oral Roberts University

I have the privilege of serving with Pastor Damazio in our city, which means I get to see firsthand how the principles in this book are actually shaping the church and the city of Portland in amazing ways! This book is biblical, practical and inspiring. It challenged me and made me grateful that pastors and leaders will get to glean from Frank's wisdom and learn how to lead God's Church with courage, insight and passion.

RICK MCKINLEY
Lead Pastor, Imago Dei Community
Author, *A Kingdom Called Desire* and *This Beautiful Mess*

Strategic Church is the perfect book to help you think differently and gain a unique perspective on how you and your church can thrive by overcoming obstacles. This is not just another "how to" book or a collection of abstract theories; these are solid principles Frank Damazio has lived out in his 30-plus years of ministry. These pages contain engaging analogies, dynamic truths and proven strategies based on a firm foundation from the Word of God that will spur you and your church to more effectively build fruitful disciples of Christ and transform lives!

ROBERT MORRIS
Senior Pastor, Gateway Church
Bestselling Author, *The Blessed Life*, *From Dream to Destiny*, *The Power of Your Words* and *The God I Never Knew*

Strategic Church is filled with Kingdom keys and treasures that will enrich both your ministry and your life. Pastor Frank writes simply, yet profoundly, with expertise and vast experience on this most vital subject. He is a teacher of teachers, a leader of leaders and a true Bible scholar with a gift for feeding and imparting to others the ways of God. *Strategic Church* is a must-read for all those inspiring to be great men and women of God in the Church of the living God. I highly recommend it.

PETER MORTLOCK
Senior Pastor, City Impact Churches

As Christians, we have the awesome honor—and the awesome challenge—of building Jesus' Church. *Strategic Church* is a manifesto and a handbook for building that Church. It will inspire you, inform you, and propel you to make God's vision a reality. Frank Damazio is a true pastor and an extraordinary teacher, and his insights into church growth will change the way you look at the Church and your role in it.

JUDAH SMITH
Lead Pastor, City Church, Seattle, Washington

Strategic Church is a book you will want to read through and meditate on. It will bring renewal and inspiration to your heart and ministry. Pastor Damazio is a brilliant leader, pastor and teacher who writes wisdom and strategies that produce results. His insights are relevant and working in our world today. After you read *Strategic Church*, you will want to go to Portland and see City Bible Church in action.

DR. CASEY TREAT
Senior Pastor, Christian Faith Center, Seattle, Washington

Strategic Church provides powerful insights into proven principles for infusing fresh life into your church. Pastor Damazio will help you understand God's biblical blueprint for being a leader who builds churches that not only change lives but also change culture. Your heart will leap as you receive wisdom from this book to transform your church into a dynamic group of people who fulfill God's great vision for His Church. An *ordinary* church can be transformed into an *extraordinary* church!

BARBARA WENTROBLE
President, International Breakthrough Ministries (IbM)
CEO, Business Owners for Christ International (BOFCI)
Author, *Prophetic Intercession*, *Praying with Authority*, *Fighting for Your Prophetic Promises*, *Removing the Veil of Deception*

I am convinced that every church leader should read *Strategic Church* in order to understand and address the many contemporary challenges that stand in front of us today. This is undoubtedly the best practical and strategic book available and will enable every church to go to the next level when implementing its well-thought-out plans. Once again, Frank has captured the heart of the need in the Church and has given us tools to address what we must do in order to reach our world. This is a must-read for everyone who has a heart to see the Church succeed in our day.

PASTOR KEN WILDE
Senior Pastor, Capital Christian Center, Meridian, Idaho
Founder and Executive Director, National Prayer Center, Washington, DC

I can't think of anyone more qualified to write on this subject than Frank Damazio. Pastor Frank is a leader to leaders and a pastor to pastors. This book is an example of why he has a voice to pastors around the world. If you are involved in ministry, in any capacity, *Strategic Church* is a must-read!

CHAD VEACH
United Generation Team Leader, Puyallup Foursquare Church, Washington

In this wonderful book, Pastor Frank has done an incredible job of unpacking the elements that shape a worshiping church—and that's just one chapter. This book will help you understand how to mobilize people to pray, how to relate to culture, how to train leaders, and so much more. It's a must-read for every leader who is serious about building a church that sees lives transformed.

DARLENE ZSCHECH
Songwriter
Co-pastor, Hope Unlimited Church

Contact Information

Twitter: **@frankdamazio**
Facebook: **Pastor Frank Damazio**

Pastor Frank online:
(blogs, sermon notes, pastor-leader resources)
www.frankdamazio.com

For *Strategic Church* study materials and more, visit
www.mystrategicchurch.com

Send inquiries to:
9200 NE Fremont St.
Portland, OR 97220
503.255.2224
www.frankdamazio.com